AF556364

BANK REGULATIONS

BANK REGULATIONS

By

S.K. Singh

DISCOVERY PUBLISHING HOUSE PVT. LTD.
NEW DELHI-110 002

First Published-2009

ISBN 978-81-8356-447-2

Published by:

DISCOVERY PUBLISHING HOUSE PVT. LTD.

4831/24, Ansari Road, Prahlad Street,
Darya Ganj, New Delhi-110002 (India)
Phone: 23279245 • Fax: 91-11-23253475
E-mail: dphbooks@rediffmail.com
dphtemp@indiatimes.com
Website: www.discoverypublishinghouse.com

Printed at:

Sachin Printers, Delhi

Contents

Preface

Bank regulations are another side of government regulations, which subject banks to certain requirements, restrictions and guidelines. The main objectives of bank regulation and its emphasis, varies between jurisdiction, namely: prudential, system risk reduction, avoiding misuse of banks, to protect banking, confidentially and credit allocation.

Banks that mobilise and allocate savings efficiently, allocate capital to endeavours, with the highest expected business returns, exert sound governance, over funded firms and foster innovation and growth.

Regulation is mostly focused on privacy, disclosure, fraud prevention, money laundering, usury lending and promoting lending to lower-income individuals. These regulations require banks to maintain a minimum reserve that cannot be loaned. The regulation of banks are key elements of a financial safety net.

This book is focused on the rationale for banking regulations. Hopefully, it would be accorded a warm welcome, among all quarters of readership. For further enhancement of the usability of the work, we look forward to positive and enlightening feedback, from esteemed readers!

General Principles of Bank Regulation

Bank regulations are a form of government regulation which subject banks to certain requirements, restrictions and guidelines.

Banking regulations can vary widely across nations and jurisdictions. Here is the description of general principles of bank regulation throughout the world.

Minimum Requirements

Requirements are imposed on banks in order to promote the objectives of the regulator. The most important minimum requirement in banking regulation is minimum capital ratios.

Supervisory Review

Banks are required to be issued with a bank licence by the regulator in order to carry on business as a bank, and the regulator supervises licensed banks for compliance with the requirements and responds to breaches of the requirements through obtaining undertakings, giving directions, imposing penalties or revoking the bank's licence.

Market Discipline

The regulator requires banks to publicly disclose financial and other information, and depositors and other creditors are able to use this information to assess the level of risk and to make investment decisions. As a result of this, the bank is subject to market discipline and the regulator can also use market pricing information as an indicator of the bank's financial health.

Objectives of Bank Regulation

The objectives of bank regulation, and the emphasis, varies between jurisdiction. The most common objectives are:

1. *Prudential:* To reduce the level of risk bank creditors are exposed to (i.e. to protect depositors).
2. *Systemic Risk Reduction:* To reduce the risk of disruption resulting from adverse trading conditions for banks causing multiple or major bank failures.
3. *Avoid Misuse of Banks:* To reduce the risk of banks being used for criminal purposes, e.g. laundering the proceeds of crime.
4. To protect banking confidentiality.
5. *Credit Allocation:* To direct credit to favoured sectors.

Capital Requirement

The capital requirement is a bank regulation, which sets a framework on how banks and depository institutions must handle their capital. The categorisation of assets and capital is highly standardised so that it can be risk weighted. Internationally, the Basel Committee on Banking Supervision housed at the Bank for International Settlements influence each country's banking capital requirements. In 1988, the Committee decided to introduce a capital measurement system commonly referred to as the Basel Capital Accords (Basel Accord). This framework is now being replaced by a new and significantly more complex capital adequacy framework commonly known as Basel II. While Basel II significantly alters the calculation of the risk weights, it leaves alone the calculation of the capital. The capital ratio is the percentage of a bank's capital to its risk-weighted assets. Weights are defined by risk-sensitivity ratios whose calculation is dictated under the relevant Accord.

Each national regulator normally has a very slightly different way of calculating bank capital, designed to meet the common requirements within their individual national legal framework. Brazil limits bank lending to 10 times the bank's capital, adjusted to inflation. Most developed countries and Basel I and II, stipulate lending limits as a multiple of a banks capital eroded by the yearly inflation rate.

The 5 C's of Credit, Character, Cash Flow, Collateral, Conditions and Capital, have been substituted by one single criterion. While the international standards of bank capital were laid down in the 1988 Basel I accord, Basel II makes significant alterations to the interpretation, if not the calculation, of the capital requirement.

Examples of national regulators implementing Basel II include the FSA in the UK, BAFIN in Germany, and OSFI in Canada.

An example of a national regulator implementing Basel I, but not Basel II, is in the United States. Depository institutions are subject to risk-based capital guidelines issued by the Board of Governors of the Federal Reserve System (FRB). These guidelines are used to evaluate capital adequacy based primarily on the perceived credit risk associated with balance sheet assets, as well as certain off-balance sheet exposures such as unfunded loan commitments, letters of credit, and derivatives and foreign exchange contracts.

The risk-based capital guidelines are supplemented by a leverage ratio requirement. To be adequately capitalised under federal bank regulatory agency definitions, a bank holding company must have a Tier 1 capital ratio of at least 4 per cent, a combined Tier 1 and Tier 2 capital ratio of at least 8 per cent, and a leverage ratio of at least 4 per cent, and not be subject to a directive, order, or written agreement to meet and maintain specific capital levels. To be well-capitalised under federal bank regulatory agency definitions, a bank holding company must have a Tier 1 capital ratio of at least 6 per cent, a combined Tier 1 and Tier 2 capital ratio of at least 10 per cent, and a leverage ratio of at least 5 per cent, and not be subject to a directive, order, or written agreement to meet and maintain specific capital levels. These capital ratios are reported quarterly on the Call Report or Thrift Financial Report.

Regulatory Capital

In the Basel I accord bank capital was divided into two "tiers", each with some subdivisions.

Tier 1 (core) Capital

Tier 1 capital, the more important of the two, consists largely of shareholders' equity. This is the amount paid up to originally purchase the stock (or shares) of the Bank (not the amount those shares are currently trading for on the stock exchange), retained profits and subtracting accumulated losses. In simple terms, if the original stockholders contributed $100 to buy their stock and the Bank has made $10 in profits each year since, paid out no dividends and made no losses, after 10 years the Bank's tier one capital would be $200.

Regulators have since allowed several other instruments, other than common stock, to count in tier one capital. These instruments are unique to each national regulator, but are always close in nature to common stock. These are commonly referred to as upper tier one capital.

Tier 2 (Supplementary) Capital

There are several classifications of tier 2 capital, also known as supplementary capital. In the Basel I accord, these are categorised as undisclosed reserves, revaluation reserves, general provisions, hybrid instruments and subordinated term debt.

Undisclosed Reserves

Undisclosed reserves are not common, but are accepted by some regulators where a Bank has made a profit but this has not appeared in normal retained profits or in general reserves. Most of the regulators do not allow this type of reserve because it does not reflect a true and fair picture of the results.

Revaluation Reserves

A revaluation reserve is a reserve created when a company has an asset revalued and an increase in value is brought to account. A simple example may be where a Bank owns the land and building of its headquarters and bought them for $100 a century ago. A current revaluation is very likely to show a large increase in value. The increase would be added to a revaluation reserve.

General Provisions

A general provision is created when a company is aware that a loss may have occurred but is not sure of the exact nature of that loss. Under pre-IFRS accounting standards, general provisions were commonly created to provide for losses that were expected in the future. As these did not represent incurred losses, regulators tended to allow them to be counted as capital.

Hybrid Instruments

Hybrids are instruments that have some characteristics of both debt and shareholders' equity. Provided these are close to equity in nature, in that they are able to take losses on the face value without triggering a liquidation of the bank, they may be counted as capital.

Subordinated-term Debt

Subordinated-term debt is debt that is not redeemable (it cannot be called upon to be repaid) for a set (usually long) term and ranks lower than (it will only be paid out after) ordinary depositors of the bank.

Common Capital Ratios

- Tier 1 capital ratio = Tier 1 capital / Risk-adjusted assets >= 6 per cent.
- Total capital (Tier 1 and Tier 2) ratio = Total capital (Tier 1 and Tier 2) / Risk-adjusted assets >=10 per cent.
- Leverage ratio = Tier 1 capital / Average total consolidated assets >=5 per cent.
- Common stockholders' equity ratio = Common stockholders' equity / Balance sheet assets.

Example

Listed below are the capital ratios in Citigroup at the end of 2003:

Ratios

At year-end	*2003*
Tier 1 capital	8.91 %
Total capital (Tier 1 and Tier 2)	12.00%
Leverage [(1)]	5.56%
Common stockholders' equity	7.67%

(1) Tier 1 capital divided by adjusted average assets.

Components of Capital Under Regulatory Guidelines

In millions of dollars at year-end	*2003*
Tier 1 capital	
Common stockholders' equity	$96,889
Qualifying perpetual preferred stock	1,125
Qualifying mandatorily redeemable securities of subsidiary trusts	6,257
Minority interest	1,158
Less: Net unrealised gains on securities available-for-sale [(1)]	(2,908)
Accumulated net gains on cash flow hedges, net of tax (751) (1,242)	(751)
Intangible assets [(2)]	
Goodwill	(27,581)
Other disallowed intangible assets	(6,725)
50% investment in certain subsidiaries [(3)]	(45)
Other	(548)
Total Tier 1 capital	**66,871**
Tier 2 capital	
Allowance for credit losses [(4)]	9,545
Qualifying debt [(5)]	13,573
Unrealised marketable equity securities gains [(1)]	399
Less: 50% investment in certain subsidiaries [(3)]	(45)
Total Tier 2 capital	**23,472**
Total capital (Tier 1 and Tier 2)	**$90,343**
Risk-adjusted assets [(6)]	**$750,293**

(1) Tier 1 capital excludes unrealised gains and losses on debt securities available-for-sale in accordance with regulatory risk-based capital guidelines. The federal bank regulatory agencies permit institutions to include in Tier 2 capital up to 45 per cent of pre-tax net unrealised holding gains on

available-for-sale equity securities with readily determinable fair values. Institutions are required to deduct from Tier 1 capital net unrealised holding losses on available-for-sale equity securities with readily determinable fair values, net of tax.

(2) The increase in intangible assets is primarily due to the acquisition of the Sears credit card portfolio in November 2003.

(3) Represents unconsolidated banking and finance subsidiaries.

(4) Includable up to 1.25 per cent of risk-adjusted assets. Any excess allowance is deducted from risk-adjusted assets.

(5) Includes qualifying subordinated debt in an amount not exceeding 50 per cent of Tier 1 capital.

(6) Includes risk-weighted credit equivalent amounts, net of applicable bilateral netting agreements, of $39.1 billion for interest rate, commodity and equity derivative contracts and foreign exchange contracts, as of December 31, 2003, compared to $31.5 billion as of December 31, 2002. Market risk-equivalent assets included in risk-adjusted assets amounted to $40.6 billion and $30.6 billion at December 31, 2003 and 2002, respectively. Risk-adjusted assets also includes the effect of other "off-balance sheet" exposures such as unused loan commitments and "letters of credit" and reflects deductions for certain intangible assets and any excess allowance for credit losses.

Reserve Requirement

The reserve requirement (or required reserve ratio) is a bank regulation that sets the minimum reserves each bank must hold to customer deposits and notes. These reserves are designed to satisfy withdrawal demands, and would normally be in the form of fiat currency stored in a bank vault (vault cash), or with a central bank.

The reserve ratio is sometimes used as a tool in monetary policy, influencing the country's economy, borrowing, and interest rates. Western central banks rarely alter the reserve requirements because it would cause immediate liquidity problems for banks with low excess reserves; they prefer to use open market operations to implement their monetary policy.

The People's Bank of China does use changes in reserve requirements as an inflation-fighting tool, and raised the reserve requirement nine times in 2007. As of 2006, the required reserve ratio in the United States was 10 per cent on transaction deposits (component of money supply "M1"), and zero on time deposits and all other deposits.

An institution that holds reserves in excess of the required amount is said to hold excess reserves.

Effects on Money Supply

Reserve requirements affect the potential of the banking system to create transaction deposits. If the reserve requirement is 10 per cent, for example, a bank that receives a $100 deposit may lend out $90 of that deposit. If the borrower then writes a check to someone who deposits the $90, the bank receiving that deposit can lend out $81. As the process continues, the banking system can expand the change in excess reserves of $90 into a maximum of $1,000 of money ($100+$90+81+$72.90+...=$1,000), e.g. $100/0.10=$1,000. In contrast, with a 20 per cent reserve requirement, the banking system would be able to expand the initial $100 deposit into a maximum of ($100+$80+$64+$51.20+...=$500), e.g. $100/0.20=$500. Thus, higher reserve requirements should result in reduced money creation and, in turn, in reduced economic activity.

Reserve requirements apply only to transaction accounts, which are components of M1, a narrowly defined measure of money. Deposits that are components of M2 and M3 (but not M1), such as savings accounts and time deposits such as CDs, have no reserve requirements and therefore can expand without regard to reserve levels.

Furthermore, the Federal Reserve operates in a way that permits banks to acquire the reserves they need to meet their requirements from the money market, so long as they are willing to pay the prevailing price (the federal funds rate) for borrowed reserves. Consequently, reserve requirements currently play a relatively limited role in money creation in the United States.

Reserve Ratios

A *cash reserve ratio* (or CRR) is the percentage of bank reserves to deposits and notes. The cash reserve ratio is also known as the *cash asset ratio* or *liquidity ratio*. In the United States, the Board of Governors of the Federal Reserve System requires zero per cent fractional reserves from depository institutions having net transactions accounts of up to $9.3 million. Depository institutions having over $9.3 million, and up to $43.9 million in net transaction accounts must have fractional reserves totalling three per cent (3%) of that amount. Finally, depository institutions having over $43.9 million in net transaction accounts must have fractional reserves totalling ten per cent (10%) of that amount. However, under current policy, these numbers do not apply to time deposits from domestic corporations, or deposits from foreign corporations or governments, called "non-personal time deposits" and "euro-currency liabilities," respectively. For these account classes, the fractional reserve requirement is zero per cent regardless of net account value.

The Bank of England holds to a voluntary reserve ratio system. In 1998, the average cash reserve ratio across the entire United Kingdom banking system was 3.1 per cent. Other countries have required reserve ratios (or RRRs) that are statutorily enforced:

Country	*Required Reserve Ratio/%*	*Note*
Australia	None	
Canada	None	
Mexico	None	
New Zealand	None	
Sweden	None	
United Kingdom	None	
Eurozone	2.00	
Slovakia	2.00	
Switzerland	2.50	
Chile	4.50	
Pakistan	7.00	
Latvia	8.00	
India	7.50	Cut from 8.50%, effective from 2008-10-11

Contd...

Country	*Required Reserve Ratio/%*	*Note*
Burundi	8.50	
Hungary	8.75	
Ghana	9.00	
United States	10.00	
Sri Lanka	10.00	
Bulgaria	12.00	Raised from 8%, effective from 2007-01-09
China	17.50	Raised from 16.5%, effective from 2008-06-25
Estonia	15.00	
Zambia	17.50	
Croatia	19.00	
Tajikistan	20.00	
Suriname	35.00	
Jordan	80.00	

In some countries, the cash reserve ratios have decreased over time:

Country	*1968*	*1978*	*1988*	*1998*
United Kingdom	20.5	15.9	5.0	3.1
Turkey	58.3	62.7	30.8	18.0
Germany	19.0	19.3	17.2	11.9
United States	12.3	10.1	8.5	10.3

(Ratios are expressed in percentage points.)

Bank for International Settlements

The Bank for International Settlements (or BIS) is an international organisation of central banks which *"fosters international monetary and financial cooperation and serves as a bank for central banks."* The BIS carries out its work through subcommittees, the secretariats it hosts, and through its annual General Meeting of all members. It also provides banking services, but only to central banks, or to international organisations like itself. Based in Basel, Switzerland, the BIS was established by the Hague agreements of 1930. The name of the BIS in German: Bank fur Internationalen Zahlungsausgleich (BIZ), in French: Banque des Reglements Internationaux (BRI), in Italian: Banca dei Regolamenti Internazionali (BRI), in Spanish (not an official BIS language): Banco de Pagos Internacionales (BPI). It has representative offices in Hong Kong and Mexico City.

Organisation of Central Banks

As an organisation of central banks, the BIS seeks to make monetary policy more predictable and transparent among its 55 member central banks. While monetary policy is determined by each sovereign nation, it is subject to central and private banking scrutiny and potentially to speculation that affects foreign exchange rates and especially the fate of export economies. Failures to keep monetary policy in line with reality and make monetary reforms in time, preferably as a simultaneous policy among all 55 member banks and also involving the International Monetary Fund, have historically led to losses in the billions as banks try to maintain a policy using open market methods that have proven to be unrealistic. Central banks do not unilaterally "set" rates, rather they set goals and intervene using their massive financial resources and regulatory powers to achieve monetary targets they set. One reason to coordinate policy closely is to ensure that this does not become too expensive and that opportunities for private arbitrage exploiting shifts in policy or difference in policy, are rare and quickly removed.

Two aspects of monetary policy have proven to be particularly sensitive, and the BIS therefore has two specific goals: to regulate capital adequacy and make reserve requirements transparent.

Regulates Capital Adequacy

Capital adequacy policy applies to equity and capital assets. These can be overvalued in many circumstances. Accordingly the BIS requires bank capital/asset ratio to be above a prescribed minimum international standard, for the protection of all central banks involved. The BIS' main role is in setting capital adequacy requirements. From an international point of view, ensuring capital adequacy is the most important problem between central banks, as speculative lending based on inadequate underlying capital and widely varying liability rules causes economic crises as "bad money drives out good" (Gresham's Law).

Encourages Reserve Transparency

Reserve policy is also important, especially to consumers and the domestic economy. To insure liquidity and limit liability to the larger economy, banks cannot create money in specific industries or regions without limit. To make bank depositing and borrowing safer for customers and reduce risk of bank runs, banks are required to set aside or "reserve".

Reserve policy is harder to standardise as it depends on local conditions and is often fine-tuned to make industry-specific or region-specific changes, especially within large developing nations. For instance, the People's Bank of China requires urban banks to hold 7 per cent reserves while letting rural banks continue to hold only 6 per cent, and simultaneously telling all banks that reserve requirements on certain overheated industries would rise sharply or penalties would be laid if investments in them did not stop completely.

The PBoC is thus unusual in acting as a national bank, focused on the country not on the currency, but its desire to control asset inflation is increasingly shared among BIS members who fear "bubbles", and among exporting countries that find it difficult to manage the diverse requirements of the domestic economy, especially rural agriculture, and an export economy, especially in manufactured goods. Effectively, the PBoC sets different reserve levels for domestic and export styles of development. Historically, the US also did this, by dividing federal monetary management into nine regions, in which the less-developed Western US had looser policies.

For various reasons it has become quite difficult to accurately assess reserves on more than simple loan instruments, and this plus the regional differences has tended to discourage standardising any reserve rules at the global BIS scale. Historically, the BIS did set some standards which favoured lending money to private landowners (at about 5 to 1) and for-profit corporations (at about 2 to 1) over loans to individuals. These distinctions reflecting classical economics were superseded by policies relying on undifferentiated market values – more in line with neoclassical economics.

Tier 1 vs. Total Capital

The BIS sets "requirements on two categories of capital, Tier 1 capital and Total capital. Tier 1 capital is the book value of its stock plus retained earnings. Tier 2 capital is loan-loss reserves plus subordinated debt. Total capital is the sum of Tier 1 and Tier 2 capital. Tier 1 capital must be at least 4 per cent of total risk-weighted assets. Total capital must be at least 8 per cent of total risk-weighted assets. When a bank creates a deposit to fund a loan, its assets and liabilities increase equally, with no increase in equity. That causes its capital ratio to drop. Thus the capital requirement limits the total amount of credit that a bank may issue. It is important to note that the capital requirement applies to assets while the bank reserve requirement applies to liabilities.

Goal: a Financial Safety Net

The relatively narrow role the BIS plays today does not reflect its ambitions or historical role.

A "well-designed financial safety net, supported by strong prudential regulation and supervision, effective laws that are enforced, and sound accounting and disclosure regimes," are among the Bank's goals. In fact they have been in its mandate since its founding in 1930 as a means to enforce the Treaty of Versailles.

The BIS has historically had less power to enforce this "safety net" than it deems necessary. Former head Andrew Crockett had bemoaned its inability to "hardwire the credit culture," despite many specific attempts to address specific concerns such as the growth of Offshore Financial Centres (OFCs), Highly Leveraged Institutions (HLIs), Large and Complex Financial Institutions (LCFIs), deposit insurance and especially the spread of money laundering and accounting scandals.

History: Despite its recent history of taking a narrow central bank mediation role, the BIS was originally formed to facilitate money transfers arising from settling an obligation arising from a peace treaty. After World War I, the need for the bank was suggested in 1929 by the Young Committee, as a means of transfer for German reparations payments. The plan was agreed in August of that year at a conference at the Hague, and a charter for the bank was drafted at the International Bankers Conference at Baden

Baden in November. The charter was adopted at a second Hague Conference on January 20, 1930.

The BIS was originally owned by both the governments and private individuals, since the United States and France had decided to sell some of their shares to private investors. BIS shares traded on stock markets, which made the bank a unique organisation: an international organisation (in the technical sense of public international law), yet with private shareholders. Many central banks had similarly started as such private institutions, for example the Bank of England was privately owned until 1946. In more recent years the BIS has forcibly bought back all shares held by private investors, and is now wholly owned by its member central banks.

Since 2004, the BIS has published its accounts in terms of Special Drawing Rights, or SDRs, replacing the Gold Franc as the bank's unit of account. As of March 31, 2007, the bank had total assets of US $409.15 billion, given a dollar/SDR exchange rate of 1.51 for March 30, 2007. Included in that total were 150 tonnes of fine gold.

Role in Banking Supervision

The BIS provides the Basel Committee on Banking Supervision with its twelve-member secretariat, and with it has played a central role in establishing the Basel Capital Accords of 1988 and 2004. There remain significant differences between US, EU and UN officials regarding the degree of capital adequacy and reserve controls that global banking now requires. Put extremely simply, the US as of 2006 favoured strong strict central controls in the spirit of the original 1988 accords, the EU was more inclined to a distributed system managed collectively with a committee able to approve some exceptions. The UN agencies especially ICLEI are firmly committed to fundamental risk measures: the so-called triple bottom line and were becoming critical of central banking as an institutional structure for ignoring fundamental risks in favour of technical risk management.

Criticism

The UN agencies are echoing a broader complaint. It has been argued by numerous critics of capitalism, including George Soros, that there is no current will to enforce any significant regulation in the present competitive financial industry. In this situation, nations effectively compete to offer less regulation.

Asserting that a stronger role for the BIS is a necessary hedge against the ideology prevailing at the International Monetary Fund, stick reserve and capital discipline are based on a non-ideological analysis of fundamental liabilities. To prevent disastrous cases like the IMF, the BIS must rationally and scientifically assess risk in order to prevent load disbursement from passing development policy trends.

Other doubts about the BIS's mandate, its programme, its effectiveness, and the desirability of any existing institution taking the lead role in accounting reform, especially in light of serious failures of money laundering law enforcement, major breaches of prudence and supervision in the United States (e.g. Enron), have led to some minor critique of the BIS in the anti-capitalism and anti-globalisation movements. This is incidental usually to critiques of the IMF and World Bank, whose role is far more visible, and which have far more discretion in their policy.

The BIS is also a frequent target of allegations by conspiracy theorists, many of whom portray it as a front organisation through which a wealthy elite controls the world. Some argue that the bank has not helped matters through a culture of secretiveness, and that lack of information always encourages some people to imagine what they do not know.

Basel Committee on Banking Supervision

The Basel Committee on Banking Supervision is an institution created by the Central Bank Governors of the Group of Ten nations. It was created in 1974 and meets regularly four times a year.

Its membership is now composed of senior representatives of bank supervisory authorities and central banks from the G-10 countries (Belgium, Canada, France, Germany, Italy, Japan, the Netherlands, Sweden, Switzerland, the United Kingdom and the United States), and representatives from Luxembourg and Spain. It usually meets at the Bank for International Settlements in Basel, where its 12 member permanent Secretariat is located.

The Basel Committee formulates broad supervisory standards and guidelines and recommends statements of best practice in banking supervision in the expectation that member authorities and other nations' authorities will take steps to implement them through their own national systems, whether in statutory form or otherwise.

The purpose of the committee is to encourage convergence towards common approaches and standards. Dieter Kerwer reports that, "the BCBS is not a classical multilateral organisation. It has no founding treaty, and it does not issue binding regulation. Rather, its main function is to act as an informal forum to find policy solutions and to promulgate standards".

Basel Accord

The Basel Accord(s) or Basle Accord(s) refers to the banking supervision Accords (recommendations on banking laws and regulations), Basel I and Basel II issued by the Basel Committee on Banking Supervision (BCBS). They are called the Basel Accords as the BCBS maintains its secretariat at the Bank of International Settlements in Basel, Switzerland and the committee normally meets there.

The Basel Committee: The Basel Committee consists of representatives from central banks and regulatory authorities of the Group of Ten (economic) countries, plus others (specifically Luxembourg and Spain). The committee does not have the authority to enforce recommendations, although most member countries (and others) tend to implement the Committee's policies. This means that recommendations are enforced through national (or EU-wide) laws and regulations, rather than as a result of the committee's recommendations — thus sometime may pass between recommendations and implementation as law at the national level.

Spelling

The Basel Committee is named after the Swiss town of Basel. In early publications, the committee sometimes used the English spelling "Basle" or the French spelling "Bale," names that are sometimes still used in the press. More recently, the Committee has deferred to the predominantly German population of the region and used the spelling "Basel."

Banknotes

Banknote (often known as a bill, paper money or simply a note) is a kind of negotiable instrument, a promissory note made by a bank payable to the bearer on demand, used as money, and in many jurisdictions is legal tender. Along with coins, banknotes make up the cash or bearer forms of all modern money. With the exception of non-circulating high-value or precious metal commemorative issues, coins are generally used for lower valued monetary units, while banknotes are used for higher values.

Advantages

Originally, precious and semi-precious metals were formed into coins and were used to negotiate and settle trades. Banknotes offer an alternative bearer form of money, but the advantages and disadvantages between the two forms of bearer money are complex and so in different circumstances the overall advantage can lie with either form.

The costs of using bearer money include:

1. *Manufacturing or Issue Costs:* Coins are produced by industrial manufacturing methods that process the precious or semi-precious metals, and require additions of alloy for hardness and wear resistance. By contrast bank notes are printed paper (or polymer), and typically have a lower cost of issue, especially in larger denominations, compared to coin of the same value.
2. *Wear Costs:* Coins wear and lose mass over their economic life, and eventually are scrapped. Banknotes do not lose economic value by wear, since, even if they are in poor condition, they are still a legally valid claim on the issuing bank. However, banks of issue do have to pay the cost of replacing banknotes in poor condition.
3. *Opportunity Cost of Capital:* Coins have economic value and are a form of non-financial capital, however they do not pay interest. Banknotes have economic value but are a form of financial capital, a loan to the issuing bank. The issuing bank invests its assets primarily in interest bearing loans and securities, but also needs to hold metallic reserves. Thus banknotes indirectly earn interest through the investments

made by the issuing bank, but coins do not pay interest to anyone. This foregone interest is the most important economic advantage of banknotes over coins.

4. *Cost of Transport:* Coins can be expensive to transport for high value transactions, but banknotes can be issued in large denominations that are lighter than the equivalent value in coins.
5. *Cost of Acceptance:* Coins can be checked for authenticity by weighing and other forms of examination and testing. These costs can be significant, but good quality coin design and manufacturing can help reduce these costs. Banknotes also have an acceptance cost, the costs of checking the banknote's security features and confirming acceptability of the issuing bank.

The different advantages and disadvantages between coins and banknotes imply that there may be an ongoing role for both forms of bearer money, each being used where its advantages outweigh its disadvantages.

Convertibility

The ability to exchange a note for some other kind of value is called "convertibility". For example a US silver certificate was "payable in silver on demand" from the treasury until 1965. If a note is payable on demand for a fixed unit, it is said to be fully convertible to that unit. Limited convertibility occurs when there are restrictions in the time, place, manner or amount of exchange.

A common misconception is that a bank note that is inconvertible is necessarily unbacked (so-called "fiat money"). Most of the confusion centres around the failure to distinguish between two types of convertibility:

1. Physical convertibility, where a unit of currency can be exchanged at the issuing bank for a given physical amount of something; and
2. Financial convertibility, where a unit of currency can be exchanged at the issuing bank for a unit's worth of the bank's assets.

The importance of financial convertibility can be seen by imagining that people in a community one day find themselves with more paper currency than they wish to hold – for example, when the main shopping season has ended. If the paper currency is physically convertible (for one ounce of silver, let us suppose), people will return the unwanted paper currency to the bank in exchange for silver, but the bank could head off this demand for silver by selling some of its own bonds to the public in exchange for its own paper currency. For example, if the community has 100 units of unwanted paper money, and if people intend to redeem the unwanted 100 units for silver at the bank, the bank could simply sell 100 units worth of bonds or other assets in exchange for 100 units of its own paper currency. This will soak up the unwanted paper and head off people's desire to redeem the 100 units for silver.

Thus, by conducting this type of open market operation – selling bonds when there is excess currency and buying bonds when there is too little – the bank can maintain the value of the paper currency at one ounce of silver without ever redeeming any paper currency for silver. In fact, this is essentially what all modern central banks do, and the fact that their currencies might be physically inconvertible is made irrelevant by the maintenance of financial convertibility. Note that financial convertibility cannot be maintained unless the bank has sufficient assets to back the currency it has issued. Thus, it is an illusion that any physically inconvertible currency is necessarily also unbacked.

History: Paper money originated in two forms: drafts, which are receipts for value held on account, and "bills", which were issued with a promise to convert at a later date.

Money is based on the coming to pre-eminence of some commodity as payment. The oldest monetary basis was for agricultural capital: cattle and grain. In Ancient Mesopotamia, drafts were issued against stored grain as a unit of account. A "drachma" was a weight of grain. Japan's feudal system was based on rice per year - koku.

At the same time, legal codes enforced the payment for injury in a standardised form, usually in precious metals. The development of money then comes from the role of agricultural capital and precious metals having a privileged place in the economy.

Such drafts were used for giro systems of banking as early as Ptolemaic Egypt in the first century BC.

The perception of banknotes as money has evolved over time. Originally, money was based on precious metals. Banknotes were seen as essentially an I.O.U. or promissory note: a promise to pay someone in precious metal on presentation. With the gradual removal of precious metals from the monetary system, banknotes evolved to represent credit money, or (if backed by the credit of a government) also fiat money.

First Banknotes in the World

The use of paper money as a circulating medium is intimately related to shortages of metal for coins. In ancient China coins were circular with a rectangular hole in the middle. Several coins could be strung together on a rope. Merchants in China, if they became rich enough, found that their strings of coins were too heavy to carry around easily. To solve this problem, coins were often left with a trustworthy person, and the merchant was given a slip of paper recording how much money he had with that person. If he showed the paper to that person he could regain his money. Eventually from this paper money "jiaozi" originated.

In the 600s, there were local issues of paper currency in China and by 960 the Song Dynasty, short of copper for striking coins, issued the first generally circulating notes. A note is a promise to redeem later for some other object of value, usually specie. The issue of credit notes is often for a limited duration, and at some discount to the promised amount later. The jiaozi nevertheless did not replace coins during the Song Dynasty; paper money was used alongside the coins.

The successive Yuan Dynasty was the first dynasty in China to use paper currency as the predominant circulating medium. The founder of the Yuan Dynasty, Kublai Khan, issued paper money known as Chao in his reign. The original notes during the Yuan Dynasty were restricted in area and duration as in the Song Dynasty, but in the later course of the dynasty, facing massive shortages of specie to fund their ruling in China, began printing paper money without restrictions on duration. By 1455, in an effort to rein in economic expansion and end hyperinflation, the new Ming Dynasty ended paper money, and closed much of Chinese trade.

Ming Dynasty notes are the earliest surviving paper money, of which the 1 Kuan is the most common. The note, 220 mm × 340 mm, is also one of the world's largest banknotes.

Banknotes in Europe

In Europe, the first paper money consisted of paper 'coins' issued in Protestant Leyden (today, Leiden) in the Netherlands during the Spanish siege of 1574. Over 5000 of the estimated 14,000 residents of Leyden died, mostly due to starvation. Even leather (often used to create emergency currency) was boiled and used to feed the people. So to create currency, the residents took covers and paper from hymnals and church missives and created paper planchets, which were struck using the same dies that were previously used to mint coins.

The first proper European banknotes were issued by Stockholms Banco, a predecessor of the Bank of Sweden, in 1660, although the bank ran out of coins to redeem its notes in 1664 and ceased operating in that year.

Until Louis XIV, banknotes were issued by small creditors, had limited circulation, and were not backed by the authority of the state. Economist John Law helped establish banknotes as formal currency, backed by capital consisting of French government bills and government accepted notes.

Banknotes in the Americas

Emergency paper money handwritten on playing cards was used in French Canada from 1685.

In the early-1690s, the Massachusetts Bay Colony was the first of the colonies to issue permanently circulating banknotes. The use of fixed denominations and printed banknotes came into use in the 18th century.

In the early-1700s, each of the thirteen colonies issued their own banknotes (colonial currency). Later, the Continental Congress issued continental currency to support the revolutionary war. The United States government did not print banknotes until 1862. However, almost immediately after adoption of the Constitution in 1789, Congress chartered the first Bank of the United States and authorised it to issue banknotes. The bank served as quasi central bank of the United States.

The bank closed in 1811 when Congress failed to renew its charter. In 1816, Congress chartered the second Bank of the United States. When its charter expired in 1836, the bank continue to operate under a charter granted by the Commonwealth of Pennsylvania until 1841.

In the United States, public acceptance of banknotes in replacement of precious metals was hastened in part by Executive Order 6102 in 1933. This order carried the threat of a maximum $10,000 fine and a maximum of ten years in prison for anyone who kept more than $100 of gold in preference to banknotes.

Issue of Banknotes

Generally, a central bank or treasury is solely responsible within a state or currency union for the issue of banknotes. However, this is not always the case, and historically the paper currency of countries was often handled entirely by private banks. Thus, many different banks or institutions may have issued banknotes in a given country.

In a small number of countries, private banknote issue continues to this day. For example, by virtue of the complex constitutional setup in the United Kingdom, certain commercial banks in two of the union's four constituent countries (Scotland and Northern Ireland) continue to print their own banknotes for domestic circulation, even though they are not fiat money or declared in law as legal tender anywhere. The UK's central bank, the Bank of England, prints notes which are legal tender in England and Wales; these notes are also usable as money (but not legal tender) in the rest of the UK.

In Hong Kong, three commercial banks are licensed to issue Hong Kong dollar notes. As well as commercial issuers, other organisations may have note-issuing powers; for example, until 2002 the Singapore dollar was issued by the Board of Commissioners of Currency Singapore, a government agency which was later taken over by the Monetary Authority of Singapore.

Paper Banknotes

Most banknotes are made of dense 80 to 90 grams per square metre starch paper, sometimes mixed with linen, abaca, or other textile fibres. Generally, the paper used is different from ordinary paper: it is much more resilient, resists wear and tear, and also does not contain the usual agents that make ordinary paper glow slightly under ultraviolet light.

Early Chinese banknotes were printed on paper made of mulberry bark and this fibre is used in Japanese banknote paper today.

Unlike most printing and writing paper, banknote paper is impregnated with polyvinyl alcohol or gelatin to give it extra strength.

Most banknotes are made using the mould made process in which a watermark and thread is incorporated during the paper forming process.

The thread is a simple looking security component found in most banknotes. It is, however, often rather complex in construction comprising fluorescent, magnetic, metallic and micro print elements. By combining it with watermarking technology the thread can be made to surface periodically on one side only. This is known as windowed thread and further increases the counterfeit resistance of the banknote paper. This process was invented by Portals, part of the De La Rue group in the UK.

Recently this company has introduced many new features to the banknote world including Cornerstone, Platinum and Optiks, all registered trade marks of De La Rue. Cornerstone uses watermarking to reduce the number of corner folds by strengthening this part of the note. Platinum is a special coating to reduce the dirt picked up by banknotes. Optiks is a new thread based security feature that creates a plastic window in the paper which is very hard to copy.

Durable Banknote Papers

Banknote paper with enhanced durability is a recent development, designed to meet the growing need for popular low-denomination banknotes to withstand extreme wear.

Improved Protection Against Dirt: Manufacturers of banknote paper were quick to recognise the problems associated with dirt and developed a special paper with a thin layer of varnish on the surface to repel soiling. This layer is applied directly to the substrate. The thickness and structure of the paper remain unchanged, thereby preserving the natural feel. The so-called Durable Banknote Papers, which are available in the global banknote market under brand names, such as *Long Life, Platinum, Marathon Coated, Diamone,* and *Flesure,* protect banknotes from soiling and environmental incluences, making it possible for them to remain in circulation for longer.

Increased Mechanical Stability: With new products, such as *Synthec* and *Diamone Composite,* banknote manufacturers have gone a step further and responded to the growing demand for higher mechanical stability of the paper—because the longer a banknote stays in circulation, the limper it becomes and the more easily it tears. *Synthec* substrate, for example, consists of 80 per cent cotton fibre and 20 per cent synthetic fibre, with the latter being longer and more flexible than the former. The synthetic fibres constitute a dense network within the cotton fibre structure, supporting the banknote like a kind of corset and increasing its mechanical stability. This practically doubles the useful life of the product. *Synthec* is much less sensitive to climate fluctuations than standard banknote paper. The synthetic fibres are incorporated in the banknote substrate at the sheet formation stage.

This has the advantage that all established security features—such as three dimensional watermarks, fluorescent fibres, security threads, or the innovative new *varifeye* see-through window—can be integrated into the new *Synthec* substrate, just as they would be with the standard cotton substrate. Optically variable effect inks and foil elements, such as holograms, can be applied to this substrate in the same way as with traditional banknote paper. Public confidence in the established security features, built up over decades, remains intact. To ensure that the banknotes are also protected against dirt, they are given a standard coating of varnish. By the end of 2007, *Synthec* banknotes were circulating in three countries, including an African country with different climate zones that has chosen *Synthec* as a substrate for its lowest-denomination note. In the south of the country conditions are tropical, with a rainy season that lasts for eight months, while the north is very arid and extremely hot, with temperatures reaching 41 degrees Celsius.

Counterfeiting and Security Measures on Paper Banknotes

The ease with which paper money can be created, by both legitimate authorities and counterfeiters, has led both to a temptation in times of crisis such as war or revolution to produce paper money which was not supported by precious metal or other goods, thus leading to hyperinflation and a loss of faith in the value of paper money, e.g. the Continental Currency produced by the Continental Congress during the American Revolution, the Assignats produced during the French Revolution, the paper currency produced by the Confederate States of America and the Individual States of the Confederate States of America, the financing of the First World War by the Central Powers (by 1922 1 gold Austro-Hungarian krone of 1914 was worth 14,400 paper Kronen), the devaluation of the Yugoslav Dinar in the 1990s, etc. Banknotes may also be overprinted to reflect political changes that occur faster than new currency can be printed.

In 1988, Austria produced the 5,000 Schilling banknote (Mozart), which is the first foil application (Kinegram) to a paper banknote in the history of banknote printing. The application of optical features is now in common use throughout the world.

Many countries' banknotes now have embedded holograms.

Polymer Banknotes

In 1983, Costa Rica and Haiti issued the first Tyvek and the Isle of Man issued the first Bradvek polymer (or plastic) banknotes; these were printed by the American Banknote Company and developed by DuPont. In 1988, after significant research and development by the Commonwealth Scientific and Industrial Research Organisation (CSIRO) and the Reserve Bank of Australia, Australia produced the first polymer banknote made from biaxially-oriented polypropylene (plastic), and in 1996 became the first country to have a full set of circulating polymer banknotes of all denominations. Since then, other countries to adopt circulating polymer banknotes include Bangladesh, Brazil, Brunei, Chile, Indonesia, Israel, Malaysia, Mexico, Nepal, New Zealand, Papua and New Guinea, Romania, Singapore, the Solomon Islands, Sri Lanka, Thailand, Vietnam, Western Samoa and Zambia, with other countries issuing commemorative polymer notes, including China, Kuwait, the Northern Bank of Northern Ireland, Taiwan. Other countries indicating plans to issue polymer banknotes include Nigeria. In 2005, Bulgaria issued the world's first hybrid paper-polymer banknote.

Polymer banknotes were developed to improve durability and prevent counterfeiting through incorporated security features, such as optically variable devices that are extremely difficult to reproduce.

The uptake of polymer banknotes has been strong with over 28 countries on all continents now using this innovative material. With strong durability and a high degree of security, polymer notes are becoming extremely popular. Countries such as Vietnam, Brunei, New Zealand, Papua New Guinea and Romania have all their circulating banknotes on polymer.

Other Materials

Over the years, a number of materials other than paper have been used to print banknotes. This includes various textiles, including silk, and materials such as leather.

Silk and other fibres have been commonly used in the manufacture of various banknote papers, intended to provide both additional durability and security. Crane and Company patented banknote paper with embedded silk threads in 1844 and has supplied paper to the United States Treasury since 1879. Banknotes printed on pure silk "paper" include "emergency money" (*Notgeld*) issues from a number of German towns in 1923 during a period of fiscal crisis and hyperinflation. Most notoriously, Bielefeld produced a number of silk, leather, velvet, linen and wood issues, and although these issues were produced primarily for collectors, rather than for circulation, they are in demand by collectors. Banknotes printed on cloth include a number of Communist Revolutionary issues in China from areas such as Xinjiang, or Sinkiang, in the United Islamic Republic of East

Turkestan in 1933. Emergency money was also printed in 1902 on khaki shirt fabric during the Boer War.

Leather banknotes (or coins) were issued in a number of sieges, as well as in other times of emergency. During the Russian administration of Alaska, banknotes were printed on sealskin. A number of 19th century issues are known in Germanic and Baltic states, including the towns of Dorpat, Pernau, Reval, Werro and Woisek. In addition to the Bielefeld issues, other German leather Notgeld from 1923 is known from Borna, Osterwieck, Paderborn and Posneck.

Other issues from 1923 were printed on wood, which was also used in Canada in 1763-1764 during Pontiac's Rebellion, and by the Hudson's Bay Company. In 1848, in Bohemia, wooden checkerboard pieces were used as money.

Even playing cards were used for currency in France in the early-19th century, and in French Canada from 1685 until 1757, in the Isle of Man in the beginning of the 19th century, and again in Germany after World War I.

Vending Machines and Banknotes

People are not the only economic actors who are required to accept banknotes. In the late twentieth century machines were designed to recognise banknotes of the smaller values long after they were designed to recognise coins distinct from slugs. This capability has become inescapable in economies where inflation has not been followed by introduction of progressively larger coin denominations (such as the United States, where several attempts to introduce dollar coins in general circulation have largely failed). The existing infrastructure of such machines presents one of the difficulties in changing the design of these banknotes to make them less counterfeitable, that is, by adding additional features so easily discernible by people that they would immediately reject banknotes of inferior quality, for every machine in the country would have to be updated.

Destruction

Banknotes have a limited lifetime, after which they are collected for destruction, usually recycling or shredding. A banknote is removed from the money supply by banks or other financial institutions due to everyday wear and tear from its handling. Banknote bundles are passed through a sorting machine that determines whether a particular note needs to be shredded, or are removed from the supply chain by a human inspector if they are deemed unfit for continued use – for example, if they are mutilated or torn. Counterfeit banknotes are destroyed unless they are needed for evidentiary or forensic purposes.

Contaminated banknotes are also decommissioned. A Canadian government report indicates:

> "Types of contaminants include: notes found on a corpse, stagnant water, contaminated by human or animal body fluids such as urine, feces, vomit, infectious blood, fine hazardous powders from detonated explosives, dye pack and/or drugs..."

These are removed from circulation primarily to prevent the spread of diseases.

When taken out of circulation, Australian bank notes are melted down and mixed together to form plastic garbage bins.

Paper Money Collecting as a Hobby

Banknote collecting, or Notaphily, is a rapidly growing area of numismatics. Although generally not as widespread as coin and stamp collecting, the hobby is increasingly expanding. Prior to the 1990s, currency collecting was a relatively small adjunct to coin collecting, but the practice of currency auctions, combined with larger public awareness of paper money have caused a boom in interest and values of rare banknotes.

In the 1950s, Robert Friedberg published the landmark book *Paper Money of the United States*. Friedberg devised an organising number system of all types of US banknotes; the system is widely accepted among collectors and dealers to this day, and the volume has been regularly updated.

Another pioneer of cataloguing banknotes was Albert Pick, a well-known German notaphilist (born 15 May 1922 in Cologne) who published a number of catalogues of European paper money, and, in 1974, the first *Standard Catalogue of World Paper Money*. His collection of over 180,000 banknotes was eventually housed at the

Bavarian Mortgages and Exchange Bank (Bayerischen Hypotheken-und Wechselbank, now HypoVereinsbank). This catalogue underwent several incarnations, and currently is published as a three volume group. Volume I, called Specialised Issues, includes notes issued by local authorities, which circulated in a limited area. Volume II called General Issues covers notes issued on a national scope, dated 1368 through 1960. Volume III covers Modern Issues dated 1960 to present. Each of the volumes is updated regularly, with Volume III now updated every year, Volumes I and II every 3 or so years. While Pick no longer edits the catalogues (since 1994 the honour has passed to George S. Cuhaj), the catalogues are still commonly referred to as 'Pick Catalogues' and dealers and collectors alike refer to banknotes by their 'Pick number.' Current issues of the three volumes include:

- *Standard Catalogue of World Paper Money:* Specialised Issues (10th Ed. Vol. 1) by George S. Cuhaj. Paperback – 1200 pages. (January 2006).
- *Standard Catalogue of World Paper Money:* General Issues to 1368-1960 (11th Ed. Vol. 2) by George S. Cuhaj (Editor). (December 2006).
- *Standard Catalogue of World Paper Money:* Modern Issues, 1961-present (14th Ed. Vol. 3) by George S. Cuhaj. (June 2008).

For years, the mode of collecting banknotes was through a handful of mail order dealers who issued price lists and catalogues. In the early-1990s, it became more common for rare notes to be sold at various coin and currency shows via auction. The illustrated catalogues and "event nature" of the auction practice seemed to fuel a sharp rise in overall awareness of paper money in the numismatic community. Entire advanced collections are often sold at one time, and to this day single auctions can generate well in excess of $1 million dollars in gross sales. Today, eBay has surpassed auctions in terms of highest volume of sales of banknotes. However, as of 2005, rare banknotes still sell for much less than comparable rare coins. There is wide consensus in the paper money collecting arena that this disparity is diminishing as paper money prices continue to rise at a rapid rate.

There are many different organisations and societies around the world for the hobby including the International Bank Note Society (IBNS).

Financial Prospectus

A prospectus is a legal document that institutions and businesses use to describe the securities they are offering for participants and buyers. A prospectus commonly provides investors with material information about mutual funds, stocks, bonds and other investments, such as a description of the company's business, financial statements, biographies of officers and directors, detailed information about their compensation, any litigation that is taking place, a list of material properties and any other material information. In the context of an individual securities offering, such as an initial public offering, a prospectus is distributed by underwriters or brokerages to potential investors.

United States

In a securities offering in the United States, a prospectus is required to be filed with the Securities and Exchange Commission (SEC) as part of a registration statement. The issuer may not use the prospectus to finalise sales until the registration statement has been declared effective by the SEC, meaning it appears to comply on its face with the various rules governing disclosure.

If a company has been filing periodic reports like the Form 10-K with the SEC for a certain period of time, has a market capitalisation above a certain threshold and takes certain procedural steps, it is permitted to offer securities using a simplified prospectus that incorporates information by reference to its SEC filings. In certain situations, such as when the offering is not required to be registered with the SEC, a prospectus is instead referred to as an "offering memorandum" or "offering circular." In the case of municipal securities offerings, which are generally exempt from most of the federal securities laws, municipal issuers typically prepare an analogous form of disclosure document known as an "official statement." Prospectuses are generally prepared with the assistance of the underwriter acting as issue manager (also called a *bookrunning manager*). They also explain the Assets and Liabilities.

United Kingdom

Publication of information in relation to the issue of securities in the United Kingdom is governed by the Prospectus Rules, which implement the European law Prospectus Directive. A prospectus must be published where certain types of securities either are offered to the public or are requested for admission on a regulated market. In the United Kingdom, the only regulated market is London Stock Exchange full list. The Alternative Investment Market (AIM) does not constitute a regulated market, nor does the Professional Securities Market (PSM) for issues of debt securities. There are numerous exceptions to the requirement to publish a prospectus, although an exempt company may still be required to publish listing particulars where it is seeking admission of its shares to the full list or an admission document where it is seeking admission of its shares to AIM.

The prospectus must be approved by the competent authority in the United Kingdom, which is currently the Financial Services Authority in its capacity as the United Kingdom Listing Authority. If the purpose of the prospectus is to induce people to engage in an investment activity, it will also need to be issued or approved by an 'authorised person', or it will constitute an unlawful financial promotion under section 21 of the Financial Services and Markets Act 2000.

Credit Rating Agency

A credit rating agency (CRA) is a company that assigns credit ratings for issuers of certain types of debt obligations as well as the debt instruments themselves. In some cases, the servicers of the underlying debt are also given ratings. In most cases, the issuers of securities are companies, special purpose entities, state and local governments, non-profit organisations, or national governments issuing debt-like securities (i.e. bonds) that can be traded on a secondary market. A credit rating for an issuer takes into consideration the issuer's credit worthiness (i.e. its ability to pay back a loan), and affects the interest rate applied to the particular security being issued. (In contrast to CRAs, a company that issues credit scores for individual credit-worthiness is generally called a *credit bureau* or *consumer credit reporting agency*).

Credit Rating Agencies for Corporations and Government Entities

Agencies that assign credit ratings for corporations include:

- A. M. Best (US).
- Baycorp Advantage (Australia).
- Dominion Bond Rating Service (Canada).
- Fitch Ratings (US).
- Japan Credit Rating Agency (Japan).
- Malaysian Rating Corporation (Malaysia).
- Moody's (US).
- Standard and Poor's (US).
- Pacific Credit Rating (Peru).
- Rating Agency Malaysia (Malaysia).
- Egan-Jones Ratings Company (US).
- Capital Intelligence Ltd. (Cyprus).

Uses of Ratings

Credit ratings are used by investors, issuers, investment banks, broker-dealers, and governments. For investors, credit rating agencies increase the range of investment alternatives and provide independent, easy-to-use measurements of relative credit risk; this generally increases the efficiency of the market, lowering costs for both borrowers and lenders. This in turn increases the total supply of risk capital in the economy, leading to stronger growth. It also opens the capital markets to categories of borrower who might otherwise be shut out altogether: small governments, start-up companies, hospitals, and universities.

Ratings Use by Bond Issuers

Issuers rely on credit ratings as an independent verification of their own credit-worthiness and the resultant value of the instruments they issue. In most cases, a significant bond issuance must have at least one rating from a respected CRA for the issuance to be successful (without such a rating, the issuance may be undersubscribed or the price offered by investors too low for the issuer's purposes). Studies by the Bond Market Association note that many institutional investors now prefer that a debt issuance have at least three ratings.

Issuers also use credit ratings in certain structured finance transactions. For example, a company with a very high credit rating wishing to undertake a particularly risky research project could create a legally separate entity with certain assets that would own and conduct the research work. This "special purpose entity" would then assume all of the research risk and issue its own debt securities to finance the research. The SPE's credit rating likely would be very low, and the issuer would have to pay a high rate of return on the bonds issued. However, this risk would not lower the parent company's overall credit rating because the SPE would be a legally separate entity. Conversely, a company with a low credit rating might be able to borrow on better terms if it were to form an SPE and transfer significant assets to that subsidiary and issue secured debt securities. That way, if the venture were to fail, the lenders would have recourse to the assets owned by the SPE. This would lower the interest rate the SPE would need to pay as part of the debt offering.

The same issuer also may have different credit ratings for different bonds. This difference results from the bond's structure, how it is secured, and the degree to which the bond is subordinated to other debt. Many larger CRAs offer "credit rating advisory services" that essentially advise an issuer on how to structure its bond offerings and SPEs so as to achieve a given credit rating for a certain debt tranche. This creates a potential conflict of interest, of course, as the CRA may feel obligated to provide the issuer with that given rating if the issuer followed its advice on structuring the offering. Some CRAs avoid this conflict by refusing to rate debt offerings for which its advisory services were sought.

Ratings Use by Investment Banks and Broker-dealers

Investment banks and broker-dealers also use credit ratings in calculating their own risk portfolios (i.e. the collective risk of all of their investments). Larger banks and broker-dealers conduct their own risk calculations, but rely on CRA ratings as a "check" (and double-check or triple-check) against their own analyses.

Ratings Use by Government Regulators

Regulators use credit ratings as well, or permit ratings to be used for regulatory purposes. For example, under the Basel II agreement of the Basel Committee on Banking Supervision, banking regulators can allow banks to use credit ratings from certain approved CRAs (called *ECAIs* or *External Credit Assessment Institutions*) when calculating their net capital reserve requirements. In the United States, the Securities and Exchange Commission (SEC) permits investment banks and broker-dealers to use credit ratings from "Nationally Recognised Statistical Rating Organisations" (or NRSROs) for similar purposes. The idea is that banks and other financial institutions should not need to keep in reserve the same amount of capital to protect the institution against (for example) a run on the bank, if the financial institution is heavily invested in highly liquid and very "safe" securities (such as US government bonds or short-term commercial paper from very stable companies).

CRA ratings are also used for other regulatory purposes as well. The US SEC, for example, permits certain bond issuers to use a shortened prospectus form when issuing bonds if the issuer is older, has issued bonds before, and has a credit rating above a certain level. SEC regulations also require that money market funds (mutual funds that mimic the safety and liquidity of a bank savings deposit, but without FDIC insurance) comprise only securities with a very high NRSRO rating. Likewise, insurance regulators use credit ratings to ascertain the strength of the reserves held by insurance companies.

Under both Basel II and SEC regulations, not just any CRA's ratings can be used for regulatory purposes. (If this were the case, it would present an obvious moral hazard, since an issuer, insurance company, or investment bank would have a strong incentive to seek out a CRA with the most lax standards, with potentially dire consequences for overall financial stability.) Rather, there is a vetting process of varying sorts. The Basel II guidelines (paragraph 91, *et al.*), for example, describe certain criteria that bank regulators should look to when permitting the ratings from a particular CRA to be used. These include "objectivity," "independence," "transparency," and others. Banking regulators from a number of jurisdictions have since issued their own discussion papers on this subject, to further define how these terms will be used in practice.

In the United States, since 1975, NRSRO recognition has been granted through a "No Action Letter" sent by the SEC staff. Following this approach, if a CRA (or investment bank or broker-dealer) were interested in using the ratings from a particular CRA for regulatory purposes, the SEC staff would research the market to determine whether ratings from that particular CRA are widely used and considered "reliable and credible." If the SEC staff determines that this is the case, it sends a letter to the CRA indicating that if a regulated entity were to rely on the CRA's ratings, the SEC staff will not recommend enforcement action against that entity. These "No Action" letters are made public and can be relied upon by other regulated entities, not just the entity making the original request. The SEC has since sought to further define the criteria it uses when making this assessment, and in March 2005 published a proposed regulation to this effect.

On September 29, 2006, US President George W. Bush signed into law the "Rating Reform Act of 2006". This law requires the US Securities and Exchange Commission to clarify how NRSRO recognition is granted, eliminates the "No Action Letter" approach and makes NRSRO recognition a Commission (rather than SEC staff) decision, and requires NRSROs to register with, and be regulated by, the SEC. On Feb. 2, 2007, the SEC proposed a rule on "Oversight of Credit Rating Agencies Registered as Nationally Recognised Statistical Rating Organisations" that would implement the CRA Reform Act.

Recognising CRAs' role in capital formation, some governments have attempted to jump-start their domestic rating-agency businesses with various kinds of regulatory relief or encouragement. This may, however, be counterproductive, if it dulls the market mechanism by which agencies compete, subsidising less-capable agencies and penalising agencies that devote resources to higher-quality opinions.

Ratings Use in Structured Finance

Credit rating agencies may also play a key role in structured financial transactions. Unlike a "typical" loan or bond issuance, where a borrower offers to pay a certain return on a loan, structured financial transactions may be viewed as either a series of loans with different characteristics, or else a number of small loans of a similar type packaged together into a series of "buckets" (with the "buckets" or different loans called "*tranches*"). Credit ratings often determine the interest rate or price ascribed to a particular tranche, based on the quality of loans or quality of assets contained within that grouping.

Companies involved in structured financing arrangements often consult with credit rating agencies to help them determine how to structure the individual tranches so that each receives a desired credit rating. For example, a firm may wish to borrow a large sum of money by issuing debt securities. However, the amount is so large that the return investors may demand on a single issuance would be prohibitive. Instead, it decides to issue three separate bonds, with three separate credit ratings — A (medium low risk), BBB (medium risk), and BB (speculative) (using Standard and Poor's rating system). The firm expects that the effective interest rate it pays on the A-rated bonds will be much less than the rate it must pay on the BB-rated bonds, but that, overall, the amount it must pay for the total capital it raises will be less than it would pay if the entire amount were raised from a single bond offering. As this transaction is devised, the firm may consult with a credit rating agency to see how it must structure each tranche — in other words, what types of assets must be used to secure the debt in each tranche — in order for that tranche to receive the desired rating when it is issued.

There has been criticism in the wake of large losses in the collateralised debt obligation (CDO) market that occurred despite being assigned top ratings by the CRAs. For instance, losses on $340.7 million worth of collateralised debt obligations (CDO) issued by Credit Suisse Group added up to about $125 million, despite being rated AAA or Aaa by Standard and Poor's, Moody's Investors Service and Fitch Group.

The rating agencies respond that their advice constitutes only a "point in time" analysis, that they make clear that they never promise or guarantee a certain rating to a tranche, and that they also make clear that any change in circumstance regarding the risk factors of a particular tranche will invalidate their analysis and result in a different credit rating. In addition, some CRAs do not rate bond issuances upon which they have offered such advice.

Complicating matters, particularly where structured finance transactions are concerned, the rating agencies state that their ratings are opinions regarding the likelihood that a given debt security will fail to be serviced over a given period of time, and not an opinion on the volatility of that security and certainly not the wisdom of investing in that security. In the past, most highly rated (AAA or Aaa) debt securities were characterised low volatility and high liquidity – in other words, the price of a highly rated bond did not fluctuate greatly day-to-day, and sellers of such securities could easily find buyers. However, where structured transactions that involve the bundling of hundreds or thousands of similar (and similarly rated) securities tend to concentrate similar risk in such a way that even a slight change on a chance of default can have an enormous effect on the price of the bundled security. This means that even though a rating agency could be correct in its opinion that the chance of default of a structured product is very low, even a slight change in the market's perception of the risk of that product can have a disproportionate effect on the product's market price, with the result that an ostensibly AAA or Aaa-rated security can collapse in price even without there being any default (or significant chance of default). This possibility raises significant regulatory issues because the use of ratings in securities and banking regulation assumes that high ratings correspond with low volatility and high liquidity.

Criticism

Credit rating agencies have been subject to the following criticisms:

- Credit rating agencies do not downgrade companies promptly enough. For example, Enron's rating remained at investment grade four days before the company went bankrupt, despite the fact that credit rating agencies had been aware of the company's problems for months. Some finance scholars have documented in empirical studies that yield spreads of corporate bonds start to expand as credit quality deteriorates but before a rating downgrade, implying that the market often leads a downgrade and questioning the informational value of credit ratings. This has led to suggestions that, rather than rely on CRA ratings in financial regulation, financial regulators should instead require banks, broker-dealers and insurance firms (among others) to use credit spreads when calculating the risk in their portfolio.
- Large corporate rating agencies have been criticised for having too familiar a relationship with company management, possibly opening themselves to undue influence or the vulnerability of being misled. These agencies meet frequently in person with the management of many companies, and advise on actions the company should take to maintain a certain rating. Furthermore, because information about ratings changes from the larger CRAs can spread so quickly (by word of mouth, e-mail, etc.), the larger CRAs charge debt issuers, rather than investors, for their ratings. This has led to accusations that these CRAs are plagued by conflicts of interest that might inhibit them from providing accurate and honest ratings. At the same time, more generally, the largest agencies (Moody's and Standard and Poor's) are often seen as agents of globalisation and/or "Anglo-American" market forces, that drive companies to consider how a proposed activity might effect their credit rating, possibly at the expense of employees, the environment, or long-term research and development. These accusations are not entirely consistent: on one hand, the larger CRAs are accused of being too cosy with the companies they rate, and on the other hand they

are accused of being too focused on a company's "bottom line" and unwilling to listen to a company's explanations for its actions.

- The lowering of a credit score by a CRA can create a vicious cycle, as not only interest rates for that company would go up, but other contracts with financial institutions may be affected adversely, causing an increase in expenses and ensuing decrease in credit worthiness. In some cases, large loans to companies contain a clause that makes the loan due in full if the companies' credit rating is lowered beyond a certain point (usually a "speculative" or "junk bond" rating). The purpose of these "ratings triggers" is to ensure that the bank is able to lay claim to a weak company's assets before the company declares bankruptcy and a receiver is appointed to divide up the claims against the company. The effect of such ratings triggers, however, can be devastating: under a worst-case scenario, once the company's debt is downgraded by a CRA, the company's loans become due in full; since the troubled company likely is incapable of paying all of these loans in full at once, it is forced into bankruptcy (a so-called "death spiral"). These rating triggers were instrumental in the collapse of Enron. Since that time, major agencies have put extra effort into detecting these triggers and discouraging their use, and the US Securities and Exchange Commission requires that public companies in the United States disclose their existence.
- Agencies are sometimes accused of being oligopolists, because barriers to market entry are high and rating agency business is itself reputation-based (and the finance industry pays little attention to a rating that is not widely recognised). Of the large agencies, only Moody's is a separate, publicly held corporation that discloses its financial results without dilution by non-ratings businesses. The high profit on Moody's revenues (>50 per cent gross margin), which are consistent with the high barriers to entry, do nothing to allay market fears of monopoly pricing.
- Credit Rating Agencies have made errors of judgement in rating structured products, particularly in assigning AAA

ratings to structured debt, which in a large number of cases has subsequently been downgraded or defaulted. This has led to problems for several banks whose capital requirements depend on the rating of the structured assets they hold, as well as large losses in the banking industry. AAA rated mortgage securities trading at only 80 cents in the dollar, implying a greater than 20 per cent chance of default, and 8.9 per cent of AAA rated structured CDOs are being considered for downgrade by Fitch, which expects most to downgrade to an average of BBB to BB. These levels of reassessment are surprising for AAA rated bonds, which have the same rating class as US government bonds.

As part of the Sarbanes-Oxley Act of 2002, Congress ordered the US SEC to develop a report, titled Report on the Role and Function of Credit Rating Agencies in the Operation of the Securities Marketsdetailing how credit ratings are used in US regulation and the policy issues this use raises. Partly as a result of this report, in June 2003, the SEC published a "concept release" called Rating Agencies and the Use of Credit Ratings under the Federal Securities Laws that sought public comments on many of the issues raised in its report. Public comments on this concept release have also been published on the SEC's website.

In December 2004, the International Organisation of Securities Commissions (IOSCO) published a Code of Conduct for CRAs that, among other things, is designed to address the types of conflicts of interest that CRAs face. All of the major CRAs have agreed to sign on to this Code of Conduct and it has been praised by regulators ranging from the European Commission to the US Securities and Exchange Commission.

Anti-money Laundering

Anti-money laundering (AML) is a term mainly used in the financial and legal industries to describe the legal controls that require financial institutions and other regulated entities to prevent or report money laundering activities. Anti-money laundering guidelines came into prominence globally after the September 11, 2001 attacks and the subsequent enactment of the USA PATRIOT Act.

Today, all financial institutions globally are required to monitor, investigate and report transactions of a suspicious nature to the financial intelligence unit of the central bank in the respective country. For example, a bank must perform due diligence by having proof of a customer's identity and that the use, source and destination of funds do not involve money laundering. United States federal law related to money laundering is implemented under the Bank Secrecy Act of 1970 as amended by anti-money laundering acts up to the present. Many people have confused Anti-Money Laundering (AML) with Anti-Terrorist Financing (ATF). Under the Bank Secrecy Act of USA, Money Laundering and Terrorist Financing are classified into two different categories when financial institutions file Suspicious Activities Reports (SAR) to Financial Crimes Enforcement Network (FinCEN) which is a US government agency.

To effectively implement AML and ATF measures, the US government encourages financial institutions to work together for AML and ATF purposes in accordance with Section 314(b) of the USA PATRIOT Act. However, since financial institutions are required by law to protect the privacy of their clients, section 314(b) cooperation has not been generally adopted by financial institutions. To overcome this obstacle, the United Crimes Elimination Network (UCEN) has been established by AML and ATF professionals to achieve this global cooperation goal in compliance with the privacy laws of most countries.

Steps

Money laundering involves three independent and often simultaneous steps:

1. Placement – Physically placing bulk cash proceeds.
2. Layering – Separating the proceeds of criminal activity from their origins through layers of complex financial transactions.
3. Integration – Providing an apparently legitimate explanation for the illicit proceeds.

Additional Information

An entire industry has developed around providing software to analyse transactions in an attempt to identify transactions or patterns of transactions, that may constitute illegal financial activity. Financial institutions face penalties for failing to properly file CTR (Cash Transaction Report) and SAR (Suspicious Activity Report) reports, including heavy fines and regulatory restrictions, even to the point of charter revocation. These software applications effectively monitor bank customer transactions on a daily basis and, using customer historical information and account profile, provide a whole picture to the bank management. Transaction monitoring can include cash deposits and withdrawals, wire transfers, credit card activity, cheques (checks), share (securities) dealing and ACH activity. In the bank circles, these applications are known as BSA software or AML software.

Different standards exist in different countries and dependent on the activity demand, different action. For example; in the US a deposit of US $10,000 or more requires a CTR, in Europe it is EUR 15,000, in Switzerland it is CHF 25,000, in many countries there is no CTR requirement. Suspicion of AML activity in the US requires the submittance of a SAR, while in Switzerland a SAR will only get filed if that activity can be proved. As a result, thousands of SARs are filed daily in the US, while in Switzerland the rate is closer to one or two per year.

The United Nations Office on Drugs and Crime maintains the *International Money Laundering Information Network,* a website that provides information and software for anti-money laundering data collection and analysis.

Costs

The financial services industry has become increasingly vocal about the rising costs of anti-money laundering regulation, and the limited benefits that appears to bring. As one commentator expresses the issue:

> "It seems that the bigger the figure for money laundering the more likely it is to be quoted. Indeed, there is even a tendency to 'talk up' the figures as smaller estimates would not only invalidate the logic of the approach (of strict anti-money laundering regulation) but would possibly deter the levels of

> investment necessary for its operational impact. Without facts, legislation has been driven on rhetoric, driving by ill-guided activism responding to the need to be "see to be doing something" rather than by an objective understanding of its impact on predicate crime. The social panic approach is justified by the language used – we talk of the battle against terrorism or the war on drugs..."

The Economist newspaper has become increasingly vocal in its criticism of such regulation, particularly with reference to countering terrorist financing, referring to it as a "costly failure".

Business Process Management

Business process management (BPM) is a method of efficiently aligning an organisation with the wants and needs of clients. It is a holistic management approach that promotes business effectiveness and efficiency while striving for innovation, flexibility and integration with technology. As organisations strive for attainment of their objectives, BPM attempts to continuously improve processes – the process to define, measure and improve your processes - a 'process optimisation' process.

Overview

A business process is a collection of related, structured activities that produce a service or product that meet the needs of a client. These processes are critical to any organisation as they generate revenue and often represent a significant proportion of costs.

BPM articles and pundits often discuss BPM from one of two viewpoints: people and technology.

People

BPM is considered by some to be a philosophy. BPM alignment to the customer means that customer-facing staff are best suited to understand customer needs and must be empowered to make improvements.

Technology

BPM System (BPMS) is sometimes seen as the whole of BPM. Some see that information moves between enterprise software packages and immediately think of Service Oriented Architecture (SOA); while others believe that modelling is the only way to create the 'perfect' process, so they think of modelling as BPM.

Both of these concepts go into the definition of Business Process Management. For instance, the size and complexity of daily tasks often requires the use of technology to model efficiently. Bringing the power of technology to staff is part of the BPM credo. Many thought BPM as the bridge between Information Technology (IT) and Business.

BPMS could be industrial specific and can be driven by a software such as Agilent OpenLAB BPM. Some other products may focus on Enterprise Resource Planning and warehouse management. Validation of BPMS is another technical issue which vendors and users need to be aware of, if regulatory compliances are mandatory. The task could be performed either by an authenticated third party or by user themselves. In either way, validation documentation need to be generated. The validation document usually can either be published officially or well retained by users.

Business Process Management Life Cycle

The activities which constitute business process management can be grouped into five categories: design, modelling, execution, monitoring, and optimisation.

Design: Process Design encompasses both the identification of existing processes and designing the "to-be" process. Areas of focus include: representation of the process flow, the actors within it, alerts and notifications, escalations, Standard Operating Procedures, Service Level Agreements, and task handover mechanisms.

Good design reduces the number of problems over the lifetime of the process. Whether or not existing processes are considered, the aim of this step is to ensure that a correct and efficient theoretical design is prepared.

The proposed improvement could be in human to human, human to system, and system to system workflows, and might target regulatory, market, or competitive challenges faced by the businesses.

Modelling: Modelling takes the theoretical design and introduces combinations of variables, for instance, changes in the cost of materials or increased rent, that determine how the process might operate under different circumstances.

It also involves running "what-if analysis" on the processes: What if I have 75 per cent of resources to do the same task? What if I want to do the same job for 80 per cent of the current cost?

Execution: One way to automate processes is to develop or purchase an application that executes the required steps of the process; however, in practice, these applications rarely execute all the steps of the process accurately or completely. Another approach is to use a combination of software and human intervention; however this approach is more complex, making documenting process difficult.

As a response to these problems, software has been developed that enables the full business process (as developed in the process design activity) to be defined in a computer language which can be directly executed by the computer. The system will either use services in connected applications to perform business operations (e.g. calculating a repayment plan for a loan) or, when a step is too complex to automate, will message a human requesting input. Compared to either of the previous approaches, directly executing a process definition can be more straightforward and therefore easier to improve.

However, automating a process definition requires flexible and comprehensive infrastructure which typically rules out implementing these systems in a legacy IT environment.

Business rules have been used by systems to provide definitions for governing behaviour, and a business rule engine can be used to drive process execution and resolution.

Monitoring: Monitoring encompasses the tracking of individual processes so that information on their state can be easily seen and statistics on the performance of one or more processes provided.

An example of the tracking is being able to determine the state of a customer order (e.g. ordered arrived, awaiting delivery, invoice paid) so that problems in its operation can be identified and corrected.

In addition, this information can be used to work with customers and suppliers to improve their connected processes. Examples of the statistics are the generation of measures on how quickly a customer order is processed or how many orders were processed in the last month. These measures tend to fit into three categories: cycle time, defect rate and productivity.

The degree of monitoring depends on what information the business wants to evaluate and analyse and how business wants it to be monitored, in real time or *ad hoc.* Here, business activity monitoring (BAM) extends and expands the monitoring tools in generally provided by BPMS.

Process mining is a collection of methods and tools related to process monitoring. The aim of process mining is to analyse event logues extracted through process monitoring and to compare them with an 'a priori' process model. Process mining allows process analysts to detect discrepancies between the actual process execution and the a priori model as well as to analyse bottlenecks.

Optimisation: Process optimisation includes retrieving process performance information from modelling or monitoring phase and identifying the potential or actual bottlenecks and potential rooms for cost savings or other improvements and then applying those enhancements in the design of the process thus continuing the value cycle of business process management.

Future Developments

Although the initial focus of BPM was on the automation of mechanistic business processes, it has since been extended to integrate human-driven processes in which human interaction takes place in series or parallel with the mechanistic processes. A common form is where individual steps in the business process which require human intuition or judgement to be performed are assigned to the appropriate members of an organisation (as with workflow systems).

More advanced forms such as human interaction management are in the complex interaction between human workers in performing a workgroup task. In this case many people and system interact in structured, *ad hoc*, and sometimes completely dynamic ways to complete one to many transactions.

BPM can be used to understand organisations through expanded views that would not otherwise be available to organise and present. These views include the relationships of processes to each other which, when included in the process model, provide for advanced reporting and analysis that would not otherwise be available. BPM is regarded by some as the backbone of enterprise content management.

Business Process Management in Practice

Whilst the steps can be viewed as a cycle, economic or time constraints are likely to limit the process to one or more iterations.

In addition, organisations often start a BPM project or programme with the objective to optimise an area which has been identified as an area for improvement.

In financial sector, BPM is critical to make sure the system delivers a quality service while the regulatory compliance is also not compromised.

Use of Software

Some say that not all activities can be effectively modelled with BPMS, and so some processes are best left alone. Taking this viewpoint, the value in BPMS is not in automating very simple or very complex tasks, it is in modelling processes where there is the most opportunity.

The alternate view is that a complete process modelling language, supported by a BPMS, is needed; the purpose is not purely automation to replace manual tasks, but to enhance manual tasks with computer assisted automation.

In this sense, the argument over whether BPM is about replacing human activity with automation or simply analysing for greater understanding of process is a sterile debate; all processes modelled using BPMS must be executable in order to bring to life the software application that the human users interact with at run time.

Standardisation

Currently, the international standards for the task have only limited to the application for IT sectors and ISO/IEC 15944 covers the operational aspects of the business.

However, some corporations with the culture of good business practices do use standard operating procedures to regulate their operational process.

Financial Regulations

Financial regulations are a form of regulation or supervision, which subjects financial institutions to certain requirements, restrictions and guidelines, aiming to maintain the integrity of the financial system. This may be handled by either a government or non-government organisation.

Aims of Regulations

The specific aims of financial regulators are usually:

- To enforce applicable laws.
- To prosecute cases of market misconduct, such as insider trading.
- To licence providers of financial services.
- To protect clients, and investigate complaints.
- To maintain confidence in the financial system.

Authority by Country

The following is a shortlisting of regulatory authorities in various jurisdictions:

- US Securities and Exchange Commission (SEC), USA.
- Securities and Exchange Surveillance Commission (SESC), Japan.
- Investment Dealers Association of Canada (IDA), Canada.

- Irish Financial Services Regulatory Authority, Ireland.
- Financial Services Authority (FSA), UK.
- Autorite des marches financiers (AMF), France.
- Financial Supervisory Commission (FSC), Taiwan.
- China Securities Regulatory Commission (CSRC), People's Republic of China.
- China Insurance Regulatory Commission (CIRC), People's Republic of China.
- China Banking Regulatory Commission (CBRC), People's Republic of China.
- Securities and Exchange Commission of Pakistan, Pakistan.
- Comision Nacional Bancaria y de Valores, Mexico.
- Security and Exchange Board of India, India.

Unique Jurisdictions

In Australia, the Australian Prudential Regulation Authority (APRA) supervises banks and insurers. Australian Securities and Investments Commission (ASIC) is responsible for enforcing financial services and corporations laws.

ISO 4217

ISO 4217 is the international standard describing three-letter codes (also known as the currency code) to define the names of currencies established by the International Organisation for Standardisation (ISO). The ISO 4217 code list is the established norm in banking and business all over the world for defining different currencies, and in many countries the codes for the more common currencies are so well known publicly, that exchange rates published in newspapers or posted in banks use only these to define the different currencies, instead of translated currency names or ambiguous currency symbols. ISO 4217 codes are used on airline tickets and international train tickets to remove any ambiguity about the price.

The first two letters of the code are the two letters of ISO 3166-1 alpha-2 country codes (which are also used as the basis for national top-level domains on the internet) and the third is usually the initial of the currency itself. So Japan's currency code becomes

JPY– JP for Japan and Y for yen. This eliminates the problem caused by the names dollar, franc and pound being used in dozens of different countries, each having significantly differing values. Also, if a currency is revalued, the currency code's last letter is changed to distinguish it from the old currency. In some cases, the third letter is the initial for "new" in that country's language, to distinguish it from an older currency that was revalued; the code often long outlasts the usage of the term "new" itself. Examples of this include the Mexican peso (MXN) and the Turkish lira (TRY). Other changes can be seen, however; the Russian ruble, for example, changed from RUR to RUB, where the B comes from the third letter in the word "ruble".

There is also a three-digit code number assigned to each currency, in the same manner as there is also a three-digit code number assigned to each country as part of ISO 3166. This numeric code is usually the same as the ISO 3166 numeric code. For example, USD (US Dollar) has code 840 which is also the numeric code for US (United States).

The standard also defines the relationship between the major currency unit and any minor currency unit. Often, the minor currency unit has a value that is 1/100 of the major unit, but 1/1000 is also common. Some currencies do not have any minor currency unit at all. In others, the major currency unit has so little value that the minor unit is no longer generally used (e.g. the Japanese *sen*, 1/100th of a yen). This is indicated in the standard by the currency exponent. For example, USD has exponent 2, while JPY has exponent 0. Mauritania does not use a decimal division of units, setting 1 ouguiya (UM) = 5 khoums, and Madagascar has 1 ariary = 5 iraimbilanja.

ISO 4217 includes codes not only for currencies, but also for precious metals (gold, silver, palladium and platinum; by definition expressed per one troy ounce, as compared to "1 USD") and certain other entities used in international finance, e.g. Special Drawing Rights. There are also special codes allocated for testing purposes (XTS), and to indicate no currency transactions (XXX). These codes all begin with the letter "X". The precious metals use "X" plus the metal's chemical symbol; silver, for example, is XAG. ISO 3166 never assigns country codes beginning with "X" while these codes are assigned for privately customised use only (reserved, never for official codes), so ISO 4217 can use "X" codes for non-country-specific currencies without risk of clashing with future country codes.

Supranational currencies, such as the East Caribbean dollar, the CFP franc, the CFA franc BEAC and the CFA franc BCEAO are normally also represented by codes beginning with an "X". The euro is represented by the code EUR (EU is included in the ISO 3166-1 reserved codes list to represent the European Union). The predecessor to the euro, the European Currency Unit, had the code XEU.

History: In 1973, the ISO Technical Committee 68 decided to develop codes for the representation of currencies and funds for use in any application of trade, commerce or banking. At the 17th session (February 1978) of the related UN/ECE Group of Experts agreed that the three-letter alphabetic codes for International Standard ISO 4217, "Codes for the representation of currencies and funds", would be suitable for use in international trade.

Over time, new currencies are created and old currencies are discontinued. Frequently, these changes are due to new governments (through war or a new Constitution), treaties between countries standardising on a currency, or revaluation of the currency due to excessive inflation. As a result, the list of codes must be updated from time to time. The ISO 4217 Maintenance Agency (MA), the British Standards Institution, is responsible for maintaining the list of codes.

ISO 6166: ISO 6166 defines the structure of an International Securities Identifying Number (ISIN). An ISIN uniquely identifies a fungible security. Securities with which ISINs can be used are Equities, Fixed income and ETF's only.

ISINs consist of two alphabetic characters, which are the ISO 3166-1 alpha-2 code for the issuing country, nine alpha-numeric digits (the National Securities Identifying Number, or NSIN, which identifies the security), and one numeric check digit. The NSIN is issued by a national numbering agency (NNA) for that country. Regional substitute NNAs have been allocated the task of functioning as NNAs in those countries where NNAs have not yet been established.

ISINs are slowly being introduced worldwide. At present, many countries have adopted ISINs as a secondary measure of identifying securities, but as yet only some of those countries have moved to using ISINs as their primary means of identifying securities.

NNAs cooperate through the Association of National Numbering Agencies (ANNA). ANNA also functions as the ISO 6166 Maintenance Agency (MA).

ISO 9362: ISO 9362 (also known as SWIFT-BIC, BIC code, SWIFT ID or SWIFT code) is a standard format of Bank Identifier Codes approved by the International Organisation for Standardisation (ISO). It is the unique identification code of a particular bank. These codes are used when transferring money between banks, particularly for international wire transfers, and also for the exchange of other messages between banks. The codes can sometimes be found on account statements.

The overlapping issue between ISO 9362 and ISO 13616 is discussed in the article International Bank Account Number (also called IBAN).

The SWIFT code is 8 or 11 characters, made up of:

- 4 characters – bank code (only letters).
- 2 characters – ISO 3166-1 alpha-2 country code (only letters).
- 2 characters – location code (letters and digits) (if the second character is '1', then it denotes a passive participant in the SWIFT network).
- 3 characters – branch code, optional ('XXX' for primary office) (letters and digits).

Where an 8-digit code is given, it may be assumed that it refers to the primary office.

SWIFT Standards, a division of The Society for Worldwide Interbank Financial Telecommunication (SWIFT), handles the registration of these codes. For this reason, Bank Identifier Codes (BICs) are often called SWIFT addresses or codes.

There are over 7,500 "live" codes (for partners actively connected to the BIC network) and an estimated 10,000 additional BIC codes which can be used for manual transactions.

Examples: Deutsche Bank is an international bank, with its head office in Frankfurt, Germany. The SWIFT code for its primary office is DEUTDEFF:

- DEUT identifies Deutsche Bank.
- DE is the country code for Germany.
- FF is the code for Frankfurt.

Deutsche Bank uses an extended code of 11 digits and has assigned branches or processing areas individual extended codes. This allows the payment to be directed to a specific office. For example, DEUTDEFF500 would direct the payment to an office of Deutsche Bank in Bad Homburg.

Nedbank is a primarily South African bank, with its head office in Johannesburg. The SWIFT code for its primary office is NEDSZAJJ:

- NEDS identifies Nedbank.
- ZA is the country code for South Africa.
- JJ is the code for Johannesburg.

Nedbank has not implemented the extended code of 11 digits and all SWIFT transfers to its accounts are directed to the primary office for processing. Those transfer interfaces that require an 11 digit code would enter NEDSZAJJXXX.

12-character SWIFTNet FIN Address Based on BIC: To identify endpoints on its network, SWIFT also uses 12-character codes that are derived from the BIC of the institution. Such a code consists of the BIC8, followed by 1-character code that identifies the Logical Terminal (LTC), or "local destination", and the 3-character branch code. These 'BIC12's are not part of the ISO standard, and are only relevant in the context of the messaging platform.

ISO 10962: ISO 10962 is the CFI (Classification of Financial Instruments) code maintained by the International Organisation for Standardisation (ISO). It is an alphabetical code consisting of 6 letters. The first letter is the category, the second is the group, and the remaining letters show special attributes of the group. The letter X always means *Not Applicable/Undefined*. Here are some of the possible codes:

- E = Equities:
  - S = Shares (common/ordinary):
    - § 1: Voting Right;
    - § V = Voting;
    - § N = Non-voting;
    - § R = Restricted voting;
    - § E = Enhanced voting;
    - § 2: Ownership/transfer restrictions;
    - § T = Restrictions;
    - § U = Free;
    - § 3: Payment status;
    - § O = Nil paid;
    - § P = Partly paid;
    - § F = Fully paid;
    - § 4: Form:
    - § B = Bearer;
    - § R = Registered;
    - § N = Bearer/Registered;
    - § Z = Bearer depository receipt;
    - § A = Registered depository receipt;
    - § P = Preferred Shares;
    - § C = Convertible preferred shares;
    - § U = Units (units trusts/mutual funds);
    - § M = Others.
- D = Debt Instruments:
  - B = Bonds;
  - C = Convertible bonds;
  - M = Others;

- T = Medium-term Notes;
- W = Bonds With Warrants Attached;
- Y = Money Market Instruments.

- R = Entitlements (Rights):
  - A = Allotment Rights;
  - M = Others (Miscellaneous);
  - S = Subscription rights;
  - W = Warrants.
- O = Options:
  - C = Call Options:
    - § 1: Exercise Style;
    - § A = American;
    - § E = European;
    - § 2: Underlying Asset;
    - § S = Stock;
    - § I = Index;
    - § D = Debt;
    - § C = Currency;
    - § O = Option;
    - § F = Future;
    - § T = Commodity;
    - § W = Swap;
    - § B = Basket;
    - § M = Other;
    - § 3: Delivery;
    - § C = Cash;
    - § P = Physical;
    - § 4: Standard/Non-standard;
    - § S = Standard;
    - § N = Non-standard.
  - P = Put Options:
    - § Same as *Call.*

- F = Futures:
  - C = Commodities Futures:
    - § 1: Underlying Asset;
    - § A = Agricultural;
    - § E = Extraction;
    - § I = Industrial;
    - § S = Service;
    - § 2: Delivery;
    - § C = Cash;
    - § P = Physical;
    - § 3: Standard/Non-standard;
    - § S = Standard;
    - § N = Non-standard;
    - § 4: not used;
    - § X = not used.
  - F = Financial Futures:
    - § 1: Underlying Asset;
    - § S = Stock;
    - § I = Index;
    - § D = Debt;
    - § C = Currency;
    - § O = Option;
    - § F = Future;
    - § T = Commodity;
    - § W = Swap;
    - § B = Basket;
    - § M = Other;
    - § 2: Delivery;
    - § C = Cash;
    - § P = Physical;
    - § 3: Standard/Non-standard;
    - § S = Standard;

§ N = Non-standard;

§ 4: not used;

§ X = not used.

- M = Others (Miscellaneous):
  - o M = Other Assets (Miscellaneous);
  - o R = Referential Instruments.

Example:

- ESNTPB is Equities/Shares/Non-voting/Restrictions/Partly paid/Bearer.
- OPASPS is Options/Put/American/Stock/Physical/Standard.

Monetary Policy

Monetary policy is the process by which the government, central bank, or monetary authority of a country controls (i) the supply of money, (ii) availability of money, and (iii) cost of money or rate of interest, in order to attain a set of objectives oriented towards the growth and stability of the economy. Monetary theory provides insight into how to craft optimal monetary policy.

Monetary policy is generally referred to as either being an expansionary policy, or a contractionary policy, where an expansionary policy increases the total supply of money in the economy, and a contractionary policy decreases the total money supply. Expansionary policy is traditionally used to combat unemployment in a recession by lowering interest rates, while contractionary policy involves raising interest rates in order to combat inflation. Monetary policy should be contrasted with fiscal policy, which refers to government borrowing, spending and taxation.

Overview

Monetary policy rests on the relationship between the rates of interest in an economy, that is the price at which money can be borrowed, and the total supply of money. Monetary policy uses a variety of tools to control one or both of these, to influence outcomes like economic growth, inflation, exchange rates with other currencies and unemployment. Where currency is under a monopoly of issuance, or where there is a regulated system of issuing currency through banks which are tied to a central bank, the monetary authority has the ability to alter the money supply and thus influence the interest rate (in order to achieve policy goals). The beginning of monetary policy as such comes from the late-19th century, where it was used to maintain the gold standard.

A policy is referred to as contractionary if it reduces the size of the money supply or raises the interest rate. An expansionary policy increases the size of the money supply, or decreases the interest rate. Furthermore, monetary policies are described as follows: accommodative, if the interest rate set by the central monetary authority is intended to create economic growth; neutral, if it is intended neither to create growth nor combat inflation; or tight if intended to reduce inflation.

There are several monetary policy tools available to achieve these ends: increasing interest rates by fiat; reducing the monetary base; and increasing reserve requirements. All have the effect of contracting the money supply; and, if reversed, expand the money supply. Since the 1970s, monetary policy has generally been formed separately from fiscal policy. Even prior to the 1970s, the Bretton Woods system still ensured that most nations would form the two policies separately.

Within almost all modern nations, special institutions (such as the Bank of England, the European Central Bank, the Federal Reserve System in the United States, the Bank of Japan or Nippon Ginko, the Bank of Canada or the Reserve Bank of Australia) exist which have the task of executing the monetary policy and often independently of the executive. In general, these institutions are called central banks and often have other responsibilities such as supervising the smooth operation of the financial system.

The primary tool of monetary policy is open market operations. This entails managing the quantity of money in circulation through the buying and selling of various credit instruments, foreign currencies or commodities. All of these purchases or sales result in more or less base currency entering or leaving market circulation.

Usually, the short-term goal of open market operations is to achieve a specific short-term interest rate target. In other instances, monetary policy might instead entail the targeting of a specific exchange rate relative to some foreign currency or else relative to gold. For example, in the case of the USA the Federal Reserve targets the federal funds rate, the rate at which member banks lend to one another overnight; however, the monetary policy of China is to target the exchange rate between the Chinese renminbi and a basket of foreign currencies.

The other primary means of conducting monetary policy include: (i) Discount window lending (i.e. lender of last resort); (ii) Fractional deposit lending (i.e. changes in the reserve requirement); (iii) Moral suasion (i.e. cajoling certain market players to achieve specified outcomes); (iv) "Open mouth operations" (i.e. talking monetary policy with the market).

History of Monetary Policy

Monetary policy is primarily associated with interest rate and credit. For many centuries, there were only two forms of monetary policy: i) Decisions about coinage; ii) Decisions to print paper money to create credit. Interest rates, while now thought of as part of monetary authority, were not generally coordinated with the other forms of monetary policy during this time. Monetary policy was seen as an executive decision, and was generally in the hands of the authority with seigniorage, or the power to coin. With the advent of larger trading networks came the ability to set the price between gold and silver, and the price of the local currency to foreign currencies. This official price could be enforced by law, even if it varied from the market price.

With the creation of the Bank of England in 1694, which acquired the responsibility to print notes and back them with gold, the idea of monetary policy as independent of executive action began to be established. The goal of monetary policy was to maintain the value of the coinage, print notes which would trade at par to specie, and prevent coins from leaving circulation. The establishment of central banks by industrialising nations was associated then with the desire to maintain the nation's peg to the gold standard, and to trade in a narrow band with other gold-backed currencies. To accomplish this end, central banks as part of the gold standard began setting the interest rates that they charged, both their own borrowers, and other banks who required liquidity. The maintenance of a gold standard required almost monthly adjustments of interest rates.

During the 1870-1920 period the industrialised nations set up central banking systems, with one of the last being the Federal Reserve in 1913. By this point the understanding of the central bank as the "lender of last resort" was understood. It was also increasingly understood that interest rates had an effect on the entire economy, in no small part because of the marginal revolution in economics, which focused on how many more, or how many fewer, people would make a decision based on a change in the economic trade-offs. It also became clear that there was a business cycle, and economic theory began understanding the relationship of interest rates to that cycle. (Nevertheless, steering a whole economy by influencing the interest rate has often been described as trying to steer an oil tanker with a canoe paddle.) Research by Cass Business School has also suggested that perhaps it is the central bank policies of expansionary and contractionary policies that are causing the economic cycle; evidence can be found by looking at the lack of cycles in economies before central banking policies existed.

The advancement of monetary policy as a pseudo-scientific discipline has been quite rapid in the last 150 years, and it has increased especially rapidly in the last 50 years. Monetary policy has grown from simply increasing the monetary supply enough to keep up with both population growth and economic activity. It must now take into account such diverse factors as:

- Short-term interest rates;
- Long-term interest rates;
- Velocity of money through the economy;
- Exchange rates;
- Credit quality;
- Bonds and equities (corporate ownership and debt);
- Government versus private sector spending/savings;
- International capital flows of money on large scales;
- Financial derivatives such as options, swaps, futures contracts, etc.

A small but vocal group of people advocate for a return to the gold standard (the elimination of the dollar's fiat currency status and even of the Federal Reserve Bank). Their argument is basically that monetary policy is fraught with risk and these risks will result in drastic harm to the populace should monetary policy fail. Others see another problem with our current monetary policy. The problem for them is not that our money has nothing physical to define its value, but that fractional reserve lending of that money as a debt to the recipient, rather than a credit, causes all but a small proportion of society (including all governments) to be perpetually in debt.

In fact, many economists disagree with returning to a gold standard. They argue that doing so would drastically limit the money supply, and throw away 100 years of advancement in monetary policy. The sometimes complex financial transactions that make big business (especially international business) easier and safer would be much more difficult if not impossible. Moreover, shifting risk to different people/companies that specialise in monitoring and using risk can turn any financial risk into a known dollar amount and therefore make business predictable and more profitable for everyone involved.

Trends in Central Banking

The central bank influences interest rates by expanding or contracting the monetary base, which consists of currency in circulation and banks' reserves on deposit at the central bank. The primary way that the central bank can affect the monetary base is by open market operations or sales and purchases of second hand government debt, or by changing the reserve requirements. If the central bank wishes to lower interest rates, it purchases government debt, thereby increasing the amount of cash in circulation or crediting banks' reserve accounts. Alternatively, it can lower the interest rate on discounts or overdrafts (loans to banks secured by suitable collateral, specified by the central bank).

If the interest rate on such transactions is sufficiently low, commercial banks can borrow from the central bank to meet reserve requirements and use the additional liquidity to expand their balance sheets, increasing the credit available to the economy.

Lowering reserve requirements has a similar effect, freeing up funds for banks to increase loans or buy other profitable assets.

A central bank can only operate a truly independent monetary policy when the exchange rate is floating. If the exchange rate is pegged or managed in any way, the central bank will have to purchase or sell foreign exchange. These transactions in foreign exchange will have an effect on the monetary base analogous to open market purchases and sales of government debt; if the central bank buys foreign exchange, the monetary base expands, and vice versa. But even in the case of a pure floating exchange rate, central banks and monetary authorities can at best "lean against the wind" in a world where capital is mobile.

Accordingly, the management of the exchange rate will influence domestic monetary conditions. In order to maintain its monetary policy target, the central bank will have to sterilise or offset its foreign exchange operations. For example, if a central bank buys foreign exchange (to counteract appreciation of the exchange rate), base money will increase. Therefore, to sterilise that increase, the central bank must also sell government debt to contract the monetary base by an equal amount. It follows that turbulent activity in foreign exchange markets can cause a central bank to lose control of domestic monetary policy when it is also managing the exchange rate.

In the 1980s, many economists began to believe that making a nation's central bank independent of the rest of executive government is the best way to ensure an optimal monetary policy, and those central banks which did not have independence began to gain it. This is to avoid overt manipulation of the tools of monetary policies to effect political goals, such as re-electing the current government. Independence typically means that the members of the committee which conducts monetary policy have long, fixed terms. Obviously, this is a somewhat limited independence.

In the 1990s, central banks began adopting formal, public inflation targets with the goal of making the outcomes, if not the process, of monetary policy more transparent. In other words, a central bank may have an inflation target of 2 per cent for a given year, and if inflation turns out to be 5 per cent, then the central bank will typically have to submit an explanation.

The Bank of England exemplifies both these trends. It became independent of government through the Bank of England Act 1998 and adopted an inflation target of 2.5 per cent RPI (now 2 per cent of CPI).

The debate rages on about whether monetary policy can smooth business cycles or not. A central conjecture of Keynesian economics is that the central bank can stimulate aggregate demand in the short run, because a significant number of prices in the economy are fixed in the short run and firms will produce as many goods and services as are demanded (in the long run, however, money is neutral, as in the neoclassical model). There is also the Austrian school of economics, which includes Friedrich von Hayek and Ludwig von Mises's arguments, but most economists fall into either the Keynesian or neoclassical camps on this issue.

Developing Countries

Developing countries may have problems establishing an effective operating monetary policy. The primary difficulty is that few developing countries have deep markets in government debt. The matter is further complicated by the difficulties in forecasting money demand and fiscal pressure to levy the inflation tax by expanding the monetary base rapidly. In general, the central banks in many developing countries have poor records in managing monetary policy. This is often because the monetary authority in a developing country is not independent of government, so good monetary policy takes a backseat to the political desires of the government or are used to pursue other non-monetary goals. For this and other reasons, developing countries that want to establish credible monetary policy may institute a currency board or adopt dollarisation. Such forms of monetary institutions thus essentially tie the hands of the government from interference and, it is hoped, that such policies will import the monetary policy of the anchor nation.

Recent attempts at liberalising and reforming the financial markets (particularly the recapitalisation of banks and other financial institutions in Nigeria and elsewhere) are gradually providing the latitude required in order to implement monetary policy frameworks by the relevant central banks.

Types of Monetary Policy

In practice, all types of monetary policy involve modifying the amount of base currency (M0) in circulation. This process of changing the liquidity of base currency through the open sales and purchases of (government-issued) debt and credit instruments is called open market operations.

Constant market transactions by the monetary authority modify the supply of currency and this impacts other market variables such as short-term interest rates and the exchange rate.

The distinction between the various types of monetary policy lies primarily with the set of instruments and target variables that are used by the monetary authority to achieve their goals.

Monetary Policy	*Target Market Variable*	*Long-term Objective*
Inflation Targeting	Interest rate on overnight debt	A given rate of change in the CPI
Price Level Targeting	Interest rate on overnight debt	A specific CPI number
Monetary Aggregates	The growth in money supply	A given rate of change in the CPI
Fixed Exchange Rate	The spot price of the currency	The spot price of the currency
Gold Standard	The spot price of gold	Low inflation as measured by the gold price
Mixed Policy change	Usually interest rates	Usually unemployment + CPI

The different types of policy are also called monetary regimes, in parallel to exchange rate regimes. A fixed exchange rate is also an exchange rate regime; The Gold standard results in a relatively fixed regime towards the currency of other countries on the gold standard and a floating regime towards those that are not. Targeting inflation, the price level or other monetary aggregates implies floating exchange rate unless the management of the relevant foreign currencies is tracking the exact same variables (such as a harmonised consumer price index).

Inflation Targeting

Under this policy approach the target is to keep inflation, under a particular definition such as Consumer Price Index, within a desired range.

The inflation target is achieved through periodic adjustments to the Central Bank interest rate target. The interest rate used is generally the interbank rate at which banks lend to each other overnight for cash flow purposes. Depending on the country this particular interest rate might be called the cash rate or something similar.

The interest rate target is maintained for a specific duration using open market operations. Typically the duration that the interest rate target is kept constant will vary between months and years. This interest rate target is usually reviewed on a monthly or quarterly basis by a policy committee.

Changes to the interest rate target are made in response to various market indicators in an attempt to forecast economic trends and in so doing keep the market on track towards achieving the defined inflation target. For example, one simple method of inflation targeting called the Taylor rule adjusts the interest rate in response to changes in the inflation rate and the output gap. The rule was proposed by John B. Taylor of Stanford University.

The inflation targeting approach to monetary policy approach was pioneered in New Zealand. It is currently used in Australia, Canada, Chile, the Eurozone, New Zealand, Norway, Iceland, Poland, Sweden, South Africa, Turkey, and the United Kingdom.

Price Level Targeting

Price level targeting is similar to inflation targeting except that CPI growth in one year is offset in subsequent years such that over time the price level on aggregate does not move.

Something similar to price level targeting was tried by Sweden in the 1930s, and seems to have contributed to the relatively good performance of the Swedish economy during the Great Depression. As of 2004, no country operates monetary policy based on a price level target.

Monetary Aggregates

In the 1980s, several countries used an approach based on a constant growth in the money supply. This approach was refined to include different classes of money and credit (M0, M1, etc.). In the USA, this approach to monetary policy was discontinued with the selection of Alan Greenspan as Fed Chairman.

This approach is also sometimes called monetarism.

While most monetary policy focuses on a price signal of one form or another, this approach is focused on monetary quantities.

Fixed Exchange Rate

This policy is based on maintaining a fixed exchange rate with a foreign currency. There are varying degrees of fixed exchange rates, which can be ranked in relation to how rigid the fixed exchange rate is with the anchor nation.

Under a system of fiat fixed rates, the local government or monetary authority declares a fixed exchange rate but does not actively buy or sell currency to maintain the rate. Instead, the rate is enforced by non-convertibility measures (e.g. capital controls, import/export licences, etc.). In this case, there is a black market exchange rate where the currency trades at its market/unofficial rate.

Under a system of fixed-convertibility, currency is bought and sold by the central bank or monetary authority on a daily basis to achieve the target exchange rate. This target rate may be a fixed level or a fixed band within which the exchange rate may fluctuate until the monetary authority intervenes to buy or sell as necessary to maintain the exchange rate within the band. (In this case, the fixed exchange rate with a fixed level can be seen as a special case of the fixed exchange rate with bands where the bands are set to zero.)

Under a system of fixed exchange rates maintained by a currency board every unit of local currency must be backed by a unit of foreign currency (correcting for the exchange rate). This ensures that the local monetary base does not inflate without being backed by hard currency and eliminates any worries about a run on the local currency by those wishing to convert the local currency to the hard (anchor) currency.

Under dollarisation, foreign currency (usually the US dollar, hence the term "dollarisation") is used freely as the medium of exchange either exclusively or in parallel with local currency. This outcome can come about because the local population has lost all faith in the local currency, or it may also be a policy of the government (usually to rein in inflation and import credible monetary policy).

These policies often abdicate monetary policy to the foreign monetary authority or government as monetary policy in the pegging nation must align with monetary policy in the anchor nation to maintain the exchange rate. The degree to which local monetary policy becomes dependent on the anchor nation depends on factors such as capital mobility, openness, credit channels and other economic factors.

Managed Float

Officially, the Indian Rupee (INR) exchange rate is supposed to be 'market determined'. In reality, the Reserve Bank of India (RBI) trades actively on the INR/USD with the purpose of controlling the volatility of the Rupee – US Dollar exchange rate– within a narrow bandwidth. (i.e pegs it to the US Dollar).

Other rates – like the INR/Pound or the INR/JPY – have volatilities which reflect the volatilities of the US/Pound and the US/JPY, respectively.

The pegged exchange rate is accompanied by an elaborate system of capital controls.

- On the current account, there are no currency conversion restrictions hindering buying or selling foreign exchange (though trade barriers do exist).
- On the capital account, "foreign institutional investors" have convertibility to bring money in and out of the country and buy securities (subject to an elaborate maze of quantitative restrictions).
- Local firms are able to take capital out of the country in order to expand globally.
- Local households have quantitative restrictions (which are being relaxed in recent times) in their ability to do global diversification. (Example while local firms can buy real estate– individuals may not). However, they are able to purchase items (mainly consumer items – say a laptop) and

services reasonably freely (there are quantitative restrictions). Most of these transactions happen through credit cards through the internet.

Owing to an enormous expansion of the current account and the capital account, India is increasingly moving into *de facto* convertibility. However, it still cannot be considered a fully convertible currency.

The INR is not a highly traded currency – beyond India. It is traded by way of Forwards through inter bank transactions (Again the US Dollar exchange rate determines the INR/other Crosses exchange rate).

As any currency traded in the international market – the INR does trade at a market determined premium/discount for the forward months.

Gold Standard

The gold standard is a system in which the price of the national currency as measured in units of gold bars and is kept constant by the daily buying and selling of base currency to other countries and nationals. (i.e. open market operations). The selling of gold is very important for economic growth and stability.

The gold standard might be regarded as a special case of the "Fixed Exchange Rate" policy. And the gold price might be regarded as a special type of "Commodity Price Index".

Today this type of monetary policy is not used anywhere in the world, although a form of gold standard was used widely across the world prior to 1971.

Mixed Policy

In practice, a mixed policy approach is most like "inflation targeting". However, some consideration is also given to other goals such as economic growth, unemployment and asset bubbles.

This type of policy was used by the Federal Reserve in 1998.

Monetary Base

Monetary policy can be implemented by changing the size of the monetary base. This directly changes the total amount of money circulating in the economy. A central bank can use open market operations to change the monetary base. The central bank would buy/sell bonds in exchange for hard currency. When the central bank disburses/collects this hard currency payment, it alters the amount of currency in the economy, thus altering the monetary base.

Reserve Requirements

The monetary authority exerts regulatory control over banks. Monetary policy can be implemented by changing the proportion of total assets that banks must hold in reserve with the central bank. Banks only maintain a small portion of their assets as cash available for immediate withdrawal; the rest is invested in illiquid assets like mortgages and loans. By changing the proportion of total assets to be held as liquid cash, the Federal Reserve changes the availability of loanable funds. This acts as a change in the money supply.

Discount Window Lending

Many central banks or finance ministries have the authority to lend funds to financial institutions within their country. By calling in existing loans or extending new loans, the monetary authority can directly change the size of the money supply.

Interest Rates

The contraction of the monetary supply can be achieved indirectly by increasing the nominal interest rates. Monetary authorities in different nations have differing levels of control of economy-wide interest rates. In the United States, the Federal Reserve can set the discount rate, as well as achieve the desired Federal funds rate by open market operations. This rate has significant effect on other market interest rates, but there is no perfect relationship. In the United States open market operations are a relatively small part of the total volume in the bond market.

In other nations, the monetary authority may be able to mandate specific interest rates on loans, savings accounts or other financial assets. By raising the interest rate(s) under its control, a monetary authority can contract the money supply, because higher interest rates encourage savings and discourage borrowing. Both of these effects reduce the size of the money supply.

Currency Board

A currency board is a monetary arrangement which pegs the monetary base of a country to that of an anchor nation. As such, it essentially operates as a hard fixed exchange rate, whereby local currency in circulation is backed by foreign currency from the anchor nation at a fixed rate. Thus, to grow the local monetary base an equivalent amount of foreign currency must be held in reserves with the currency board. This limits the possibility for the local monetary authority to inflate or pursue other objectives. The principal rationales behind a currency board are threefold: (i) To import monetary credibility of the anchor nation; (ii) To maintain a fixed exchange rate with the anchor nation; (iii) To establish credibility with the exchange rate (the currency board arrangement is the hardest form of fixed exchange rates outside of dollarisation).

In theory, it is possible that a country may peg the local currency to more than one foreign currency; although, in practice this has never happened (and it would be a more complicated to run than a simple single-currency currency board).

The currency board in question will no longer issue fiat money but instead will only issue a set number of units of local currency for each unit of foreign currency it has in its vault. The surplus on the balance of payments of that country is reflected by higher deposits local banks hold at the central bank as well as (initially) higher deposits of the (net) exporting firms at their local banks. The growth of the domestic money supply can now be coupled to the additional deposits of the banks at the central bank that equals additional hard foreign exchange reserves in the hands of the central bank. The virtue of this system is that questions of currency stability no longer apply. The drawbacks are that the country no longer has the ability to set monetary policy according to other domestic considerations, and that the fixed exchange rate will, to a large extent, also fix a country's terms of trade, irrespective of economic differences between it and its trading partners.

Hong Kong operates a currency board, as does Bulgaria. Estonia established a currency board pegged to the Deutschmark in 1992 after gaining independence, and this policy is seen as a mainstay of that country's subsequent economic success. Argentina abandoned its currency board in January 2002 after a severe recession. This emphasised the fact that currency boards are not irrevocable, and hence may be abandoned in the face of speculation by foreign exchange traders.

Currency boards have advantages for small, open economies which would find independent monetary policy difficult to sustain. They can also form a credible commitment to low inflation.

A gold standard is a special case of a currency board where the value of the national currency is linked to the value of gold instead of a foreign currency.

Monetary Policy Theory

It is important for policy-makers to make credible announcements and degrade interest rates as they are non-important and irrelevant in regarding to monetary policies. If private agents (consumers and firms) believe that policy-makers are committed to lowering inflation, they will anticipate future prices to be lower than otherwise (how those expectations are formed is an entirely different matter; compare for instance rational expectations with adaptive expectations). If an employee expects prices to be high in the future, he or she will draw up a wage contract with a high wage to match these prices. Hence, the expectation of lower wages is reflected in wage-setting behaviour between employees and employers (lower wages since prices are expected to be lower) and since wages are in fact lower, there is no demand pull inflation because employees are receiving a smaller wage and there is no cost push inflation because employers are paying out less in wages.

In order to achieve this low-level of inflation, policy-makers must have *credible* announcements; that is, private agents must believe that these announcements will reflect actual future policy. If an announcement about low-level inflation targets is made but not believed by private agents, wage-setting will anticipate high-level inflation and so wages will be higher and inflation will rise. A high wage will increase a consumer's demand (demand pull inflation) and a firm's costs (cost push inflation), so inflation rises. Hence, if a policy-maker's announcements regarding monetary policy are not credible, policy will not have the desired effect.

If policy-makers believe that private agents anticipate low inflation, they have an incentive to adopt an expansionist monetary policy (where the marginal benefit of increasing economic output outweighs the marginal cost of inflation); however, assuming private agents have rational expectations, they know that policy-makers have this incentive. Hence, private agents know that if they anticipate low inflation, an expansionist policy will be adopted that causes a rise in inflation. Consequently, (unless policy-makers can make their announcement of low inflation *credible*), private agents expect high inflation. This anticipation is fulfilled through adaptive expectation (wage-setting behaviour); so, there is higher inflation (without the benefit of increased output). Hence, unless credible announcements can be made, expansionary monetary policy will fail.

Announcements can be made credible in various ways. One is to establish an independent central bank with low inflation targets (but no output targets). Hence, private agents know that inflation will be low because it is set by an independent body. Central banks can be given incentives to meet their targets (for example, larger budgets, a wage bonus for the head of the bank) in order to increase their reputation and signal a strong commitment to a policy goal. Reputation is an important element in monetary policy implementation. But the idea of reputation should not be confused with commitment. While a central bank might have a favourable reputation due to good performance in conducting monetary policy, the same central bank might not have chosen any particular form of commitment (such as targeting a certain range for inflation). Reputation plays a crucial role in determining how much would markets believe the announcement of a particular commitment to a policy goal but both concepts should not be assimilated.

Also, note that under rational expectations, it is not necessary for the policy-maker to have established its reputation through past policy actions; as an example, the reputation of the head of the central bank might be derived entirely from her or his ideology, professional background, public statements, etc. In fact, it has been argued that in order to prevent some pathologies related to the time-inconsistency of monetary policy implementation (in particular excessive inflation), the head of a central bank should have a larger distaste for inflation than the rest of the economy on average. Hence the reputation of a particular central bank is not necessary tied to past performance, but rather to particular institutional arrangements that the markets can use to form inflation expectations.

Monetary Policy Used by Various Nations

- Australia – Inflation targeting.
- Brazil – Inflation targeting.
- Canada – Inflation targeting.
- Chile – Inflation targeting.
- China – Targets a currency basket.
- Eurozone – Inflation Targeting.
- Hong Kong – Currency board (fixed to US dollar).
- India – Inflation targeting.
- New Zealand – Inflation targeting.
- Singapore – Exchange rate targeting.
- Turkey – Inflation targeting.
- United Kingdom – Inflation Targeting, alongside secondary targets on 'output and employment'.
- United States – Mixed policy (and since the 1980s it is well fitted/described by the "Taylor rule" which shows that the Fed funds rate responds to shocks in inflation and output).

Money Market

In finance, the money market is the global financial market for short-term borrowing and lending. It provides short-term liquidity funding for the global financial system. The money market is where short-term obligations such as Treasury bills, commercial paper and bankers' acceptances are bought and sold.

The money market consists of financial institutions and dealers in money or credit who wish to either borrow or lend. Participants borrow and lend for short periods of time, typically up to thirteen months. Money market trades in short-term financial instruments commonly called "paper." This contrasts with the capital market for longer-term funding, which is supplied by bonds and equity.

The core of the money market consists of banks borrowing and lending to each other, using commercial paper, repurchase agreements and similar instruments. These instruments are often benchmarked (i.e. priced over and above) to the London Interbank Offered Rate (LIBOR).

Finance companies, such as GMAC, typically fund themselves by issuing large amounts of asset-backed commercial paper (ABCP) which is secured by the pledge of eligible assets into an ABCP conduit. Examples of eligible assets include auto loans, credit card receivables, residential/commercial mortgage loans, mortgage-backed securities and similar financial assets. Certain large corporations with strong credit ratings, such as General Electric, issue commercial paper on their own credit. Other large corporations arrange for banks to issue commercial paper on their behalf via commercial paper lines.

In the United States, federal, state and local governments all issue paper to meet funding needs. States and local governments issue municipal paper, while the US Treasury issues Treasury bills to fund the US public debt.

- Trading companies often purchase bankers' acceptances to be tendered for payment to overseas suppliers;
- Retail and institutional money market funds;
- Banks;
- Central banks;
- Cash management programmes;
- Arbitrage ABCP conduits, which seek to buy higher yielding paper, while themselves selling cheaper paper.

Common Money Market Instruments

- *Bankers' Acceptance:* A draft issued by a bank that will be accepted for payment, effectively the same as a cashier's check.
- *Certificate of Deposit:* A time deposit at a bank with a specific maturity date; large-denomination certificates of deposits can be sold before maturity.

- *Repurchase Agreements:* Short-term loans—normally for less than two weeks and frequently for one day – arranged by selling securities to an investor with an agreement to repurchase them at a fixed price on a fixed date.
- *Commercial Paper:* Unsecured promissory notes with a fixed maturity of one to 270 days; usually sold at a discount from face value.
- *Eurodollar Deposit:* Deposits made in US dollars at a bank or bank branch located outside the United States.
- *Federal Agency Short-term Securities(in the US):* Short-term securities issued by government sponsored enterprises such as the Farm Credit System, the Federal Home Loan Banks and the Federal National Mortgage Association.
- *Federal Funds(in the US):* Interest-bearing deposits held by banks and other depository institutions at the Federal Reserve; these are immediately available funds that institutions borrow or lend, usually on an overnight basis. They are lent for the federal funds rate.
- *Municipal Notes(in the US):* Short-term notes issued by municipalities in anticipation of tax receipts or other revenues.
- *Treasury Bills:* Short-term debt obligations of a national government that are issued to mature in three to twelve months.
- *Money Market Mutual Funds:* Pooled short maturity, high quality investments which buy money market securities on behalf of retail or institutional investors.
- *Foreign Exchange Swaps:* Exchanging a set of currencies in spot date and the reversal of the exchange of currencies at a predetermined time in the future.

Securities and Exchange Board of India

Securities and Exchange Board of India (SEBI) is the Regulator for the Securities Market in India. Originally set up by the Government of India in 1988, it acquired statutory form in 1992 with SEBI Act 1992 being passed by the Indian Parliament.

SEBI is headquartered in the popular business district of Bandra-Kurla Complex in Mumbai, and has Northern, Eastern and Southern regional offices in New Delhi, Kolkata and Chennai. It is in the news that a new Western Regional Office has been proposed at Ahmedabad.

Functions and Responsibilities

SEBI has to be responsive to the needs of three groups, which constitute the market:

- The issuers of securities.
- The investors.
- The market intermediaries.

SEBI has three functions rolled into one body quasi-legislative, quasi-judicial and quasi-executive. It drafts regulations in its legislative capacity, it conducts investigation and enforcement action in its executive function and it passes rulings and orders in its judicial capacity. Though this makes it very powerful, there is an appeals process to create accountability. There is a Securities Appellate Tribunal which is a three member tribunal.

SEBI has enjoyed success as a regulator by pushing systemic reforms aggressively and successively (e.g. the quick movement towards making the markets electronic and paperless rolling settlement on T+2 basis). SEBI has been active in seting up the regulations as required under law.

Mutual Fund

A mutual fund is a professionally managed type of collective investments that pools money from many investors and invests it in stocks, bonds, short-term money market instruments, and/or other securities. The mutual fund will have a fund manager that trades the pooled money on a regular basis.

Since 1940, there have been three basic types of investment companies in the United States: open-end funds, also known in the US as mutual funds; unit investment trusts (UITs); and closed-end funds. Similar funds also operate in Canada. However, in the rest of the world, *mutual fund* is used as a generic term for various types of collective investment vehicles, such as unit trusts, open-ended investment companies (OEICs), unitised insurance funds, and undertakings for collective investments in transferable securities (UCITS).

The Backdrop

Massachusetts Investors Trust (now MFS Investment Management) was founded on March 21, 1924, and, after one year, it had 200 shareholders and $392,000 in assets. The entire industry, which included a few closed-end funds represented less than $10 million in 1924.

The stock market crash of 1929 hindered the growth of mutual funds. In response to the stock market crash, Congress passed the

Securities Act of 1933 and the Securities Exchange Act of 1934. These laws require that a fund be registered with the Securities and Exchange Commission (SEC) and provide prospective investors with a prospectus that contains required disclosures about the fund, the securities themselves, and fund manager. The SEC helped draft the Investment Company Act of 1940, which sets forth the guidelines with which all SEC-registered funds today must comply.

With renewed confidence in the stock market, mutual funds began to blossom. By the end of the 1960s, there were approximately 270 funds with $48 billion in assets. The first retail index fund, First Index Investment Trust, was formed in 1976 and headed by John Bogle, who conceptualised many of the key tenets of the industry in his 1951 senior thesis at Princeton University. It is now called the Vanguard 500 Index Fund and is one of the world's largest mutual funds, with more than $100 billion in assets.

A key factor in mutual-fund growth was the 1975 change in the Internal Revenue Code allowing individuals to open individual retirement accounts (IRAs). Even people already enrolled in corporate pension plans could contribute a limited amount (at the time, up to $2,000 a year). Mutual funds are now popular in employer-sponsored "defined-contribution" retirement plans such as (401[k]s) and 403(b)s as well as IRAs including Roth IRAs.

As of October 2007, there were 8,015 mutual funds that belonged to the Investment Company Institute (ICI), a national trade association of investment companies in the United States, with combined assets of $12.356 trillion.

Usage

Since the Investment Company Act of 1940, a mutual fund is one of three basic types of investment companies available in the United States.

Mutual funds can invest in many kinds of securities. The most common are cash instruments, stock, and bonds, but there are hundreds of subcategories. Stock funds, for instance, can invest primarily in the shares of a particular industry, such as technology or utilities. These are known as sector funds. Bond funds can vary according to risk (e.g. high-yield junk bonds or investment-grade corporate bonds), type of issuers (e.g. government agencies, corporations, or municipalities), or maturity of the bonds (short- or long-term). Both stock and bond funds can invest in primarily US securities (domestic funds), both US and foreign securities (global funds), or primarily foreign securities (international funds).

Most mutual funds' investment portfolios are continually adjusted under the supervision of a professional manager, who forecasts cash flows into and out of the fund by investors, as well as the future performance of investments appropriate for the fund and chooses those which he or she believes will most closely match the fund's stated investment objective. A mutual fund is administered under an advisory contract with a management company, which may hire or fire fund managers.

Mutual funds are subject to a special set of regulatory, accounting, and tax rules. In the US, unlike most other types of business entities, they are not taxed on their income as long as they distribute 90 per cent of it to their shareholders and the funds meet certain diversification requirements in the Internal Revenue Code. Also, the type of income they earn is often unchanged as it passes through to the shareholders. Mutual fund distributions of tax-free municipal bond income are tax-free to the shareholder. Taxable distributions can be either ordinary income or capital gains, depending on how the fund earned those distributions. Net losses are not distributed or passed through to fund investors.

Net Asset Value

The *net asset value*, or NAV, is the current market value of a fund's holdings, less the fund's liabilities, usually expressed as a per-share amount. For most funds, the NAV is determined daily, after the close of trading on some specified financial exchange, but some funds update their NAV multiple times during the trading day. The public offering price, or POP, is the NAV plus a sales charge. Open-end funds sell shares at the POP and redeem shares at the NAV, and so process orders only after the NAV is determined. Closed-end funds (the shares of which are traded by investors) may trade at a higher or lower price than their NAV; this is known as a *premium* or *discount*, respectively. If a fund is divided into multiple classes of shares, each class will typically have its own NAV, reflecting differences in fees and expenses paid by the different classes.

Some mutual funds own securities which are not regularly traded on any formal exchange. These may be shares in very small or bankrupt companies; they may be derivatives; or they may be private investments in unregistered financial instruments (such as stock in a non-public company). In the absence of a public market for these securities, it is the responsibility of the fund manager to form an estimate of their value when computing the NAV. How much of a fund's assets may be invested in such securities is stated in the fund's prospectus.

Average Annual Return

US mutual funds use SEC form N-1A to report the average annual compounded rates of return for 1-year, 5-year and 10-year periods as the "average annual total return" for each fund. The following formula is used:

$$P(1+T)^n = ERV$$

Where:

P = a hypothetical initial payment of $1,000.

T = average annual total return.

n = number of years.

ERV = ending redeemable value of a hypothetical $1,000 payment made at the beginning of the 1-, 5-, or 10-year periods at the end of the 1-, 5-, or 10-year periods (or fractional portion).

Turnover

Turnover is a measure of the fund's securities transactions, usually calculated over a year's time, and usually expressed as a percentage of net asset value.

This value is usually calculated as the value of all transactions (buying, selling) divided by 2 divided by the fund's total holdings; i.e. the fund counts one security sold and another one bought as one "turnover". Thus turnover measures the replacement of holdings.

In Canada, under NI 81-106 (required disclosure for investment funds) turnover ratio is calculated based on the lesser of purchases or sales divided by the average size of the portfolio (including cash).

Expenses and TER's

Mutual funds bear expenses similar to other companies. The fee structure of a mutual fund can be divided into two or three main components: management fee, non-management expense, and 12b-1/non-12b-1 fees. All expenses are expressed as a percentage of the average daily net assets of the fund.

Management Fees: The management fee for the fund is usually synonymous with the contractual investment advisory fee charged for the management of a fund's investments. However, as many fund companies include administrative fees in the advisory fee component, when attempting to compare the total management expenses of different funds, it is helpful to define management fee as equal to the contractual advisory fee + the contractual administrator fee. This "levels the playing field" when comparing management fee components across multiple funds.

Contractual advisory fees may be structured as "flat-rate" fees, i.e. a single fee charged to the fund, regardless of the asset size of the fund. However, many funds have contractual fees which include breakpoints, so that as the value of a fund's assets increases, the advisory fee paid decreases. Another way in which the advisory fees remain competitive is by structuring the fee so that it is based on the value of all of the assets of a group or a complex of funds rather than those of a single fund.

Non-management Expenses: Apart from the management fee, there are certain non-management expenses which most funds must pay. Some of the more significant (in terms of amount) non-management expenses are: transfer agent expenses (this is usually the person you get on the other end of the phone line when you want to purchase/sell shares of a fund), custodian expense (the fund's assets are kept in custody by a bank which charges a custody fee), legal/audit expense, fund accounting expense, registration expense (the SEC charges a registration fee when funds file registration statements with it), board of directors/ trustees expense (the disinterested members of the board who oversee the fund are usually paid a fee for their time spent at meetings), and printing and postage expense (incurred when printing and delivering shareholder reports).

12b-1/Non-12b-1 Service Fees: 12b-1 service fees/shareholder servicing fees are contractual fees which a fund may charge to cover the marketing expenses of the fund. Non-12b-1 service fees are marketing/shareholder servicing fees which do not fall under SEC rule 12b-1. While funds do not have to charge the full contractual 12b-1 fee, they often do. When investing in a front-end load or no-load fund, the 12b-1 fees for the fund are usually 0.250 per cent (or 25 basis points). The 12b-1 fees for back-end and level-load share classes are usually between 50 and 75 basis points but may be as much as 100 basis points. While funds are often marketed as "no-load" funds, this does not mean they do not charge a distribution expense through a different mechanism. It is expected that a fund listed on an online brokerage site will be paying for the "shelf-space" in a different manner even if not directly through a 12b-1 fee.

Investor Fees and Expenses

Fees and expenses borne by the investor vary based on the arrangement made with the investor's broker. Sales loads (or contingent deferred sales loads (CDSL)) are not included in the fund's total expense ratio (TER) because they do not pass through the statement of operations for the fund. Additionally, funds may charge early redemption fees to discourage investors from swapping money into and out of the fund quickly, which may force the fund to make bad trades to obtain the necessary liquidity. For example, Fidelity Diversified International Fund (FDIVX) charges a 1 per cent fee on money removed from the fund in less than 30 days.

Brokerage Commissions

An additional expense which does not pass through the statement of operations and cannot be controlled by the investor is brokerage commissions. Brokerage commissions are incorporated into the price of the fund and are reported usually 3 months after the fund's annual report in the statement of additional information. Brokerage commissions are directly related to portfolio turnover (portfolio turnover refers to the number of times the fund's assets are bought and sold over the course of a year). Usually the higher the rate of the portfolio turnover, the higher the brokerage commissions. The advisors of mutual fund companies are required to achieve "best execution" through brokerage arrangements so that the commissions charged to the fund will not be excessive.

Open-end Fund

The term *mutual fund* is the common name for what is classified as an open-end investment company by the SEC. Being open-ended means that, at the end of everyday, the fund issues new shares to investors and buys back shares from investors wishing to leave the fund.

Mutual funds must be structured as corporations or trusts, such as business trusts, and any corporation or trust will be classified by the SEC as an investment company if it issues securities and primarily invests in non-government securities. An investment company will be classified by the SEC as an open-end investment company if they do not issue undivided interests in specified securities (the defining characteristic of unit investment trusts or UITs) and if they issue redeemable securities. Registered investment companies that are not UITs or open-end investment companies are closed-end funds. Neither UITs nor closed-end funds are mutual funds (as that term is used in the US).

Exchange-traded Funds

A relatively recent innovation, the exchange-traded fund or ETF, is often structured as an open-end investment company. ETFs combine characteristics of both mutual funds and closed-end funds. ETFs are traded throughout the day on a stock exchange, just like closed-end funds, but at prices generally approximating the ETF's net asset value. Most ETFs are index funds and track stock market indexes. Shares are issued or redeemed by institutional investors in large blocks (typically of 50,000). Most investors purchase and sell shares through brokers in market transactions. Because the institutional investors normally purchase and redeem in kind transactions, ETFs are more efficient than traditional mutual funds (which are continuously issuing and redeeming securities and, to effect such transactions, continually buying and selling securities and maintaining liquidity positions) and therefore tend to have lower expenses.

Exchange-traded funds are also valuable for foreign investors who are often able to buy and sell securities traded on a stock market, but who, for regulatory reasons, are limited in their ability to participate in traditional US mutual funds.

Equity Funds

Equity funds, which consist mainly of stock investments, are the most common type of mutual fund. Equity funds hold 50 per cent of all amounts invested in mutual funds in the United States. Often equity funds focus investments on particular strategies and certain types of issuers.

Capitalisation

Fund managers and other investment professionals have varying definitions of mid-cap, and large-cap ranges. The following ranges are used by Russell Indexes:

- Russell Microcap Index – micro-cap ($54.8-539.5 million).
- Russell 2000 Index – small-cap ($182.6 million-1.8 billion).
- Russell Midcap Index – mid-cap ($1.8-13.7 billion).
- Russell 1000 Index – large-cap ($1.8-386.9 billion).

Growth vs Value

Another distinction is made between growth funds, which invest in stocks of companies that have the potential for large capital gains, and value funds, which concentrate on stocks that are undervalued. Value stocks have historically produced higher returns; however, financial theory states this is compensation for their greater risk. Growth funds tend not to pay regular dividends. Income funds tend to be more conservative investments, with a focus on stocks that pay dividends. A balanced fund may use a combination of strategies, typically including some level of investment in bonds, to stay more conservative when it comes to risk, yet aim for some growth.

Index Funds versus Active Management

An index fund maintains investments in companies that are part of major stock (or bond) indices, such as the S&P 500, while an actively managed fund attempts to outperform a relevant index through superior stock-picking techniques. The assets of an index fund are managed to closely approximate the performance of a particular published index. Since the composition of an index changes infrequently, an index fund manager makes fewer trades, on average, than does an active fund manager. For this reason, index funds generally have lower trading expenses than actively managed funds, and typically incur fewer short-term capital gains which must be passed on to shareholders. Additionally, index funds do not incur expenses to pay for selection of individual stocks (proprietary selection techniques, research, etc.) and deciding when to buy, hold or sell individual holdings. Instead, a fairly simple computer model can identify whatever changes are needed to bring the fund back into agreement with its target index.

Certain empirical evidence seems to illustrate that mutual funds do not beat the market and actively managed mutual funds underperform other broad-based portfolios with similar characteristics. One study found that nearly 1,500 US mutual funds underperformed the market in approximately half of the years between 1962 and 1992. Moreover, funds that performed well in the past are not able to beat the market again in the future.

Bond Funds

Bond funds account for 18 per cent of mutual fund assets. Types of bond funds include term funds, which have a fixed set of time (short-, medium-, or long-term) before they mature. Municipal bond funds generally have lower returns, but have tax advantages and lower risk. High-yield bond funds invest in corporate bonds, including high-yield or junk bonds. With the potential for high yield, these bonds also come with greater risk.

Money Market Funds

Money market funds hold 26 per cent of mutual fund assets in the United States. Money market funds entail the least risk, as well as lower rates of return. Unlike certificates of deposit (CDs), money market shares are liquid and redeemable at any time.

Funds of Funds

Funds of funds (FoF) are mutual funds which invest in other underlying mutual funds (i.e. they are funds comprised of other funds). The funds at the underlying level are typically funds which an investor can invest in individually. A fund of funds will typically charge a management fee which is smaller than that of a normal fund because it is considered a fee charged for asset allocation services. The fees charged at the underlying fund level do not pass through the statement of operations, but are usually disclosed in the fund's annual report, prospectus, or statement of additional information. The fund should be evaluated on the combination of the fund-level expenses and underlying fund expenses, as these both reduce the return to the investor.

Most FoFs invest in affiliated funds (i.e. mutual funds managed by the same advisor), although some invest in funds managed by other (unaffiliated) advisors. The cost associated with investing in an unaffiliated underlying fund is most often higher than investing in an affiliated underlying because of the investment management research involved in investing in fund advised by a different advisor. Recently, FoFs have been classified into those that are actively managed (in which the investment advisor reallocates frequently among the underlying funds in order to adjust to changing market conditions) and those that are passively managed (the investment advisor allocates assets on the basis of on an allocation model which is rebalanced on a regular basis).

The design of FoFs is structured in such a way as to provide a ready mix of mutual funds for investors who are unable to or unwilling to determine their own asset allocation model. Fund companies such as TIAA-CREF, American Century Investments, Vanguard, and Fidelity have also entered this market to provide investors with these options and take the "guess work" out of selecting funds. The allocation mixes usually vary by the time the investor would like to retire: 2020, 2030, 2050, etc. The more distant the target retirement date, the more aggressive the asset mix.

Hedge Funds

Hedge funds in the United States are pooled investment funds with loose SEC regulation and should not be confused with mutual funds. Some hedge fund managers are required to register with SEC as investment advisers under the Investment Advisers Act. The Act does not require an adviser to follow or avoid any particular investment strategies, nor does it require or prohibit specific investments. Hedge funds typically charge a management fee of 1 per cent or more, plus a "performance fee" of 20 per cent of the hedge fund's profits. There may be a "lock-up" period, during which an investor cannot cash in shares. A variation of the hedge strategy is the 130-30 fund for individual investors.

Mutual Funds vs Other Investments

Mutual funds offer several advantages over investing in individual stocks. For example, the transaction costs are divided among all the mutual fund shareholders, which allows for cost-effective diversification. Investors may also benefit by having a third party (professional fund managers) apply expertise and dedicate time to manage and research investment options, although there is dispute over whether professional fund managers can, on average, outperform simple index funds that mimic public indexes. Whether actively managed or passively indexed, mutual funds are not immune to risks. They share the same risks associated with the investments made. If the fund invests primarily in stocks, it is usually subject to the same ups and downs and risks as the stock market.

Share Classes

Many mutual funds offer more than one class of shares. For example, you may have seen a fund that offers "Class A" and "Class B" shares. Each class will invest in the same pool (or investment portfolio) of securities and will have the same investment objectives and policies. But each class will have different shareholder services and/or distribution arrangements with different fees and expenses. These differences are supposed to reflect different costs involved in servicing investors in various classes; for example, one class may be sold through brokers with a front-end load, and another class may be sold direct to the public with no load but a "12b-1 fee" included in the class's expenses (sometimes referred to as "Class C" shares). Still a third class might have a minimum investment of $10,000,000 and be available only to financial institutions (a so-called "institutional" share class). In some cases, by aggregating regular investments made by many individuals, a retirement plan (such as a 401(k) plan) may qualify to purchase "institutional" shares (and gain the benefit of their typically lower expense ratios) even though no members of the plan would qualify individually. As a result, each class will likely have different performance results.

A multi-class structure offers investors the ability to select a fee and expense structure that is most appropriate for their investment goals (including the length of time that they expect to remain invested in the fund).

Load and Expenses

A front-end load or sales charge is a commission paid to a broker by a mutual fund when shares are purchased, taken as a percentage of funds invested. The value of the investment is reduced by the amount of the load. Some funds have a deferred sales charge or back-end load. In this type of fund an investor pays no sales charge when purchasing shares, but will pay a commission out of the proceeds when shares are redeemed depending on how long they are held. Another derivative structure is a level-load fund, in which no sales charge is paid when buying the fund, but a back-end load may be charged if the shares purchased are sold within a year.

Load funds are sold through financial intermediaries such as brokers, financial planners, and other types of registered representatives who charge a commission for their services. Shares of front-end load funds are frequently eligible for breakpoints (i.e. a reduction in the commission paid) based on a number of variables. These include other accounts in the same fund family held by the investor or various family members, or committing to buy more of the fund within a set period of time in return for a lower commission "today".

It is possible to buy many mutual funds without paying a sales charge. These are called no-load funds. In addition to being available from the fund company itself, no-load funds may be sold by some discount brokers for a flat transaction fee or even no fee at all. (This does not necessarily mean that the broker is not compensated for the transaction; in such cases, the fund may pay brokers' commissions out of "distribution and marketing" expenses rather than a specific sales charge. The purchaser is, therefore, paying the fee indirectly through the fund's expenses deducted from profits).

No-load funds include both index funds and actively managed funds. The largest mutual fund families selling no-load index funds are Vanguard and Fidelity, though there are a number of smaller mutual fund families with no-load funds as well. Expense ratios in some no-load index funds are less than 0.2 per cent per year versus the typical actively managed fund's expense ratio of about 1.5 per cent per year. Load funds usually have even higher expense ratios when the load is considered. The expense ratio is the anticipated annual cost to the investor of holding shares of the fund. For example, on a $100,000 investment, an expense ratio of 0.2 per cent means $200 of annual expense, while a 1.5 per cent expense ratio would result in $1,500 of annual expense. These expenses are before any sales commissions paid to purchase the mutual fund.

Many fee-only financial advisors strongly suggest no-load funds such as index funds. If the advisor is not of the fee-only type but is instead compensated by commissions, the advisor may have a conflict of interest in selling high-commission load funds.

Venture Capital

Venture capital (also known as VC or Venture) is a type of private equity capital typically provided to immature, high-potential, growth companies in the interest of generating a return through an eventual realisation event such as an IPO or trade sale of the company. Venture capital investments are generally made as cash in exchange for shares in the invested company.

Venture capital typically comes from institutional investors and high net worth individuals and is pooled together by dedicated investment firms.

A venture capitalist (also known as a VC) is a person or investment firm that makes venture investments, and these venture capitalists are expected to bring managerial and technical expertise as well as capital to their investments. A venture capital fund refers to a pooled investment vehicle (often an LP or LLC) that primarily invests the financial capital of third-party investors in enterprises that are too risky for the standard capital markets or bank loans.

Venture capital is most attractive for new companies with limited operating history that are too small to raise capital in the public markets and are too immature to secure a bank loan or complete a debt offering. In exchange for the high risk that venture capitalists assume by investing in smaller and less mature companies, venture capitalists usually get significant control over company decisions, in addition to a significant portion of the company's ownership (and consequently value).

History

With few exceptions, private equity in the first half of the 20th century was the domain of wealthy individuals and families. The Vanderbilts, Whitneys, Rockefellers and Warburgs were notable investors in private companies in the first half of the century. In 1938, Laurance S. Rockefeller helped finance the creation of both Eastern Air Lines and Douglas Aircraft and the Rockefeller family had vast holdings in a variety of companies. Eric M. Warburg founded E.M. Warburg & Co. in 1938, which would ultimately become Warburg Pincus, with investments in both leveraged buyouts and venture capital.

Origins of Modern Private Equity

Before World War II, venture capital investments (originally known as "development capital") were primarily the domain of wealthy individuals and families. It was not until after World War II that what is considered today to be true private equity investments began to emerge marked by the founding of the first two venture capital firms in 1946: American Research and Development Corporation. (ARDC) and J.H. Whitney & Company.

ARDC was founded by Georges Doriot, the "father of venture capitalism" (former dean of Harvard Business School), with Ralph Flanders and Karl Compton (former president of MIT), to encourage private sector investments in businesses run by soldiers who were returning from World War II. ARDC's significance was primarily that it was the first institutional private equity investment firm that raised capital from sources other than wealthy families although it had several notable investment successes as well. ARDC is credited with the first major venture capital success story when its 1957 investment of $70,000 in Digital Equipment Corporation (DEC) would be valued at over $355 million after the company's initial public offering in 1968 (representing a return of over 500 times on its investment and an annualised rate of return of 101 per cent). Former employees of ARDC went on to found several prominent venture capital firms including Greylock Partners (founded in 1965 by Charlie Waite and Bill Elfers) and Morgan, Holland Ventures, the predecessor of Flagship Ventures (founded in 1982 by James Morgan). ARDC continued investing until 1971 with the retirement of Doriot. In 1972, Doriot merged ARDC with Textron after having invested in over 150 companies.

J. H. Whitney & Company was founded by John Hay Whitney and his partner Benno Schmidt. Whitney had been investing since the 1930s, founding Pioneer Pictures in 1933 and acquiring a 15 per cent interest in Technicolour Corporation with his cousin Cornelius Vanderbilt Whitney. By far Whitney's most famous investment was in Florida Foods Corporation. The company developed an innovative method for delivering nutrition to American soldiers, which later came to be known as Minute Maid orange juice and was sold to The Coca-Cola Company in 1960. J. H. Whitney & Company continues to make investments in leveraged buyout transactions and raised $750 million for its sixth institutional private equity fund in 2005.

Early Venture Capital and the Growth of Silicon Valley

One of the first steps towards a professionally-managed venture capital industry was the passage of the Small Business Investment Act of 1958. The 1958 Act officially allowed the US Small Business Administration (SBA) to licence private "Small Business Investment Companies" (SBICs) to help the financing and management of the small entrepreneurial businesses in the United States.

During the 1960s and 1970s, venture capital firms focused their investment activity primarily on starting and expanding companies. More often than not, these companies were exploiting breakthroughs in electronic, medical or data-processing technology. As a result, venture capital came to be almost synonymous with technology finance.

It is commonly noted that the first venture-backed start-up is Fairchild semi-conductor (which produced the first commercially practical integrated circuit), funded in 1959 by what would later become Venrock Associates. Venrock was founded in 1969 by Laurance S. Rockefeller, the fourth of John D. Rockefeller's six children as a way to allow other Rockefeller children to develop exposure to venture capital investments.

It was also in the 1960s that the common form of private equity fund, still in use today, emerged. Private equity firms organised limited partnerships to hold investments in which the investment professionals served as general partner and the investors, who were passive limited partners, put up the capital. The compensation structure, still in use today, also emerged with limited partners paying an annual management fee of 1-2per cent and a carried interest typically representing up to 20 per cent of the profits of the partnership.

The growth of the venture capital industry was fuelled by the emergence of the independent investment firms on Sand Hill Road, beginning with Kleiner, Perkins, Caufield and Byers and Sequoia Capital in 1972. Located, in Menlo Park, CA, Kleiner Perkins, Sequoia and later venture capital firms would have access to the burgeoning technology industries in the area. By the early-1970s, there were many semi-conductor companies based in the Santa Clara Valley as well as early computer firms using their devices and programming and service companies. Throughout the 1970s, a group of private equity firms, focused primarily on venture capital investments, would be founded that would become the model for later leveraged buyout and venture capital investment firms. In 1973, with the number of new venture capital firms increasing, leading venture capitalists formed the National Venture Capital Association (NVCA). The NVCA was to serve as the industry trade group for the venture capital industry. Venture capital firms suffered a temporary downturn in 1974, when the stock market crashed and investors were naturally wary of this new kind of investment fund.

It was not until 1978 that venture capital experienced its first major fund-raising year, as the industry raised approximately $750 million. With the passage of the Employee Retirement Income Security Act (ERISA) in 1974, corporate pension funds were prohibited from holding certain risky investments including many investments in privately held companies. In 1978, the US Labour Department relaxed certain of the ERISA restrictions, under the "prudent man rule," thus allowing corporate pension funds to invest in the asset class and providing a major source of capital available to venture capitalists.

Venture Capital in the 1980s

The public successes of the venture capital industry in the 1970s and early-1980s (e.g. Digital Equipment Corporation, Apple, Genentech) gave rise to a major proliferation of venture capital investment firms. From just a few dozen firms at the start of the decade, there were over 650 firms by the end of the 1980s, each searching for the next major "home run". While the number of firms multiplied, the capital managed by these firms increased only 11 per cent from $28 billion to $31 billion over the course of the decade.

The growth the industry was hampered by sharply declining returns and certain venture firms began posting losses for the first time. In addition to the increased competition among firms, several other factors impacted returns. The market for initial public offerings cooled in the mid-1980s before collapsing after the stock market crash in 1987 and foreign corporations, particularly from Japan and Korea, flooded early stage companies with capital.

In response to the changing conditions, corporations that had sponsored in-house venture investment arms, including General Electric and Paine Webber either sold off or closed these venture capital units. Additionally, venture capital units within Chemical Bank and Continental Illinois National Bank, among others, began shifting their focus from funding early stage companies towards investments in more mature companies. Even industry founders J.H. Whitney & Company and Warburg Pincus began to transition towards leveraged buyouts and growth capital investments.

The Venture Capital Boom and the Internet Bubble (1995 to 2000)

By the end of the 1980s, venture capital returns were relatively low, particularly in comparison with their emerging leveraged buyout cousins, due in part to the competition for hot startups, excess supply of IPOs and the inexperience of many venture capital fund managers. Growth in the venture capital industry remained limited through the 1980s and the first half of the 1990s increasing from $3 billion in 1983 to just over $4 billion more than a decade later in 1994.

After a shakeout of venture capital mangers, the more successful firms retrenched, focusing increasingly on improving operations at their portfolio companies rather than continuously making new investments. Results would begin to turn very attractive, successful and would ultimately generate the venture capital boom of the 1990s. Former Wharton Professor Andrew Metrick refers to these first 15 years of the modern venture capital industry beginning in 1980 as the "pre-boom period" in anticipation of the boom that would begin in 1995 and last through the bursting of the Internet bubble in 2000.

The late-1990s were a boom time for the venture capital, as firms on Sand Hill Road in Menlo Park and Silicon Valley benefited from a huge surge of interest in the nascent Internet and other computer technologies. Initial public offerings of stock for technology and other growth companies were in abundance and venture firms were reaping large windfalls.

The Bursting of the Internet Bubble and the Private Equity Crash (2000 to 2003)

The Nasdaq crash and technology slump that started in March 2000 shook virtually the entire venture capital industry as valuations for start-up technology companies collapsed. Over the next two years, many venture firms had been forced to write-off their large proportions of their investments and many funds were significantly "under water" (the values of the fund's investments were below the amount of capital invested). Venture capital investors sought to reduce size of commitments they had made to venture capital funds and in numerous instances, investors sought to unload existing commitments for cents on the dollar in the secondary market. By mid-2003, the venture capital industry had shrivelled to about half its 2001 capacity. Nevertheless, Pricewaterhouse Coopers' MoneyTree Survey shows that total venture capital investments held steady at 2003 levels through the second quarter of 2005.

Although the post-boom years represent just a small fraction of the peak levels of venture investment reached in 2000, they still represent an increase over the levels of investment from 1980 through 1995. As a percentage of GDP, venture investment was 0.058 per cent per cent in 1994, peaked at 1.087 per cent (nearly 19x the 1994 level) in 2000 and ranged from 0.164 per cent to 0.182 per cent in 2003 and 2004. The revival of an Internet-driven environment in 2004 through 2007 helped to revive the venture capital environment. However, as a percentage of the overall private equity market, venture capital has still not reached its mid-1990s level, let alone its peak in 2000.

However, venture capital funds, which were responsible for much of the fund-raising volume in 2000 (the height of the dot-com bubble), raised only $25.1 billion in 2006, a 2 per cent decline from 2005 and a significant decline from its peak.

Structure of Venture Capital Firms

Venture capital firms are typically structured as partnerships, the general partners of which serve as the managers of the firm and will serve as investment advisors to the venture capital funds raised. Venture capital firms in the United States may also be structured as limited liability companies, in which case the firm's managers are known as managing members. Investors in venture capital funds are known as limited partners. This constituency comprises both high net worth individuals and institutions with large amounts of available capital, such as state and private pension funds, university financial endowments, foundations, insurance companies, and pooled investment vehicles, called fund of funds or mutual funds.

Roles within Venture Capital Firms

Within the venture capital industry, the general partners and other investment professionals of the venture capital firm are often referred to as "venture capitalists" or "VCs". Typical career backgrounds vary, but broadly speaking venture capitalists come from either an operational or a finance background. Venture capitalists with an operational background tend to be former founders or executives of companies similar to those which the partnership finances or will have served as management consultants. Venture capitalists with finance backgrounds tend to have investment banking or other corporate finance experience.

Although the titles are not entirely uniform from firm to firm, other positions at venture capital firms include:

- *Venture Partners:* Venture partners are expected to source potential investment opportunities (bring in deals) and typically are compensated only for those deals with which they are involved.
- *Entrepreneur-in-residence (EIR):* EIRs are experts in a particular domain and perform due diligence on potential deals. EIRs are engaged by venture capital firms temporarily (six to 18 months) and are expected to develop and pitch start-up ideas to their host firm (although neither party is bound to work with each other). Some EIR's move on to executive positions within a portfolio company.
- *Principal:* This is a mid-level investment professional position, and often considered a "partner-track" position. Principals will have been promoted from a senior associate position or who have commensurate experience in another field such as investment banking or management consulting.
- *Associate:* This is typically the most junior apprentice position within a venture capital firm. After a few successful years, an associate may move up to the "senior associate" position and potentially principal and beyond. Associates will often have worked for 1-2 years in another field such as investment banking or management consulting.

Structure of the Funds

Most venture capital funds have a fixed life of 10 years, with the possibility of a few years of extensions to allow for private companies still seeking liquidity. The investing cycle for most funds is generally three to five years, after which the focus is managing and making follow-on investments in an existing portfolio. This model was pioneered by successful funds in Silicon Valley through the 1980s to invest in technological trends broadly but only during their period of ascendance, and to cut exposure to management and marketing risks of any individual firm or its product.

In such a fund, the investors have a fixed commitment to the fund that is initially unfunded and subsequently "called down" by the venture capital fund over time as the fund makes its investments. There are substantial penalties for a Limited Partner (or investor) that fails to participate in a capital call.

Compensation

Venture capitalists are compensated through a combination of management fees and carried interest (often referred to as a "two and 20" arrangement:

- *Management Fees:* An annual payment made by the investors in the fund to the fund's manager to pay for the private equity firm's investment operations. In a typical venture capital fund, the general partners receive an annual management fee equal to up to 2 per cent of the committed capital.
- *Carried Interest:* A share of the profits of the fund (typically 20 per cent), paid to the private equity fund's management company as a performance incentive. The remaining 80 per cent of the profits are paid to the fund's investors Strong Limited Partner interest in top-tier venture firms has led to a general trend towards terms more favourable to the venture partnership, and certain groups are able to command carried interest of 25-30 per cent on their funds.

Because a fund may run out of capital prior to the end of its life, larger venture capital firms usually have several overlapping funds at the same time; this lets the larger firm keep specialists in all stages of the development of firms almost constantly engaged. Smaller firms tend to thrive or fail with their initial industry contacts; by the time the fund cashes out, an entirely-new generation of technologies and people is ascending, whom the general partners may not know well, and so it is prudent to reassess and shift industries or personnel rather than attempt to simply invest more in the industry or people the partners already know.

Venture Capital Funding

Venture capitalists are typically very selective in deciding what to invest in; as a rule of thumb, a fund may invest in one in four hundred opportunities presented to it. Funds are most interested in ventures with exceptionally high growth potential, as only such opportunities are likely capable of providing the financial returns and successful exit event within the required timeframe (typically 3-7 years) that venture capitalists expect.

Because investments are illiquid and require 3-7 years to harvest, venture capitalists are expected to carry out detailed due diligence prior to investment. Venture capitalists also are expected to nurture the companies in which they invest, in order to increase the likelihood of reaching a IPO stage when valuations are favourable. Venture capitalists typically assist at four stages in the company's development:

- Idea generation;
- Start-up;
- Ramp up; and
- Exit.

There are typically six stages of financing offered in Venture Capital, that roughly correspond to these stages of a companies development:

- *Seed Money:* Low level financing needed to prove a new idea (Often provided by "angel investors").
- *Start-up:* Early stage firms that need funding for expenses associated with marketing and product development.
- *First-Round:* Early sales and manufacturing funds.
- *Second-Round:* Working capital for early stage companies that are selling product, but not yet turning a profit.
- *Third-Round:* Also called Mezzanine financing, this is expansion money for a newly profitable company.
- *Fourth-Round:* Also called bridge financing, 4th round is intended to finance the going public process.

Because there are no public exchanges listing their securities, private companies meet venture capital firms and other private equity investors in several ways, including warm referrals from the investors' trusted sources and other business contacts; investor conferences and symposia; and summits where companies pitch directly to investor groups in face-to-face meetings, including a variant know as "Speed Venturing", which is akin to speed-dating for capital, where the investor decides within 10 minutes whether s/he wants a follow-up meeting.

This need for high returns makes venture funding an expensive capital source for companies, and most suitable for businesses having large up-front capital requirements which cannot be financed by cheaper alternatives such as debt. That is most commonly the case for intangible assets such as software, and other intellectual property, whose value is unproven. In turn this explains why venture capital is most prevalent in the fast-growing technology and life sciences or biotechnology fields.

If a company does have the qualities venture capitalists seek including a solid business plan, a good management team, investment and passion from the founders, a good potential to exit the investment before the end of their funding cycle, and target minimum returns in excess of 40 per cent per year, it will find it easier to raise venture capital.

Main Alternatives to Venture Capital

Because of the strict requirements venture capitalists have for potential investments, many entrepreneurs seek initial funding from angel investors, who may be more willing to invest in highly speculative opportunities, or may have a prior relationship with the entrepreneur.

Furthermore, many venture capital firms will only seriously evaluate an investment in a start-up otherwise unknown to them if the company can prove at least some of its claims about the technology and/or market potential for its product or services. To achieve this, or even just to avoid the dilutive effects of receiving funding before such claims are proven, many start-ups seek to self-finance until they reach a point where they can credibly approach outside capital providers such as venture capitalists or angel investors. This practice is called "bootstrapping".

There has been some debate since the dot-com boom that a "funding gap" has developed between the friends and family investments typically in the $0 to $250,000 range and the amounts that most Venture Capital Funds prefer to invest between $1 to $2M. This funding gap may be accentuated by the fact that some successful Venture Capital funds have been drawn to raise ever-larger funds, requiring them to search for correspondingly larger investment opportunities. This 'gap' is often filled by angel investors as well as equity investment companies who specialise in investments in startups from the range of $250,000 to $1M. The National Venture Capital association estimates that the latter now invest more than $30 billion a year in the USA in contrast to the $20 billion a year invested by organised Venture Capital funds.

In industries where assets can be securitised effectively because they reliably generate future revenue streams or have a good potential for resale in case of foreclosure, businesses may more cheaply be able to raise debt to finance their growth. Good examples would include asset-intensive extractive industries such as mining, or manufacturing industries. Offshore funding is provided via specialist venture capital trusts which seek to utilise securitisation in structuring hybrid multi market transactions via an SPV (special purpose vehicle): a corporate entity that is designed solely for the purpose of the financing.

In addition to traditional venture capital and angel networks, groups have emerged which allow groups of small investors or entrepreneurs themselves to compete in a privatised business plan competition where the group itself serves as the investor through a democratic process.

Geographical Differences

Venture capital, as an industry, originated in the United States and American firms have traditionally been the largest participants in venture deals and the bulk of venture capital has been deployed in American companies. However, increasingly, non-US venture investment is growing and the number and size of non-US venture capitalists have been expanding.

Venture capital has been used as a tool for economic development in a variety of developing regions. In many of these regions, with less developed financial sectors, venture capital plays a role in facilitating access to finance for small and medium enterprises (SMEs), which in most cases would not qualify for receiving bank loans.

United States

Venture capitalists invested some $6.6 billion in 797 deals in US during the third quarter of 2006, according to the Money Tree Report by Pricewaterhousebn Coopers and the National Venture Capital Association based on data by Thomson Financial.

A National Venture Capital Association survey found that majority (69%) of venture capitalists predict that venture investments in US would level between $20-29 billion in 2007.

Canada

Canadian technology companies have attracted interest from the global venture capital community as a result, in part, of generous tax incentive through the Scientific Research and Experimental Development (SR&ED) investment tax credit programme. The basic incentive available to any Canadian corporation performing R&D is a non-refundable tax credit that is equal to 20 per cent of "qualifying" R&D expenditures (labour, material, R&D contracts, and R&D equipment). An enhanced 35 per cent refundable tax credit of available to certain (i.e. small) Canadian-controlled private corporations (CCPCs). Because the CCPC rules require a minimum of 50 per cent Canadian ownership in the company performing R&D, foreign investors who would like to benefit from the larger 35 per cent tax credit must accept minority position in the company – which might not be desirable. The SR&ED programme does not restrict the export of any technology or intellectual property that may have been developed with the benefit of SR&ED tax incentives.

Canada also has a fairly unique form of venture capital generation in its Labour Sponsored Venture Capital Corporations (LSVCC). These funds, also known as Retail Venture Capital or Labour Sponsored Investment Funds (LSIF), are generally sponsored by labour unions and offer tax breaks from government to encourage retail investors to purchase the funds. Generally, these Retail Venture Capital funds only invest in companies where the majority of employees are in Canada. However, innovative structures have been developed to permit LSVCCs to direct in Canadian subsidiaries of corporations incorporated in jurisdictions outside of Canada.

Europe

Europe has a large and growing number of active venture firms. Capital raised in the region in 2005, including buyout funds, exceeded €60 mn, of which €12.6 mn was specifically for venture investment. The European Venture Capital Association includes a list of active firms and other statistics. In 2006, the top three countries receiving the most venture capital investments were the United Kingdom (515 minority stakes sold for €1.78 bn), France (195 deals worth €875 m), and Germany (207 deals worth €428 m) according to data gathered by Library House.

European venture capital investment in the second quarter of 2007 rose 5 per cent to 1.14 billion Euros from the first quarter. However, due to bigger sized deals in early stage investments, the number of deals was down 20 per cent to 213. The second quarter venture capital investment results were significant in terms of early-round investment, where as much as 600 million Euros (about 42.8 per cent of the total capital) were invested in 126 early round deals (which comprised more than half of the total number of deals).

India

The investment of capitalists in Indian industries in the first half of 2006 was $3 billion and was expected to reach $6.5 billion at the end of the year. Most VC firms in India are either divisions or subsidiaries of Silicon Valley funds. They are primarily centred in Bangalore and Mumbai. Some VCs also operate from Delhi and other parts of the National Capital Region.

China

In China, venture funding more than doubled from $420,000 in 2002 to almost $1 million in 2003. For the first half of 2004, venture capital investment rose 32 per cent from 2003. By 2005, led by a wave of successful IPOs on the NASDAQ and revised government regulations, China-dedicated funds raised US $4 million in committed capital.

Vietnam

In Vietnam, venture funding has been increasing rapidly as Vietnamese overseas returnees and Vietnamese ex-managers of multinational companies increasingly establish new companies with ambitious growth plans. Firms such as Mekong Ventures, IDG Vietnam Ventures and DFJ-Vina Capital have pioneered investments in seed-stage and start-up stage companies in Vietnam. The $20 Million Challenge is Vietnam's first business plan contest for local entrepreneurs.

Italy

Private equity in Italy was 4.2 billion euro in 2007.

Confidential information

Unlike public companies, information regarding an entrepreneur's business is typically confidential and proprietary. As part of the due diligence process, most venture capitalists will require significant detail with respect to a company's business plan. Entrepreneurs must remain vigilant about sharing information with venture capitalists that are investors in their competitors. Most venture capitalists treat information confidentially, however, as a matter of business practice, do not typically enter into Non-disclosure Agreements because of the potential liability issues those agreements entail. Entrepreneurs are typically well-advised to protect truly proprietary intellectual property.

Limited partners of venture capital firms typically have access only to limited amounts of information with respect to the individual portfolio companies in which they are invested and are typically bound by confidentiality provisions in the fund's limited partnership agreement.

Popular Culture

Robert von Goeben and Kathryn Siegler produced a comic strip called *The VC* between the years 1997-2000 that parodied the industry, often by showing humorous exchanges between venture capitalists and entrepreneurs. Von Goeben was a partner in Redleaf Venture Management when he began writing the strip.

Mark Coggins' 2002 novel *Vulture Capital* features a venture capitalist protagonist who investigates the disappearance of the chief scientist in a biotech firm in which he has invested. Coggins also worked in the industry and was co-founder of a dot-com start-up.

Drawing on his experience as reporter covering technology for the *New York Times,* Matt Richtel produced the 2007 novel *Hooked,* in which the actions of the main character's deceased girlfriend, a Silicon Valley venture capitalist, play a key role in the plot.

In the TV series Dragon's Den, various start-up companies pitch their business plans to a panel of venture capitalists.

Selective Disclosure

Selective disclosure is a situation when a publicly traded company discloses material information to a single person, or a limited group of people or investors, as opposed to disclosing the information to all investors at the same time.

Material information is roughly defined as information that would cause a reasonable investor to make a buy or sell decision.

A problem with selective disclosure that the US Securities and Exchange Commission (SEC) sought to eliminate with Regulation Fair Disclosure (aka Regulation FD or Reg FD), is that it creates an uneven playing field for investors, allowing some investors to profit from material market moving information before others.

Possible example of selective disclosure:

> A company insider tells a small group of Wall Street analysts that the company is going to beat current analyst consensus estimates for earnings per share. If this is the first time the company disclosed such guidance, and the guidance wasn't simultaneously disseminated to all investors via a press release or publicised webcast, then the disclosure would consistitute selective disclosure.

Self-regulatory Organisation

A self-regulatory organisation (SRO) is an organisation that exercises some degree of regulatory authority over an industry or profession. The regulatory authority could be applied in addition to some form of government regulation, or it could fill the vacuum of an absence of government oversight and regulation. The ability of an SRO to exercise regulatory authority does not necessarily derive from a grant of authority from the government.

In United States securities law, a self-regulatory organisation is a defined term. The principal federal regulatory authority – the Securities and Exchange Commission (SEC) – was established by the Federal Securities Exchange Act of 1934. The SEC delegates authority to the National Association of Securities Dealers (the NASD) and to the national stock exchanges (e.g. the NYSE) to enforce certain industry standards and requirements related to securities trading and brokerage. On July 26, 2007, the SEC approved a merger of the enforcement arms of the NYSE and the NASD, to form a new SRO, the Financial Industry Regulatory Authority.

In addition, Congress created the Municipal Securities Rulemaking Board (the MSRB) as an SRO charged with adopting investor protection rules governing broker-dealers and banks that underwrite, trade and sell tax-exempt bonds, 529 college savings plans and other types of municipal securities.

The American Arbitration Association is also an SRO with official, statutory status.

Because of the prominence of the SROs in the securities industry, the term SRO is often used too narrowly to describe an organisation authorised by statute or government agency to exercise control over a certain aspect of the industry.

The National Association of Realtors (NAR) is an example of an SRO that fills the vacuum left by the absence of government oversight or regulation. The NAR sets the rules for Multiple Listing Services and how brokers use them. Another example is the American Medical Association which sets rules for ethics, conflicts, disciplinary action, and accreditation in medicine.

Short (finance)

In finance, short selling or "shorting" is the practice of selling a financial instrument that the seller does not own at the time of the sale. Short selling is done with intent of later purchasing the financial instrument at a lower price. Short-sellers attempt to profit from an expected decline in the price of a financial instrument. Short selling or "going short" is contrasted with the more conventional practice of "going long" which occurs when an investment is purchased with the expectation that its price will rise.

Typically, the short-seller will "borrow" or "rent" the securities to be sold, and later repurchase identical securities for return to the lender. If the security price falls as expected, the short-seller profits from having sold the borrowed securities for more than he or she later pays for them but if the security price rises, the short seller loses by having to pay more for them than the price at which he or she sold them. The practice is risky in that prices may rise indefinitely, even beyond the net worth of the short seller. The act of repurchasing is known as "closing" a position.

The term "short selling" or "being short" is often also used as a blanket term for strategies that allow an investor to gain from the decline in price of a security. Those strategies include buying options known as puts. A put option consists of the right to sell an asset at a given price; thus the owner of the option benefits when the market price of the asset falls. Similarly, a short position in a futures contract, or to be short on a futures contract, means the holder of the position has an obligation to sell the underlying asset at a later date, to close out the position.

Concept

To profit from a stock price going down, short sellers can borrow a security and sell it, expecting that it will be cheaper to repurchase in the future. When the seller decides that the time is right (or when the lender recalls the shares), the seller buys back the shares in order to return them to the lender. The process generally relies on the fact that securities are fungible, so that the shares returned do not need to be the same shares as were originally borrowed.

The short seller borrows from their broker, who usually in turn has borrowed the shares from some other investor who is holding his shares long; the broker itself seldom actually purchases the shares to lend to the short seller. The lender of the shares does not lose the right to sell the shares.

Short selling is the opposite of "going long." The short-seller takes a fundamentally negative, or "bearish" stance, intending to "sell high and buy low," to reverse the conventional adage. The act of buying back the shares which were sold short is called 'covering the short'. Day traders and hedge funds often use short selling to allow them to profit on trading in stocks which they believe are overvalued, just as traditional long investors attempt to profit on stocks which are undervalued by buying those stocks.

In the US, in order to sell stocks short, the seller must arrange for a broker-dealer to confirm that it is able to make delivery of the shorted securities. This is referred to as a "locate." Brokers have a variety of means to borrow stocks in order to facilitate locates and make good delivery of the shorted security.

The vast majority of stock borrowed by US brokers come from loans made by the leading custody banks and fund management companies. Sometimes brokers are able to borrow stocks from their customers who own "long" positions. In these cases, if the customer has fully paid for the long position, the broker cannot borrow the security without the express permission of the customer, and the broker must provide the customer with collateral and pay a fee to the customer.

In cases where the customer has not fully paid for the long position (meaning the customer borrowed money from the broker in order to finance the purchase of the security), the broker will not need to inform the customer that the long position is being used to effect delivery of another client's short sale.

Most brokers will allow retail customers to borrow shares to short a stock only if one of their own customers has purchased the stock on margin. Brokers will go through the "locate" process outside their own firm to obtain borrowed shares from other brokers only for their large institutional customers.

Stock exchanges such as the NYSE or the NASDAQ typically report the "short interest" of a stock, which gives the number of shares that have been sold short as a per cent of the total float. Alternatively, these can also be expressed as the short interest ratio, which is the number of shares sold short as a multiple of the average daily volume. These can be useful tools to spot trends in stock price movements.

Example

For example, assume that shares in XYZ Company currently sell for $10 per share. A short seller would borrow 100 shares of XYZ Company, and then immediately sell those shares for a total of $1000. If the price of XYZ shares later falls to $8 per share, the short seller would then buy 100 shares back for $800, return the shares to their original owner (paying a fee for having borrowed the shares) and make a $200 profit (minus the fee for having borrowed the shares). This practice has the potential for losses as well. For example, if the shares of XYZ that one borrowed and sold in fact went up to $25, the short seller would have to buy back all the shares at $2500, losing $1500. Because a short is the opposite of a long (normal) transaction, everything is the mirror opposite compared to the typical trade: the profit is limited but the loss is unlimited. Since the stock cannot be repurchased at a price lower than zero, the maximum gain is the difference between the current stock price and zero. However, because there is no ceiling on how much the stock price can go up (thereby costing short transactions money in order to buy the stocks back), an investor can theoretically lose an arbitrarily large amount of money if a stock continues to rise. Also, in actual practice, as the price of XYZ Company began to rise, the short seller would eventually receive a margin call from the brokerage, demanding that the short seller either cover his short position or provide additional cash in order to meet the margin requirement for XYZ Company stock.

History

The first case of selling short dates back to 1609 and concerns Dutch trader Isaac Le Maire, a big share holder of the Vereenigde Oostindische Compagnie (VOC). In 1602, he invested about 85,000 guilders in the VOC. By 1609 the, VOC still was not paying dividend, and Le Maire's ships on the Baltic routes were under constant threats of attack by English ships due to trading conflicts between the British and the VOC. Le Maire decided to sell his shares and sold even more than he had. The notables speak of an outrageous act and this led to the first real stock exchange regulations: a ban on short selling. The ban was revoked a couple of years later.

Short selling has been a target of ire since at least the eighteenth century when England banned it outright. It was perceived as a magnifying effect in the violent downturn in the Dutch tulip market in the seventeenth century.

The term "short" was in use from at least the mid-nineteenth century. It is commonly understood that "short" is used because the short seller is in a deficit position with his brokerage house. Jacob Little was known as The Great Bear of Wall Street who began shorting stocks in the United States in 1822.

Short sellers were blamed for the Wall Street Crash of 1929. Regulations governing short selling were implemented in the United States in 1929 and in 1940. Political fallout from the 1929 crash led Congress to enact a law banning short sellers from selling shares during a downtick; this was known as the uptick rule, and was in effect until 2007. President Herbert Hoover condemned short sellers and even J. Edgar Hoover said he would investigate short sellers for their role in prolonging the Depression. Legislation introduced in 1940 banned mutual funds from short selling (this law was lifted in 1997). A few years later, in 1949, Alfred Winslow Jones founded a fund (that was unregulated) that bought stocks while selling other stocks short, hence hedging some of the market risk, and the hedge fund was born.

Some typical examples of mass short-selling activity are during "bubbles", such as the Dot-com bubble. At such periods, short-sellers sell hoping for a market correction. Food and Drug Administration (FDA) announcements approving a drug often cause the market to react irrationally due to media attention; short sellers use the opportunity to sell into the buying frenzy and wait for the exaggerated reaction to subside before covering their position. Negative news, such as litigation against a company will also entice professional traders to sell the stock short.

During the Dot-com bubble, shorting a start-up company could backfire since it could be taken over at a higher price than what speculators shorted. Short sellers were forced to cover their positions at acquisition prices, while in many cases the firm often overpaid for the start-up.

In September of 2008 short selling was seen as a contributing factor to undesirable market volatility and subsequently was prohibited by the SEC for 799 financial companies in an effort to stabilise those companies. At the same time the UK FSA prohibited short selling for 32 financial companies. On September 22, Australia enacted even more extensive measures with a total ban of short selling. Also on September 22, the Spanish market regulator, CNMV, required investors to notify it of any short positions in financial institutions, if they exceed 0.25 per cent of a company's share capital.

Mechanism

Short selling stock consists of the following:

- An investor borrows shares. If required by law, the investor first ensures that cash or equity is on deposit with his brokerage firm as collateral for the initial short margin requirement. Some short sellers, mainly firms and hedge funds, participate in "naked short" selling, where the shorted shares are not borrowed or delivered.
- In either case the investor sells the shares and the proceeds are credited to his broker's account at the firm upon which the firm can earn interest. Generally the short seller does not earn interest on the short proceeds.
- The investor may close the position by buying back the shares (called covering). If the price has dropped, he makes a profit. If the stock advanced he takes a loss.
- Finally, the investor may return the shares to the lender or stay short indefinitely.

Securities Lending

When a security is sold, the seller is contractually obliged to deliver it to the buyer. If a seller sells a security short without owning it first, the seller needs to borrow the security from a third party to fulfil its obligation. Otherwise, the seller will "fail to deliver," the transaction will not settle, and the seller is subject to a claim from its counterparty. Certain large holders of securities, such as a custodian or investment management firm, often lend out these securities to gain extra income, a process known as securities lending.

The lender receives a fee for this service. Similarly, retail investors can sometimes make an extra fee when their broker wants to borrow their securities. This is only possible when the investor has full title of the security, so it cannot be used as collateral for margin buying.

Sources of Short Interest Data

Time delayed short interest data is available in a number of countries, including the US, the UK, Hong Kong and Spain. Some market participants (like Data Explorers Limited) believe that stock lending data provides a good proxy for short interest levels. The amount of stocks being shorted on a global basis has increased in recent years for various structural reasons (e.g. the growth of 130/30 type strategies).

Short Selling Terms

Days to Cover (DTC) is a numerical term that describes the relationship between the amount of shares in a given equity that have been short sold and the number of days of typical trading that it would require to 'cover' all short positions outstanding. For example, if there are ten million shares of XYZ Inc. that are currently short sold and the average daily volume of XYZ shares traded each day is one million, it would require ten days of trading for all short positions to be covered (10 million / 1 million).

Short Interest is a numerical term that relates the number of shares in a given equity that have been shorted divided by the total shares outstanding for the company, usually expressed as a per cent. For example, if there are ten millions shares of XYZ Inc. that are currently short sold and the total number of shares issued by the company is one hundred million, the Short Interest is 10 per cent (10 million / 100 million).

Major Lenders

- State Street Corporation (Boston).
- JP Morgan Chase (New York).
- Northern Trust (Chicago).
- Fortis (Amsterdam).
- Citibank (New York).
- Mellon Bank Corp. (Pittsburgh).
- Bank of New York (New York).
- The Bank of New York and Mellon Bank Corp. formally merged in July 2007, creating the Bank of New York Mellon Corporation.
- UBS AG (Zurich, Switzerland).

Naked Short Sale

A naked short sale is selling a security short without first ascertaining that one can borrow the security. In the US, making arrangements to borrow the securities first is often referred to as a *locate*. To prevent widespread failure to deliver securities, the US Securities and Exchange Commission (SEC) has put in place Regulation SHO, which prevents investors from selling stocks short before doing a *locate*.

Fees

When a broker facilitates the delivery of a client's short sale, the client is charged a fee for this service, usually a standard commission similar to that of purchasing a similar security.

If the short position begins to move against the holder of the short position (i.e. the price of the security begins to rise), money will be removed from the holder's cash balance and moved to his or her margin balance. If short shares continue to rise in price, and the holder does not have sufficient funds in the cash account to cover the position, the holder will begin to borrow on margin for this purpose, thereby accruing margin interest charges. These are computed and charged just as for any other margin debit.

When a security's ex-dividend date passes, the dividend is deducted from the shortholder's account and paid to the person from whom the stock was borrowed.

For some brokers, the short seller may not earn interest on the proceeds of the short sale or use it to reduce outstanding margin debt. These brokers may not pass this benefit on to the retail client unless the client is very large. This means an individual short-selling $1000 of stock will lose the interest to be earned on the $1000 cash balance in his or her account.

The Dividend

If the company distributes the dividend, the short seller is also "short the dividend". This is because he borrowed the stock shares and sold them to another investor. The investor he sold them to expects a dividend. The investor he borrowed the shares from expects a dividend also. This demonstrates that the "borrowing" is not really borrowing in the usual sense because the original shareholder has the use of the stock share, as demonstrated by the fact he still gets the dividend. (If John borrows Jim's shovel, Jim doesn't have use of his shovel any more). Not so with the type of "borrowing" going on with stocks borrowed in order to short them.

Futures and Options Contracts

When trading futures contracts, being 'short' means having the legal obligation to deliver something at the expiration of the contract, although the holder of the short position may alternately buy back the contract prior to expiration instead of making delivery. Short futures transactions are often used by producers of a commodity to fix the future price of goods they have not yet produced. Shorting a futures contract is sometimes also used by those holding the underlying asset (i.e. those with a long position) as a temporary hedge against price declines. Shorting futures may also be used for speculative trades, in which case the investor is looking to profit from any decline in the price of the futures contract prior to expiration.

An investor can also purchase a put option, giving that investor the right (but not the obligation) to sell the underlying asset (such as shares of stock) at a fixed price. In the event of a market decline, the option holder may exercise these put options, obliging the counterparty to buy the underlying asset at the agreed upon (or strike) price, which would then be higher than the current quoted spot price of the asset.

Currency

Selling short on the currency markets is different from selling short on the stock markets. Currencies are traded in pairs, each currency being priced in terms of another, so there is no possibility for any single currency to get to zero. In this way, selling short on the currency markets is identical to selling long on stocks.

Novice traders or stock traders can be confused by the failure to recognise and understand this point: a contract is always long in terms of one medium and short another.

When the exchange rate has changed the trader buys the first currency again; this time he gets more of it, and pay back the loan. Since he got more money than he had borrowed initially, he makes money. Of course, the reverse can also occur.

An example of this is as follows: Let us say a trader wants to trade with the dollar and the Indian rupee currencies. Assume that the current market rate is $1 to Rs. 50 and the trader borrows Rs. 100. With this, he buys $2. If the next day, the conversion rate becomes $1 to Rs. 51, then the trader sells his $2 and gets Rs. 102. He returns Rs. 100 and keeps the Rs. 2 profit.

One may also take a short position in a currency using futures or options; the preceding method is used to bet on the spot price, which is more directly analogous to selling a stock short.

Risk

It is important to note that buying shares (called "going long") has a very different risk profile from selling short. In the former case, losses are limited (the price can only go down to zero) but gains are unlimited (there is no limit on how high the price can go). In short selling, this is reversed, meaning the possible gains are limited (the stock can only go down to a price of zero), and the seller can lose more than the original value of the share, with no upper limit. For this reason, short selling is usually used as part of a hedge rather than as an investment in its own right.

Many short sellers place a "stop loss order" with their stockbroker after selling a stock short. This is an order to the brokerage to cover the position if the price of the stock should rise to a certain level, in order to limit the loss and avoid the problem of unlimited liability. In some cases, if the stock's price skyrockets, the stockbroker may decide to cover the short seller's position immediately and without his consent, in order to guarantee that the short seller will be able to make good on his debt of shares.

Short selling is sometimes referred to as a "negative income investment strategy" because there is no potential for dividend income or interest income. One's return is strictly from capital gains.

Short sellers must be aware of the potential for a short squeeze. When the price of a stock rises significantly, some people who are short the stock will cover their positions to limit their losses (this may occur in an automated way if the short sellers had stop-loss orders in place with their brokers); others may be forced to close their position to meet a margin call; others may be forced to cover, subject to the terms under which they borrowed the stock, if the person who lent the stock wishes to sell and take a profit. Since covering their positions involves buying shares, the short squeeze causes an ever further rise in the stock's price, which in turn may trigger additional covering. Because of this, most short sellers restrict their activities to heavily traded stocks, and they keep an eye on the "short interest" levels of their short investments. Short interest is defined as the total number of shares that have been sold short, but not yet covered.

On occasion, a short squeeze is deliberately induced. This can happen when a large investor (a company or a wealthy individual) notices significant short positions, and buys many shares, with the intent of selling the position at a profit to the short sellers who will be panicked by the initial uptick or who are forced to cover their short positions in order to avoid margin calls.

Short sellers have to deliver the securities to their broker eventually. At that point they will need money to buy them, so there is a credit risk for the broker. To reduce this, the short seller has to keep a margin with the broker.

Short sellers tend to temper overvaluation by selling into exuberance. Likewise, short sellers often provide price support by buying when negative sentiment is exacerbated during a significant price decline. Short selling can have negative implications if it causes a premature or unjustified share price collapse when the fear of cancellation due to bankruptcy becomes contagious.

Finally, short sellers must remember that they are going against the overall upward direction of the market. This, combined with interest costs, can make it unattractive to keep a short position open for a long duration.

Speculation

A seller intentionally takes on directional risk in the belief that the value of the shorted asset will fall.

Hedging

Short selling often represents a means of minimising the risk from a more complex set of transactions. Examples of this are:

- A farmer who has just planted his wheat wants to lock in the price at which he can sell after the harvest. He would take a short position in wheat futures.
- A market maker in corporate bonds is constantly trading bonds when clients want to buy or sell. This can create substantial bond positions. The largest risk is that interest rates overall move. The trader can hedge this risk by selling government bonds short against his long positions in corporate bonds. In this way, the risk that remains is credit risk of the corporate bonds.
- An options trader may short shares in order to remain delta neutral so that he is not exposed to risk from price movements in the stocks that underlie his options

Arbitrage

A short seller may be trying to benefit from market inefficiencies arising from the mispricing of certain products. Examples of this are:

- An arbitrageur who buys long futures contracts on a US Treasury security, and sells short the underlying US Treasury security.

Against the Box

One variant of selling short involves a long position. "Selling short against the box" is holding a long position on which one enters a short sell order. The term *box* alludes to the days when a safe deposit box was used to store (long) shares. The purpose of this technique is to lock in paper profits on the long position without having to sell that position (and possibly incur taxes if said position has appreciated). Whether prices increase or decrease, the short position balances the long position and the profits are locked in (less brokerage fees and short financing costs).

US investors considering entering into a "short against the box" transaction should be aware of the tax consequences of this transaction. Unless certain conditions are met, the IRS deems a "short against the box" position to be a "constructive sale" of the long position, which is a taxable event. These conditions include a requirement that the short position be closed out within 30 days of the end of the year and that the investor must hold their long position, without entering into any hedging strategies, for a minimum of 60 days after the short position has been closed.

Opinions

Short sellers are widely regarded with suspicion because, in the views of many people, they are profiting from the misfortune of others. Some businesses campaign against short sellers who target them, sometimes resulting in litigation.

Advocates of short sellers say that the practice is an essential part of the price discovery mechanism. They state that short-seller scrutiny of companies' finances has led to the discovery of instances of fraud which were glossed over or ignored by investors who had held the companies' stock long. Some hedge funds and short sellers claimed that the accounting of Enron and Tyco was suspicious months before their respective financial scandals emerged. Financial researchers at Duke University have provided statistically significant support for the assertion that short interest is an indicator of poor future stock performance and that short sellers exploit market mistakes about firms' fundamentals.

Such noted investors as Seth Klarman and Warren Buffett have said that short sellers help the market. Klarman argued that short sellers are a useful counterweight to the widespread bullishness on Wall Street, while Buffett believes that short sellers are useful in uncovering fraudulent accounting and other problems at companies. In response to the UK and US moves to ban short selling in September 18 and 19 of 2008, UBS stated:

> This can be characterised as a populist reaction of no positive value. Anyone who seriously thinks that the cause of this crisis arises from the actions of evil and manipulative speculators lacks the insight and knowledge to be allowed anywhere near the regulation of financial markets. Short selling may well exacerbate problems, but it was not the cause.

The Regulatory Response

In the US, Regulation SHO was the SEC's first update to short selling restrictions since 1938. It established "locate" and "close-out" requirements for broker-dealers, in an effort to curb naked short selling. Compliance with the regulation began on January 3, 2005.

In the US, initial public offerings (IPOs) cannot be sold short for a month after they start trading. This mechanism is in place to ensure a degree of price stability during a company's initial trading period. However, some brokerages that specialise in penny stocks (referred to colloquially as bucket shops) have used the lack of short selling during this month to pump and dump thinly traded IPOs. Canada and other countries do allow selling IPOs (including US IPOs) short.

In the UK, the Financial Services Authority has a moratorium on short selling 29 leading financial stocks, effective from 2300 GMT, 18 September 2008 until 16 January 2009.

In the US, a similar response was made by the Securities and Exchange Commission with a ban on short selling on 799 financial stocks from 19 September 2008 until 2 October 2008. Greater penalties for naked shorting, by mandating delivery of stocks at clearing time, were also introduced. Some state governors have been urging state pension bodies to refrain from lending stock for shorting purposes.

Soon thereafter, between 19 and 21 September 2008, Australia temporarily banned short selling, and later placed an indefinite ban on naked short selling. Germany, Ireland, Switzerland and

Canada banned short selling leading financial stocks, and France, The Netherlands and Belgium banned naked short selling leading financial stocks.

By contrast, Chinese regulators have responded by allowing short selling, along with a package of other market reforms.

Standardised Approach (credit risk)

The term standardised approach refers to a set of credit risk measurement techniques proposed under Basel II capital adequacy rules for banking institutions.

Under this approach the banks are required to use ratings from External Credit Rating Agencies to quantify required capital for credit risk. In many countries this is the only approach the regulators are planning to approve in the initial phase of Basel II Implementation.

The Summary of Risk Weights in Standardised Approach

There are some options in weighting risks for some claims, below are the summary as it might be likely to be implemented.

Note: For some "unrated" risk weights, banks are encouraged to use their own internal-ratings system based on Foundation IRB and Advanced IRB in Internal-Ratings Based approach with a set of formulae provided by the Basel-II accord. There exist several alternative weights for some of the following claim categories published in the original Framework text.

- Claims on Sovereigns:

Credit Assessment	AAA to AA-	A+ to A-	BBB+ to BBB-	B+ to B-	Below B-	unrated
Risk Weight	0%	20%	50%	100%	150%	100%

- Claims on the BIS, the IMF, the ECB, the EC and the MDBs

  Risk Weight: 0%.

- Claims on banks and securities companies:

Related to assessment of sovereign as banks and securities companies are regulated.

Credit Assessment	AAA to AA-	A+ to A-	BBB+ to BBB-	B+ to B-	Below B-	unrated
Risk Weight	20%	50%	100%	100%	150%	100%

- Claims on corporates:

Credit Assessment	AAA to AA-	A+ to A-	BBB+ to BB-	Below BB-	unrated
Risk Weight	20%	50%	100%	150%	100%

- Claims on retail products:

This includes credit card, overdraft, auto loans, personal finance and small business.

Risk weight: 75%.

- Claims secured by residential property:

Risk weight: 35%.

- Claims secured by commercial real estate:

Risk weight: 100%.

- Overdue loans – more than 90 days other than residential mortgage loans.

Risk weight:

150 per cent for provisions are less than 20 per cent of the outstanding amount.

100 per cent for provisions are between 20-49 per cent of the outstanding amount.

100 per cent with supervisory discretion to reduce to 50 per cent for provisions are 50 per cent and more of the outstanding amount.

- Other assets:

Risk weight: 100%.

- Cash:

Risk weight: 0%.

Stock Exchange Executive Council

The Stock Exchange Executive Council (SEEC) of the People's Republic of China was established to improve the efficiency of the securities market in mainland China.

According to research by Nottle (1993), the re-emergence of securities markets commenced under the introduction of the economic reform programme. The initiative was announced by then party Vice Premier Deng Xiaoping in 1978; under the plan market forces would be brought to bear on the economy and China's "doors would be opened" to foreign capital and entrepreneurs.

Under this economic reform, a number of experiments have been conducted in order to facilitate the development of securities markets.

1. September 1984, the first joint stock company and then one was commenced in Shanghai in 1985 and in Shenzhen in 1987.
2. Another experiment consisted of establishing securities trading markets such as, over-the-counter (OTC) market for shares and bonds was established in 1986.

To further improve the efficiency of the Chinese securities markets, eventually the Stock Exchange Executive Council (SEEC) was formed in March 1989 to create a nationwide treasury bond trading system (Securities Trading Automated Quotations System (STAQ)) which was established on December 1990.

Bank Secrecy Act

The Bank Secrecy Act of 1970 (or BSA, or otherwise known as the Currency and Foreign Transactions Reporting Act) requires USA financial institutions to assist US government agencies to detect and prevent money laundering. Specifically, the act requires financial institutions to keep records of cash purchases of negotiable instruments, and file reports of cash purchases of these negotiable instruments of $3,000 or more (daily aggregate amount), and to report suspicious activity that might signify money laundering, tax evasion, or other criminal activities.

Many banks will no longer sell negotiable instruments when purchased with cash, requiring the purchase to be withdrawn from an account at that institution. BSA was passed by the Congress of the United States in 1970. The BSA is sometimes referred to as an "anti-money laundering" law (AML) or jointly as "BSA/AML". Several anti-money laundering acts, including provisions in title III of the USA PATRIOT Act, have been enacted up to the present to amend the BSA.

Types of Reports

The BSA regulations require all financial institutions to submit five types of reports to the government:

1. *FinCEN Form 104 Currency Transaction Report (CTR):* A CTR must be filed for each deposit, withdrawal, exchange of currency, or other payment or transfer, by, through or to a financial institution, which involves a transaction in currency of more than $10,000. Multiple currency transactions must be treated as a single transaction if the financial institution has knowledge that: (a) they are conducted by or on behalf of the same person; and, (b) they result in cash received or disbursed by the financial institution of more than $10,000 (31 CFR 103.22).
2. *FinCEN Form 105 Report of International Transportation of Currency or Monetary Instruments (CMIR):* Each person (including a bank) who physically transports, mails or ships, or causes to be physically transported, mailed, shipped or received, currency, traveller's checks, and certain other monetary instruments in an aggregate amount exceeding $10,000 into or out of the United States must file a CMIR.
3. *Department of the Treasury Form 90-22.1 Report of Foreign Bank and Financial Accounts (FBAR):* Each person (including a bank) subject to the jurisdiction of the United States having an interest in, signature or other authority over, one or more bank, securities, or other financial accounts in a foreign country must file an FBAR if the aggregate value of such accounts at any point in a calendar year exceeds $5,000 (31 CFR 103.24).
4. *Treasury Department Form 90-22.47 and OCC Form 8010-9, 8010-1 Suspicious Activity Report (SAR):* Banks must file a SAR for any suspicious transaction relevant to a possible violation of law or regulation (31 CFR 103.18 " formerly 31 CFR 103.21) (12 CFR 12.11).
5. *"Designation of Exempt Person" FinCEN Form 110:* Banks must file this form to designate an exempt customer for the purpose of CTR reporting under the BSA [31 CFR 103.22(d)(3)(i)]. In addition, banks use this form biennially (every two years)

to renew exemptions for eligible non-listed business and payroll customers [31 CFR 103.22(d)(5)(i)].

It also requires any business receiving one or more related cash payments totalling $5,000 or more to file form 8300.

Currency Transaction Report (CTR)

Cash transactions in excess of $10,000 during the same business day. The amount over $10,000 can be either from one transaction or a combination of cash transactions. Filed with the Internal Revenue Service.

Monetary Instrument Log (MIL)

Cash purchases of monetary instruments, such as money orders, cashier's checks and travellers checks, totalling from $3,000 to $10,000, inclusive. This form is required to be kept on record at the financial institution, and produced at the request of examiners or audit to verify compliance. A financial institution must maintain a Monetary Instrument Log for 5 years.

Suspicious Activity Report (SAR)

Any cash transaction where the customer seems to be trying to avoid BSA reporting requirements (e.g. CTR, MIL). A SAR must also be filed if the customer's actions indicate that s/he is laundering money or otherwise violating federal criminal law. The customer must not know that a SAR is being filed. These reports are filed with the Financial Crimes Enforcement Network (FinCEN).

Sanctions

There are stiff penalties for individuals and institutions that fail to file CTRs, MILs, or SARs. There are also penalties for those that disclose to its clients that it has filed a SAR about a client. Penalties include extremely high fines and long prison sentences if found guilty.

How it Affects American Citizens

CTRs include the individual's bank account number, name, address, and Social Security Number. SAR reports, required when transactions indicate behaviour designed to elude CTRs (or many other types of suspicious activities), include somewhat more detailed information and usually include investigation efforts on the part of the financial institution to assess the validity or nature of the transactions. A single CTR filed for your account is usually of no concern to the authorities, while multiple CTRs from varying institutions or a SAR indicates that activity may be suspicious. A financial institution is not allowed to inform a business or consumer that a SAR is being filed, and all the reports mandated by the BSA are exempt from disclosure under the Freedom of Information Act.

Businesses that primarily deal in cash, such as bars and restaurants can be exempted from having their deposits and withdrawals reported as CTRs, although this exemption is rarely granted. Instead, most banks have computer systems which retains the CTR information and allows duplicate CTRs to be created seamlessly.

Additional Information

An entire industry has developed around providing software to analyse transactions in an attempt to identify transactions or patterns of transactions, called structuring, which requires a SAR filing, that qualify for reporting. Financial institutions face penalties for failing to properly file CTR and SAR reports, including heavy fines and regulatory restrictions, even to the point of charter revocation. These software applications effectively monitor bank customer transactions on a daily basis and, using customer historical information and account profile, provide a "whole picture" to the bank management. Transaction monitoring can include cash deposits and withdrawals, wire transfers and ACH activity. In the bank circles, these applications are known as "BSA software" or "Anti-money laundering software".

Bank Holding Company

A bank holding company is a company with significant ownership of one or more banks.

United States

A bank holding company, under the laws of the United States, is any entity that directly or indirectly owns, controls, or has the power to vote 25 per cent or more of a class of securities of a US bank. Bank holding companies are required to register with the

Board of Governors of the Federal Reserve System. Bank holding companies are subject to the Bank Holding Company Act of 1956 (12 U.S.C. § 1841(a)(2)(A) *et seq.*).

Regulation

The Federal Reserve Board of Governors, under Regulation Y (12 C.F.R. Pt. 225) has responsibility for regulating and supervising bank holding company activities, such as establishing capital standards, approving mergers and acquisitions and inspecting the operations of such companies. This authority applies even though a bank owned by a holding company may be under the primary supervision of the Comptroller of the Currency or the Federal Deposit Insurance Corporation.

Bank Holding Company Status

New or smaller banks often restructure themselves into bank holding companies to take advantage of the greater financial flexibility this corporate and legal status permits. Becoming a bank holding company makes it easier for the firm to raise capital than as a traditional bank. The holding company can assume debt of shareholders on a tax free basis, borrow money, acquire other banks and non-bank entities more easily, and issue stock with greater regulatory ease. It also has a greater legal authority to conduct share repurchases of own stock.

The downside includes responding to an additional regulatory authorities, especially if there are more than 300 shareholders, at which point the bank holding company is forced to register with the Securities and Exchange Commission. There are also added expenses of operating with an extra layer of administration.

Bank Accounts

A bank account is a financial account with a banking institution recording the financial transactions between the customer and the bank and the resulting financial position of the customer with the bank.

Bank accounts may have a positive or *credit* balance where the bank owes money to the customer; or a negative or debit balance where the customer owes the bank money.

Broadly, accounts opened with the purpose of holding credit balances are referred to as deposit accounts; whilst accounts opened with the purpose of holding debit balances are referred to as loan accounts.

Some accounts are defined by their function rather than nature of the balance they hold. Bank accounts designed to process large numbers of transactions may offer credit and debit facilities and therefore do not sit easily with a polarised definition. These transactional accounts are called by different names in different countries: in the US and Canada, they are checking accounts, in the UK current accounts.

Types of Accounts

- Savings account;
- Transactional account;
- Low-cost account;

- Time deposit / Certificate of deposit;
- Numbered bank account;
- Negotiable Order of Withdrawal account;
- Automatic transfer service account;
- Money market deposit account;
- Individual Savings Account;
- Tax-Exempt Special Savings Account;
- Transaction deposit;
- Nostro and Vostro Account;
- Joint account;
- Automated Teller Machine (ATM).

Neutral Consumer Information

The Government of Canada maintains a database of the fees and features of bank account packages offered by various financial institutions operating in Canada. The information is periodically incorporated in comparative tables and published in booklet form. The tables are also published in PDF form on the website of the Financial Consumer Agency of Canada. The database also feeds into an interactive online tool that allows consumers to compare various bank account packages online.

Savings Account

Savings accounts are accounts maintained by retail financial institutions that pay interest but can not be used directly as money (by, for example, writing a cheque). These accounts let customers set aside a portion of their liquid assets while earning a monetary return.

Features

Savings accounts are offered by commercial banks, savings and loan associations, credit unions, building societies and mutual savings banks.

Obtaining funds held in a savings account may not be as convenient as from a demand account. For example, one may need to visit an ATM or bank branch, instead of writing a cheque or using a debit card. However, this transference is easy enough that savings accounts are often termed "near money".

Some savings accounts require funds to be kept on deposit for a minimum length of time, but most permit unlimited access to funds. In the US, Regulation D, 12 CFR 204.2(d)(2) limits the withdrawals, payments, and transfers that a savings account may perform. Banks comply with these regulations differently; some will immediately prevent the transfer from happening, while others will allow the transfer to occur but will notify the account holder upon violation of the regulation. True savings accounts do not offer cheque-writing privileges, although many institutions will call their higher-interest demand accounts or money market accounts "savings accounts."

All savings accounts offer itemised lists of all financial transactions, traditionally through a passbook, but also through a bank statement.

Regulations

In the United States, under Regulation D, 12 CFR 204.2(d)(2), the term "savings deposit" includes a deposit or an account that meets the requirements of Sec. 204.2(d)(1) and from which, under the terms of the deposit contract or by practice of the depository institution, the depositor is permitted or authorised to make up to six transfers or withdrawals per month or statement cycle of at least four weeks. The depository institution may authorise up to three of these six transfers to be made by check, draft, debit card, or similar order drawn by the depositor and payable to third parties. There is no regulation limiting number of deposits, however some banks may choose to limit deposits themselves.

Within most European countries, interest paid on deposit accounts is taxed at source. The high rates of some countries has led to the development of a significant offshore savings industry. The European Union Savings Directive has made arrangements with many offshore financial centres for either information on interest earned to be shared with EU tax authorities or for withholding tax to be deducted on interest paid on offshore accounts, because of concerns relating to potential tax evasion.

Account holders must either pay the withholding tax or disclose account holder information to relevant tax authorities.

Costs

Withdrawals from a savings account are occasionally costly and are sometimes much higher and more time-consuming than the same financial transaction being performed on a demand account. However, most savings accounts do not limit withdrawals, unlike certificates of deposit. In the United States, violations of Regulation D often involve a service charge, or even a downgrade of the account to a checking account. With online accounts, the main penalty is the time required for the Automated Clearing House to transfer funds from the online account to a "brick and mortar" bank where it can be easily accessed. During the period between when funds are withdrawn from the online bank and transferred to the local bank, no interest is earned.

Notice Deposit Account

In some countries, such as the United Kingdom and Burkina Faso, an account called the notice deposit account is available. A slight interest premium is paid, with the caveat that one must give up to 90 days notice to make a withdrawal without a fee. Often, withdrawals can be made without notice by paying a penalty equivalent to the interest earned in the notice period. This is in contrast to instant access deposit accounts, which do not require notice for withdrawals. Notice deposit accounts are not common in North America.

Transactional Account

A transactional account (North America: checking account or chequing account, United Kingdom and some other countries: current account or cheque account) is a deposit account held at a bank or other financial institution, for the purpose of securely and quickly providing frequent access to funds on demand, through a variety of different channels. Because money is available on demand these accounts are also referred to as demand accounts or demand deposit accounts.

Transactional accounts are meant neither for the purpose of earning interest nor for the purpose of savings, but for convenience of the business or personal client; hence they tend to not bear interest. Instead, a customer can deposit or withdraw any amount of money any number of times, subject to availability of funds.

Features and Access

All transactional accounts offer itemised lists of all financial transactions, either through a bank statement or a passbook. A transactional account allows the account holder to make or receive payments by:

- Cash money (coins and banknotes).
- Cheque and money order (paper instruction to pay).
- Giro (funds transfer, direct deposit).
- Direct debit (pre-authorised debit).
- Standing order (automatic funds transfer).
- ATM card or debit card (cashless direct payment at a store or merchant).
- SWIFT: International account to account transfer.

Country Specific

Certain modes of payment are country-specific:

- In the United Kingdom, BACS offers giros that clear in a matter of days while CHAPS is done on the same day.
- Canada has an E-mail Money Transfer service.
- The United States offers e-checks.
- In India, NEFT service is available to clear funds in a day.

Branch Networks

This refers to the practice of maintaining physical locations where customers can receive a wide array of banking and financial services, such locations are described as branches. They may provide access to a combination of cash machines, telephone banking, counter services and financial advice.

Cash Machines

Cash machines are electronic devices that allow bank customers to make cash withdrawals and check their account balances without the need for a human teller. Many also allow people to deposit cash or cheques, transfer money between their bank accounts, top up their mobile phones' pre-paid accounts or even buy postage stamps.

Internet Banking

Internet or Online banking describes the use of a bank's secure website to view balances and statements, perform transactions and payments, and various other facilities. This can be very useful, especially for banking outside bank hours and banking from anywhere where internet access is available. Since the internet revolution most retail banking institutions offer access to current accounts via online banking.

Telephone Banking

Telephone banking is the term applied to specific provision of banking services over the telephone. In many cases such calls are to a call centre or automated service, although some institutions continue to answer such calls in their branches. Often call centre opening times are considerably longer than branches, and some firms provide these services on a 24 hour basis.

Overdrafts

An overdraft occurs when withdrawals from a bank account exceed the available balance. This gives the account a negative balance and in effect means the account provider is providing credit. If there is a prior agreement with the account provider for an overdraft facility, and the amount overdrawn is within this authorised overdraft, then interest is normally charged at the agreed rate. If the balance exceeds the agreed facility then fees may be charged and a higher interest rate might apply.

Cost

The policy of charging a fee for doing financial transactions depends on a variety of factors, including the country and its overall interest rates for lending and for saving, as well as the size of the financial institution and the number of channels of access it offers. This is why virtual banks, operating few or no branches can afford to offer low-cost or free banking, and why, in some countries, transaction fees do not exist, but extremely high lending rates are the norm.

Financial transaction fees may be charged either per item or for a flat rate covering a certain number of transactions (usually charged on a monthly basis). Often, youths, students, senior citizens or high-valued customers do not pay fees for basic financial transactions. Some will offer free transactions for maintaining a very high average balance in their account. Other service charges are applicable for overdraft, non-sufficient funds, the use of an external interbank network, etc. In countries where there are no service charges for transaction fees, there are, on the other hand, other recurring service charges such as a debit card annual fee.

Interest

Unlike savings accounts, for which the primary reason for depositing money is to generate interest, the main function of a transactional account is transactional. Therefore, most providers either pay no interest or pay a low level of interest on credit balances.

Checking Accounts

Checking account is the name given in North America to a transactional account.

Overdrafts

In North America, overdraft protection is an optional feature of a checking account. An account holder may either apply for a permanent one, or the financial institution may, at its sole discretion, provide a temporary overdraft on an *ad hoc* basis.

Interest

In the United States, Regulation Q (12 CFR 217) and the Banking Acts of 1933 and 1935 (12 USC 371a) prohibit a member of the Federal Reserve system from paying interest on checking accounts. This restriction can be circumvented by either creating an account type such as a Negotiable Order of Withdrawal account (NOW account) which is legally not a checking account or by offering interest paying checking through a bank which is not a member of the Federal Reserve system.

High-interest NOW accounts have become prevalent throughout the industry. They pay a higher interest rate than typical NOW accounts and frequently function as loss-leaders to drive relationship banking.

In 2003, banks and credit unions began to establish maximum balances on high-interest checking accounts. This counter-traditional trend (banks have typically established minimum account balances rather than maximum account balances) developed as a way to allow financial institutions to attract multiple customer relationships while limiting the interest expense associated with each account. The first maximum-balance, high-interest checking account was offered in 2003 by a small community bank in New Mexico, Pioneer Bank.

In 2004 and 2005, several community banks in West Texas expanded the idea, and a 3rd party vendor, Banc Vue (headquartered in Austin, TX), began offering "Reward Checking" as a stand-alone product to community banks in 2005. In 2007, "High-interest Free Checking" became the primary focus of Capital One's annual marketing budget.

Current Accounts

Current account is the name given to a transactional account in the United Kingdom and countries with a UK banking heritage, offering various flexible payment methods to allow customers to distribute money directly to others. Most current accounts come with a cheque book and offer the facility to arrange standing orders, direct debits and payment via a debit card. Current accounts may also allow borrowing via an overdraft facility.

Lending: Current accounts have two different ways in which money can be lent: overdraft and offset mortgage.

Overdraft: In the UK, virtually all current accounts offer a pre-agreed overdraft facility the size of which is based upon affordability and credit history. This overdraft facility can be used at any time without consulting the bank and can be maintained indefinitely (subject to *ad hoc* reviews). Although an overdraft facility may be authorised, technically the money is repayable on demand by the bank. In reality, this is a rare occurrence as the overdrafts are profitable for the bank and expensive for the customer.

Offset Mortgage: An offset mortgage is a type of mortgage common in the United Kingdom used for the purchase of domestic property, the key principle is the reduction of interest charged by "offsetting" a credit balance against the mortgage debt. This can be achieved via one of two methods either lenders provide a single account for all transactions (often referred to as a current account mortgage) or they make multiple accounts available which allow the borrowers to notionally split their money according to purpose whilst all accounts are offset each day against the mortgage debt.

Interest: In the UK some online banks offer rates as high as many savings accounts along with free banking (no charges for transactions) as institutions which offer centralised services (telephone, internet of postal based) tend to pay higher levels of interest. The same holds true for banks within the euro currency zone.

Low-cost Account

Low-cost accounts are accounts with monthly fees of no more than C$4.00, offered in Canada. Low-cost accounts came about as a result of an agreement between the Canadian federal government and the banking sector. There are currently eight banks offering low-cost accounts to their customers.

Features

Low-cost accounts have the following features:

- Deposits free of charge;
- Debit card usage;
- Cheque-writing;
- Account statement or passbook updated at no charge;
- 8-15 debit transactions per month, with two or more in-branch; and
- Monthly fee no higher than C$4.00.

The Financial Consumer Agency of Canada publishes a booklet called Low-cost Accounts which explains the fees and features associated with these accounts.

Time Deposit

A time deposit (also known as a term deposit, particularly in Canada, Australia and New Zealand; a bond in the United Kingdom) is a money deposit at a banking institution that cannot be withdrawn for a certain "term" or period of time. When the term is over it can be withdrawn or it can be held for another term. Generally speaking, the longer the term the better the yield on the money. A certificate of deposit is a time-deposit product.

The opposite is a Demand deposit or a sight deposit which can be withdrawn at any time, without any notice or penalty; e.g. money deposited in a checking account or savings account in a bank.

A deposit of funds in a savings institution is made under an agreement stipulating that (a) the funds must be kept on deposit for a stated period of time, or (b) the institution may require a minimum period of notification before a withdrawal is made.

US Time Deposits Regulations

Note that the M2 money supply includes funds that can be used directly in payment, such as money market mutual funds and money market deposit accounts (MMDAs). MMDAs are considered by the United States Federal Reserve (the Fed) to be savings accounts and are thus exempt from reserve requirements. These large transaction accounts not being included in the M1 money supply suggests that the Fed does not pay much attention to ordinary deposits, and in July 2000, it announced that it was no longer setting target ranges for growth rates of the money supply.

Small-denomination Time Deposit

"Small" time deposits in M2 are defined as those under $100,000.

Large-denomination Time Deposit

"Large" time deposits are currently defined as deposits larger than $100,000. The term "jumbo CD" is commonly used in the United States. Some banks, recognising that customers do not want more in the bank than is covered by insurance, have lowered the "jumbo CD" minimum requirement to $95,000, so with compounded interest the total falls below the insurance limit.

Certificate of Deposit

A certificate of deposit or CD is a time deposit, a financial product commonly offered to consumers by banks, thrift institutions, and credit unions.

CDs are similar to savings accounts in that they are insured and thus virtually risk-free; they are "money in the bank" (CDs are insured by the FDIC for banks or by the NCUA for credit unions). They are different from savings accounts in that the CD has a specific, fixed term (often three months, six months, or one to five years), and, usually, a fixed interest rate. It is intended that the CD be held until maturity, at which time the money may be withdrawn together with the accrued interest.

In exchange for keeping the money on deposit for the agreed-on term, institutions usually grant higher interest rates than they do on accounts from which money may be withdrawn on demand, although this may not be the case in an inverted yield curve situation. Fixed rates are common, but some institutions offer CDs with various forms of variable rates. For example, in mid-2004, with interest rates expected to rise, many banks and credit unions began to offer CDs with a "bump-up" feature. These allow for a single readjustment of the interest rate, at a time of the consumer's choosing, during the term of the CD. Sometimes, CDs that are indexed to the stock market, the bond market, or other indices are introduced.

A few general guidelines for interest rates are:

- A larger principal should receive a higher interest rate, but may not.
- A longer term may or may not receive a higher interest rate, depending on the current yield curve.
- Smaller institutions tend to offer higher interest rates than larger ones.
- Personal CD accounts generally receive higher interest rates than business CD accounts.

- Banks and credit unions that are not insured by the FDIC or NCUA generally offer higher interest rates.

Buying a CD

CDs typically require a minimum deposit, and may offer higher rates for larger deposits. In the US, the best rates are generally offered on "Jumbo CDs" with minimum deposits of $100,000 (though some, recognising that some investors don't want more in the account than is covered by FDIC insurance, have lowered the minimum deposit to $95,000). However, there are also institutions that do the opposite and offer lower rates for their "Jumbo CDs".

The consumer who opens a CD may receive a passbook or paper certificate, but it now is common for a CD to consist simply of a book entry and an item shown in the consumer's periodic bank statements; that is, there is usually no "certificate" as such.

Interest Payout

At most institutions, the CD purchaser can arrange to have the interest periodically mailed as a check or transferred into a checking or savings account. This reduces total yield because there is no compounding. Some institutions allow the customer to select this option only at the time the CD is opened.

Closing a CD

Withdrawals before maturity are usually subject to a substantial penalty. For a five-year CD, this is often the loss of six months' interest. These penalties ensure that it is generally not in a holder's best interest to withdraw the money before maturity—unless the holder has another investment with significantly higher return or has a serious need for the money.

Commonly, institutions mail a notice to the CD holder shortly before the CD matures requesting directions. The notice usually offers the choice of withdrawing the principal and accumulated interest or "rolling it over" (depositing it into a new CD). Generally, a "window" is allowed after maturity where the CD holder can cash in the CD without penalty. In the absence of such directions, it is common for the institution to "roll over" the CD automatically, once again tying up the money for a period of time (though the

CD holder may be able to specify at the time the CD is opened not to "roll over" the CD).

CD Refinance

In the US, insured CDs are required by the Truth in Savings Regulation DD to state at the time of account opening the penalty for early withdrawal. These penalties cannot be revised by the depository prior to maturity. The penalty for early withdrawal is the deterrent to allowing depositors to take advantage of subsequent enhanced investment opportunities during the term of the CD. In rising interest rate environments the penalty may be insufficient to discourage depositors from redeeming their deposit and reinvesting the proceeds after paying the applicable early withdrawal penalty. The added interest from the new higher yielding CD may more than offset the cost of the early withdrawal penalty.

Ladders

While longer investment terms yield higher interest rates, longer terms also may result in a loss of opportunity to lock in higher interest rates in a rising-rate economy. A common mitigation strategy for this opportunity cost is the "CD ladder" strategy. In the ladder strategies, the investor distributes the deposits over a period of several years with the goal of having all one's money deposited at the longest term (and therefore the higher rate), but in a way that part of it matures annually. In this way, the depositor reaps the benefits of the longest-term rates while retaining the option to reinvest or withdraw the money in shorter-term intervals.

For example, an investor beginning a three-year ladder strategy would start by depositing equal amounts of money each into a 3-year CD, 2-year CD, and 1-year CD. From this point on, a CD will reach maturity every year, at which time the investor would reinvest at a 3-year term. After two years of this cycle, the investor would have all money deposited at a three-year rate, yet have one-third of the deposits mature every year (which can then be reinvested, augmented, or withdrawn).

The responsibility for maintaining the ladder falls on the depositor, not the financial institution. Because the ladder does not depend on the financial institution, depositors are free to distribute a ladder strategy across more than one bank, which can be advantageous as smaller banks may not offer the longer terms found at some larger banks. Although laddering is most common with CDs, this strategy may be employed on any time deposit account with similar terms.

Deposit Insurance

In the US, the amount of insurance coverage varies depending on how accounts for an individual or family are structured at the institution. The level of insurance is governed by complex FDIC and NCUA rules, available in FDIC and NCUA booklets or online. Basic Coverage is $250,000 for a single account and $500,000 for a joint account. As of April 1, 2006, Individual Retirement Accounts were insured up to $250,000.

Some institutions use a private insurance company instead of, or in addition to, the Federally backed FDIC or NCUA deposit insurance. Institutions often stop using private supplemental insurance when they find that few customers have a high enough balance level to justify the additional cost.

A programme called the "Certificate of Deposit Account Registry Service" allows investors to keep up to $50 million invested in CDs managed through one bank with full FDIC insurance. However, rates will likely not be the highest available.

Terms and Conditions

There are many variations in the terms and conditions for CDs.

In the US, the federally required "Truth in Savings" booklet, or other disclosure document that gives the terms of the CD, must be made available before the purchase. Employees of the institution are generally not familiar with this information; only the written document carries legal weight. If the original issuing institution has merged with another institution, or if the CD is closed early by the purchaser, or there is some other issue, the purchaser will need to refer to the terms and conditions document to ensure that the withdrawal is processed following the original terms of the contract.

- *The CD may be "Callable":* The terms may state that the bank or credit union can close the CD before the term ends.
- *Payment of Interest:* Interest may be paid out as it is accrued or it may accumulate in the CD.
- *Interest Calculation:* The CD may start earning interest from the date of deposit or from the start of the next month or quarter.
- *Right to Delay Withdrawals:* Institutions generally have the right to delay withdrawals for a specified period to stop a bank run.
- *Withdrawal of Principal:* May be at the discretion of the financial institution. Withdrawal of principal below a certain minimum—or any withdrawal of principal at all—may require closure of the entire CD. A US Individual Retirement Account CD may allow withdrawal of IRA Required Minimum Distributions without a withdrawal penalty.
- *Withdrawal of Interest:* May be limited to the most recent interest payment or allow for withdrawal of accumulated total interest since the CD was opened. Interest may be calculated to date of withdrawal or through the end of the last month or last quarter.
- *Penalty for Early Withdrawal:* May be measured in months of interest, may be calculated to be equal to the institution's current cost of replacing the money, or may use another formula. May or may not reduce the principal—for example, if principal is withdrawn three months after opening a CD with a six-month penalty.
- *Fees:* A fee may be specified for withdrawal or closure or for providing a certified check.
- *Automatic Renewal:* The institution may or may not commit to sending a notice before automatic rollover at CD maturity. The institution may specify a grace period before automatically rolling over the CD to a new CD at maturity.

Other Similar Products

FDIC-insured or NCUA-insured CDs are usually purchased by consumers directly from banks or credit unions. There are also "certificates of deposit" issued by various entities that do not carry insurance.

Callable CDs

A callable CD is similar to a traditional CD, except that the bank reserves the right to "call" the investment. After the initial non-callable period, the bank can buy (call) back the CD. Callable CDs pay a premium interest rate. Banks manage their interest rate risk by selling callable CDs. On the call date, the banks determine if it is cheaper to replace the investment or leave it outstanding. This is similar to refinancing a mortgage.

Brokered CDs

Many brokerage firms - known as "deposit brokers" - offer CDs. These brokerage firms can sometimes negotiate a higher rate of interest for a CD by promising to bring a certain amount of deposits to the institution.

Unlike traditional bank CDs, brokered CDs are sometimes held by a group of unrelated investors. Instead of owning the entire CD, each investor owns a piece. If several investors own the CD, the deposit broker may not list each person's name in the title but the account records should reflect that the broker is merely acting as an agent (e.g. XYZ Brokerage as Custodian for Customers). This ensures that each portion of the CD qualifies for up to $100,000 of FDIC coverage.

In some cases, the deposit broker may advertise that the CD does not have a pre-payment penalty for early withdrawal. In those cases, the deposit broker will instead try to resell the CD if the investor wants to redeem it before maturity. If interest rates have fallen since the CD was purchased, and demand is high, he/she may be able to sell the CD for a profit. But if interest rates have risen, there may be less demand for such lower-yielding CD, which means that he/she may have to sell the CD at a discount and lose some of the investor's original deposit.

Deposit brokers do not have to go through any licensing or certification procedures, and no state or federal agency licences, examines, or approves them.

Criticism

CD interest rates closely track inflation. For example, in one situation interest rates may be 15 per cent and inflation may be 15 per cent, and in another situation interest rates may be 2 per cent and inflation may be 2 per cent. Of course, these factors cancel out, so the real interest rate is the same in both cases.

This is fine as long as someone understands it. However, people may misinterpret the interest as an increase in value, and spend the interest. However, to keep the same value the rate of withdrawal must be the same as the real rate of return, in this case, zero. People may also think that the higher-rate situation is "better," when the real rate of return is actually the same.

Also, the above does not include taxes. When taxes are considered, the higher-rate situation above is worse, with a lower (more negative) real return, although the before-tax real rates of return are identical. The after-inflation, after-tax return is what's important.

Ric Edelman writes, "You don't make any money in bank accounts (in real economic terms), simply because you're not supposed to"; on the other hand, bank accounts and CDs are fine for holding cash for a short amount of time.

However, Mr. Edelman's opinions may apply only to "average" CD interest rates. In reality, some banks pay much lower than average rates while others pay much higher rates (differences of 100 per cent are not unusual, e.g. 2.50 per cent vs 5.00 per cent). Depositors can take advantage of the best FDIC-insured rates without increasing their risk whatsoever.

Furthermore, a long-term CD might have a high nominal interest rate with a relatively low real interest rate due to high inflation at the time of purchase; however inflation rates often change rapidly and the final real interest rate could be significantly higher than riskier investments.

Finally, Mr. Edelman's statement that "CD interest rates closely track inflation" is not necessarily true. For example, during a credit crunch banks are in dire need of funds and CD interest rate increases may not track inflation.

Numbered Bank Account

Numbered bank accounts are offered by Swiss banks to the majority of their clients, and are also offered by banks in some other countries such as Andorra, Austria, Gibraltar, Liechtenstein, Latvia, and Panama. Typically the account will also have a code-name attached to it for the convenience of both the banker and customer. This avoids confusion between banker and customer as to which account is being discussed. The novel feature of numbered accounts is that the customer's name does not appear on bank statements. Only the number and code-name appear. This means that if bank statements are lost or stolen, it will not be immediately obvious who is behind the account.

Although numbered accounts may seem to grant some anonymity, Swiss law now requires all banks to know the identity of their customers. However, in the case of a numbered account, the customer's identity will only be known to a small group of people in the bank, on a "need to know" basis. Additionally, the customer's name does not appear on the bank's computer, thus preserving confidentiality in the case of cybercrime.

To avoid numbered accounts being used to hide the proceeds of crime, Swiss banks have strict anti-money laundering rules and laws, which require the reporting of suspected cases to the Swiss authorities. Still, numbered accounts have been used for criminal activities, such as corrupt politicians hiding money embezzled from citizens. While it is unknown how complicit Swiss banks were in such activities, they have cooperated with subsequent governments to return the funds to the country concerned, such as the fortune of the late Ferdinand Marcos.

The Swiss Banking Association warns that Swiss "numbered accounts should not be used for international wire transfers. According to international regulations the client's name, address and account number must be given when making international wire transfers." The same is yet not true of Liechtenstein numbered accounts, but will be starting in 2009.

Numbered accounts also have more mundane uses such as hiding funds from spouses, family members, and others who would potentially try to take funds away from the owner. In some countries this might include criminals, kidnappers, and blackmailers, whilst in others it may include unknown persons who might potentially sue, e.g. in a malpractice suit. Numbered accounts have also been used for tax evasion, but following the imposition of a 15 per cent withholding income tax on interest earned by EU residents, the perceived tax benefits have been somewhat diminished.

Negotiable Order of Withdrawal Account

In the United States, a Negotiable Order of Withdrawal account (NOW account) is a deposit account that pays interest, on which checks may be written.

They are structured to comply with Regulation Q, which prohibits interest on checking accounts: NOW accounts are interest-bearing, and checks may be written on them, but legally they are not interest-bearing checking accounts.

History

In the early-1970s, smaller banks in Massachusetts created the Negotiable Order of Withdrawal account to compete with the larger commercial banks. The sesquipedalian name comes from Regulation Q, which prohibits interest on checking accounts. Payment law meant that checks were negotiable instruments so some banks sought the permission to allow depositors the ability to issue negotiable withdrawals that can be given to a third party. Once approved, the banks could pay interest because they were not technically checking accounts. Authorised on a national scale in 1981, these accounts typically pay a relatively small return, although some banks offer high-interest NOW accounts in order to attract depositors' assets.

NOW accounts are considered checkable deposits, and are counted in the Fed's M1 definition of the money supply. As such, they are considered liabilities from the bank's perspective.

Automatic Transfer Service Account

An automatic transfer service account is a deposit account that allows the transfer of funds from a savings account to a checking account in order to cover a check written or to maintain a minimum balance.

Money Market Deposit Account

A money market account is a deposit account with a relatively high rate of interest, and short notice (or no notice) required for withdrawals. In the United States, it is a style of instant access deposit subject to federal savings account regulations, such as a monthly transaction limit.

United States

In the United States, a money market deposit account is a deposit account that is considered a savings account for some purposes, but upon which checks can typically be written, subject to certain restrictions. Like a Negotiable Order of Withdrawal account, it is structured to comply with Regulation Q, which forbids paying interest on checking accounts. Thus money market deposit accounts are accounts that bear interest, and on which checks can be written, but, due to various restrictions, are not legally checking accounts, and thus do not run afoul of Regulation Q.

Typical restrictions are that a fairly high minimum balance must be maintained in order to avoid fees. With the advent of online banking, many banks are able to pay a high interest rate on a low balance, sometimes as low as $1. A debit card is often issued for making withdrawals.

In theory, the restrictions allow the bank to invest the money with more discretion, allowing a higher return. The return is often competitive with money market mutual funds, although nothing requires a bank to invest deposits in these types of accounts into the money market.

Regulations in the US

Since the account is not considered a transaction account, it is subject to the regulations on savings accounts: only six withdrawal transactions to third parties are permitted per month, only three of which may be paid by check. Banks are required to discourage customers from exceeding these limits, either by imposing high fees on customers who do so, or by closing their accounts. Banks are free to impose additional restrictions (for instance: some banks limit their customers to six total transactions). ATM transactions may or may not be counted.

Comparison with "Money Market Funds"

Although money market deposit accounts have a similar name to money market funds, they are not the same: a money market fund consists of assets held by a brokerage (or bank) on behalf of investors, while a money market deposit account is a deposit at the bank, and hence a liability of the bank towards depositors.

A money market fund is a kind of mutual fund (technically, a regulated investment company). Investors receive shares in this company, which buys securities (for example, commercial paper). There are rules on what kind of securities may be held and rules about diversification. Thus, investors have risk on the assets, but not on the bank.

A money market account is simply a liability of the bank (albeit a high-priority one). It is a note on the bank's books that it owes someone money. It has no specific assets; essentially, it is backed by the entire bank. Thus, investors have risk on the bank, but not (directly) on any assets that the bank may invest in with these deposits - in fact, the deposits will not in general match up with any particular assets: they are simply one among many liabilities of the bank.

Also, like a checking account, these accounts are insured by the FDIC or a state analogue.

Individual Savings Account

An Individual Savings Account (ISA) is a financial product available to residents in the United Kingdom. It is designed for the purpose of investment and savings with a favourable tax status.

Introduction of ISAs

ISAs were introduced on 6 April 1999, replacing the earlier Personal Equity Plans (PEPs) and Tax-Exempt Special Savings Accounts (TESSAs), which continued to exist only for money already invested in them and for interplan transfers. ISAs were explicitly designed to appeal to a broader range of the population than these earlier products, which were sometimes claimed to be exclusively for the benefit of the middle classes. However, they have been criticised as confusing. Other channels for tax-privileged savings exist that also pre-date ISAs, notably the National Savings and Investments, which is a state owned bank offering a range of non-ISA tax free accounts (in addition to its own ISAs).

Types of ISA

Up until March 2007 Budget, there were two types of ISA. Since March the limits for the 2008/9 tax year were increased, and the distinction between a mini and maxi ISA abolished:

Pre the March 2007 budget the two types of ISA were:

- Mini ISAs;
- Maxi ISAs.

Up until 5 April 2004, there were also TESSA-only ISAs or TOISAs which were created to allow the original capital (excluding interest) invested in a TESSA (up to £9,000) to be reinvested in a tax-free form. It was only possible to invest in a TOISA with the capital from a matured TESSA, and new TOISAs may be created for the complete transfer of funds from another TOISA.

New TESSAs could not be created after 5 April 1999, so the required five-year term of all TESSAs ended by 5 April 2004.

Components

An ISA can contain two components:

1. A Cash Component: A cash deposit that is similar to any other ordinary savings account, apart from the tax-free status. A TOISA must consist solely of a cash deposit.
2. A Stocks and Shares Component: The money is invested in 'qualifying investments' consisting of any combination of stock market equity investments (with no geographic restriction), public debt securities such as government or corporate bonds, or cash "awaiting investment". As a consequence, the risk profile of the ISA may be anything from low to high. The investments may also include or consist of property funds or derivatives such as options. This element may be self-invested and managed through a stockbroker, but the majority of investors invest collectively through a collective investment such as a unit trust, OEIC or investment trust.

A third component, the insurance component, was also available in both maxi and mini ISAs. However, since the 2005/06 tax year this component has not been available. Collective investment funds that once qualified for this component will have been reclassified as qualifying for either the Cash or Stocks and Shares component. The tax year in the UK is from 6th April to 5th April.

Transfer Rules

It is possible to transfer ISAs from one manager to another, however there are several points to be aware of:

- From 2008/2009, it is possible to transfer from a Cash ISA to a Stocks and Shares ISA, but not the other way round. Before 2008/2009, it was not possible to transfer between component types.
- Whether the original contributions were made to a maxi or mini has no effect on transfer.
- The transfer must be done between the managers. If a saver transfers the money manually, it will be treated as a withdrawal and they cannot invest this in an ISA if their subscription limit has already been reached.
- Transfer of an ISA from the current tax year must be total. Partial transfers are only allowed on ISAs from previous tax years.
- Cash within a TOISA is treated as a cash component, and can be transferred to a "normal" cash ISA.

Subscription Limits

There are restrictions on investing in ISAs in each tax year (6 April to the following 5 April) which affect the type of ISA that may be opened and the amount of the investment.

Any UK resident individual of at least eighteen years of age can invest in one 'maxi' ISA, with both components provided by a single financial institution. Alternatively, a person can invest in two 'mini' ISAs, one for each component. The two mini ISAs may be with two different providers if the investor wishes. TOISAs and the full transfer of ISAs created in previous years to another provider have no bearing on these restrictions. With a few exceptions, such as from an employee share ownership plan, all investor contributions must be in cash.

UK resident individuals aged between 16 and 18 can also open a cash mini ISA or a maxi ISA, but can only allocate their investment to the cash component.

The amounts which may be deposited in an ISA in a tax year are fixed by law. For all years up to and including 2007/8, the limits have been:

- For a mini-ISA:
  - Cash: up to £3,000;
  - Stocks and shares: up to £4,000.
- For a maxi-ISA: a total subscription limit of £7,000 which may be invested:
  - Cash: up to £3,000;
  - Stocks and shares: up to £7,000.

In the March 2007 Budget, the limits from the 2008/9 tax year were increased (to allow for easier division over 12 months), and the distinction between a mini and maxi ISA abolished, as follows:

- A total subscription limit of £7,200 which may be invested:
  - Cash: up to £3,600;
  - Stocks and shares: up to £7,200.

These limits may be changed by the Chancellor of the Exchequer in the Budget.

Tax Treatment

All income (dividends and interest) and all capital gains are tax-free. Interest on any cash held in the stocks and shares component is subject to a flat charge of 20 per cent.

From 6 April 1999, advance corporation tax (ACT), payable by companies when they paid dividends, was abolished. Previously, under the imputation system of taxation, recipients of a dividend were entitled to a tax credit which reflected the payment of ACT by companies. This tax credit reduced the amount of tax that was payable by the recipient of a dividend and, where the recipient's tax liability was less than the tax credit, the excess could be reclaimed (particularly by non-taxpayers, such as charities, pension funds and PEPs).

From April 1999, companies have not been required to pay ACT, and dividends are accompanied by a 'notional' 10 per cent tax credit. The ability of certain non-taxpayers to claim a repayment of this 'notional' tax credit was phased out from 6 April 1999 to 5 April 2004, effectively removing some of the originally tax-free status (although higher-rate taxpayers have no further liability which they would do on dividends held outside an ISA). The result is that a fund primarily used for income rather than capital growth is far less tax efficient (especially for non-higher-rate taxpayers) when placed in an equity fund, whereas a fund based exclusively on other asset classes (such as bonds) continues to be tax-free in terms of income as well as capital growth.

The government has guaranteed that ISAs will continue to have tax-free status in all other respects until 5 April 2010, although they may be continued beyond that date.

CAT Standards

In April 1999, the Government introduced a voluntary *CAT* standard for ISAs (standing for "Charges, Access, and Terms") to make them easier for inexperienced customers to understand and with the proposed intention that lower costs would attract more investors. It does not guarantee the investment performance or that investors would buy or be sold the right type of investment. Many products comply with the CAT standard and there is some controversy as to whether or not the CAT standard alone would reach out to many more people who would not have otherwise chosen to save.

Cash ISAs have nevertheless been beneficial to savers through providing instant access savings that require little investment, meaning that the first £3,000 of any cash savings each year will be in a tax-free environment. By way of contrast, only the interest could be withdrawn from a TESSA before its five year period had finished or the tax free status would be lost. Further, due to competition cash ISAs continue (as at September 2004) to offer the highest rates of interest, irrespective of tax status, often meaning £1 in an ISA gains a higher rate of gross interest than many thousands invested in another account with the same provider. The market is further advanced as non-taxpayers still benefit from the use of cash ISAs due to the favourable interest rates.

Many equity funds also meet the CAT standards, but the restriction on costs generally means that these funds are index funds, which require little management and simply follow a given index, such as the FTSE 100 Index.

Charges

The ISA cash component, like any savings account, is typically free of charges although some providers charge a fee for transferring to another provider.

The built-in annual "re-registering" of your ISA may attract a fee which may be automatically extracted from your account.

Collective funds in the Stocks and Shares component usually attract the same initial and annual charges as they would do if held outside an ISA.

Self Select Stocks and Shares ISAs, provided by a stockbroker, attract brokerage fees comparable to those outside an ISA. Many stockbrokers charge an additional fee for administration of the ISA.

Fund Supermarkets

Investors are only permitted to invest their Stocks and Shares component with a single financial institution in any year. For investments into collective funds, these institutions have traditionally been the fund management companies themselves. This creates a difficulty for investors wishing to diversify their investment into the collective funds of different fund management companies in the same year. It also means that investors wishing to transfer existing ISA holdings have to transfer the ISA itself between providers, which can be a time consuming process.

To avoid these problems, a number of Fund Supermarkets have been set up. These are organisations which act as ISA providers who offer access to a wider range of collective investments from a variety of fund managers. They allow investors to build a more diversified portfolio within a single ISA and to transfer their investments between funds without the complication and delay of changing ISA provider. Fund Supermarkets are promoted by many Independent Financial Advisers and have quickly become popular because they allow investors greater choice and flexibility at no extra charge. Instead of charging the investor, the Fund Supermarkets are paid by the fund managers out of their usual charges. The two largest Fund Supermarkets are Cofunds and Fidelity Funds Network.

A Fund Supermarket differs significantly from a true Self-Select ISA provided by a stockbroker. The Fund Supermarkets do not offer the entire range of ISA eligible collective funds nor do they allow investment directly into specific stocks or shares.

Tax-Exempt Special Savings Account

In the UK, the Tax-Exempt Special Savings Account (TESSA) was one of a number tax-free savings accounts. The TESSA was announced by John Major in his only Budget as Chancellor of the Exchequer in 1990 (a budget for savings). The TESSA was intended to be a low-risk complement to the personal equity plan (PEP) which would be attractive to a wider range of savers.

Qualification

An individual aged 18 or over was able to open a TESSA with a bank, building society or other financial institution from 1 January 1991 to 5 April 1999. Interest on the TESSA was free from UK income tax. The favourable tax treatment of a TESSA lasted for 5 years, and it was possible to invest up to £9,000, with a maximum investment of £3,000 invested in the first year and £1,800 in each of the second to fifth years (although, if the maximum was invested in the first four years, only £600 could be added in the fifth year). Withdrawals were permitted within the first 5 years: tax relief was clawed back if any of the invested capital was taken out; withdrawals of interest did not trigger a clawback of the tax relief.

Development

'Follow-on' TESSAs were introduced in 1995 to permit all of the capital (but not the tax-free interest) from an original TESSA to be 'rolled over' into a new TESSA. Other than permitting all of the capital in the original account to be invested in the first year, which could easily exceed the usual £3,000 first-year limit, a 'follow-on' TESSA was subject to the same conditions as any other TESSA.

Phasing Out

TESSAs were replaced from 1999 by individual savings accounts (ISAs). The final TESSAs matured on 5 April 2004, but the original capital (but not the tax-free interest) could again be 'rolled over' into a new notional income tax-free investment through use of a TESSA only ISA (TOISA). The TOISA was a form of cash ISA which can be opened using either capital that was originally invested in a TESSA and that has not been withdrawn, or with funds transferred from another TOISA.

From 6th April 2007, there was no practical difference between TOISAs and cash ISAs and transfers into cash ISAs have been permitted. On 5th April 2008, TOISAs ceased being legally distinct and are now completely interchangeable with cash ISAs.

Transaction Deposits

In the United States transactions deposit is a term used by the Federal Reserve for checkable deposits and other accounts that can be used directly as cash without withdrawal limits or restrictions. They are the only bank deposits that require the bank to keep reserves at the central bank. This is in contrast to "time deposits" (aka term deposits).

Regulatory Deposits

Transaction accounts include all deposits against which the account holder is permitted to make withdrawals by negotiable or transferable instruments, payment orders of withdrawal, or telephone or pre-authorised transfers for the purpose of making payments to third persons or others. However, accounts subject to the rules that permit no more than six pre-authorised, automatic, or other transfers per month (of which no more than three may be by check, draft, debit card, or similar order payable directly to third parties) are savings deposits, not transaction accounts.

Nostro and Vostro Account

Nostro and Vostro (Middle Italian, from Latin, noster and voster; English, ours and yours) are accounting terms used to distinguish an account you hold for another entity from an account another entity holds for you. The entities in question are almost always, but need not be, banks.

Origins

It helps to recall that the term account refers to a record of transactions, whether current, past or future, and whether in money, or shares, or other countable commodities. Originally a bank account just meant the record kept by a banker of the money they were holding on behalf of a customer, and how that changed as the customer made deposits and withdrawals (the money itself probably being in the form of specie, such as gold and silver coin).

Some customers will keep their own records of their transactions, for instance, so they can check for errors by the bank. That record kept by the customer is also an account, of the money the bank is holding for them. And when that customer is another bank, since they also keep other accounts (of the money they are holding for their customers) there is a need to clearly differentiate between these two types of accounts.

The terms Nostro and Vostro remove the potential ambiguity when referring to these two separate accounts of the same balance and set of transactions. Speaking from the bank's point-of-view:

- A Nostro is our account of our money, held by you;
- A Vostro is our account of your money, held by us.

Note that all "bank accounts" as the term is normally understood, including personal or corporate chequing, loan, and savings accounts, are treated as Vostro's by the bank. They also regard as Vostro purely internal funds such as Treasury, Trading and Suspense accounts; although there is no "you" in the sense of an external customer, the money is still "held by us".

Interestingly, a bank customer who keeps a parallel record of their chequing account or credit card at home in order to, say, verify their statements, is in theory keeping a Nostro account.

Conventions

A bank counts a Nostro account with a credit balance as a cash asset in its balance sheet. Conversely, a Vostro account with a credit balance (i.e. a deposit) is a liability, and a Vostro with a debit balance (a loan) is an asset. Thus in many banks a credit entry on an account (CR) is regarded as negative movement, and a debit (DR) is positive – the reverse of usual commercial accounting conventions.

With the advent of computerised accounting, Nostro's and Vostro's just need to have opposite signs within any one banks accounting system; that is, if a Nostro in credit has a positive sign, then a Vostro in credit must have a negative sign. This allows for a reconciliation by summing all accounts to zero (a Trial Balance) – the basic premise of Double-Entry Bookkeeping.

Typical Usage

Nostro accounts are mostly commonly used for currency settlement, where a bank or other financial institution needs to hold balances in a currency other than its home accounting unit.

For Example: First National Bank of *A* does some transactions (loans, foreign exchange, etc.) in B$, but banks in A will only handle payments in A$. So FNB of A opens a B$ account at foreign bank Credit Mutuel de B, and instructs all counterparties to settle transactions in B$ at "account no. 123456 in name of *FNBA*, at *CMB*, *X* Branch". FNBA maintains its own records of that account, for reconciliation; this is its Nostro account. CMB's record of the same account is the Vostro account.

Now, FNBA sells A$1,000,000 to C (a counterparty who has an A$ account with FNBA, and a B$ account with CMB) for a nett consideration of B$2,000,000. FNBA will make the following entries in its own accounting system:

(Internal) FX A$ Trading Account	1,000,000 DR	A$ Account in name of C	1,000,000 CR
B$ Nostro at CMB (FNBA's Nostro)	2,000,000 DR	(Internal) FX B$ Trading Account	2,000,000 CR

Over at CMB, they record the following transaction:

B$ Account in name of C	2,000,000 DR	B$ Account in name of FNBA (FNBA's Vostro)	2,000,000 CR

[This is somewhat simplified; in reality C may not have an account with FNBA's corresponding bank, and will make settlement by cheque or some form of EFT. In this case CMB will make entries on several other accounts, such as a Teller's receiving account, or a clearing account with the third bank that the cheque was written on.]

Personal Account

A personal account is an account for use by an individual for their own needs. It is a relative term to differentiate the said accounts from those accounts for corporate or business use. The term "personal account" may be used generically for financial accounts at banks and for service accounts such as accounts with the phone company, or even for e-mail accounts.

Banking

In banking in the United States, "personal account" refers to one's account at the bank that is used for non-business purposes. Most likely, the service at the bank is comprised of one of two kinds of accounts or sometimes both – a savings account and a checking account.

Banks differentiate their services for personal accounts from business accounts by setting lower minimum balance requirements, lower fees, free checks, free ATM usage, free debit card (Check card) usage, etc. The term does not apply to any one service or limit the banks from providing the same services to non-individuals.

At the turn of the 21st century, many banks started offering free checking, a checking account with no minimum balance, a free check book, and no hidden fees. This encouraged those Americans who would otherwise live from check to check, to open their "personal" account at financial institutions. For businesses that issue corporate checks to employees, this enables reduction in the amount of paperwork.

Automated Teller Machine

An automated teller machine (ATM) is a computerised telecommunications device that provides the customers of a financial institution with access to financial transactions in a public space without the need for a human clerk or bank teller. On most modern ATMs, the customer is identified by inserting a plastic ATM card with a magnetic stripe or a plastic smartcard with a chip, that contains a unique card number and some security information, such as an expiration date or CVC (CVV). Security is provided by the customer entering a personal identification number (PIN). They are sometimes referred to as "ATM machines", an example of RAS Syndrome.

Using an ATM, customers can access their bank accounts in order to make cash withdrawals (or credit card cash advances) and check their account balances as well as purchasing mobile cell phone pre-paid credit. ATMs are known by various casual terms including automated banking machine, money machine, bank machine, cash machine, hole-in-the-wall, cashpoint, Bancomat (in various countries in Europe and Russia), Multibanco (after a registered trade mark, in Portugal), and Any Time Money (in India).

History

The first mechanical cash dispenser was developed and built by Luther George Simjian and installed in 1939 in New York City by the City Bank of New York, but removed after 6 months due to the lack of customer acceptance.

Thereafter, the history of ATMs paused for over 25 years, until De La Rue developed the first electronic ATM, which was installed first in Enfield Town in North London, United Kingdom on 27 June 1967 by Barclays Bank. This instance of the invention is credited to John Shepherd-Barron, although various other engineers were awarded patents for related technologies at the time. Shepherd-Barron was awarded an OBE in the 2005 New Year's Honours List. The first person to use the machine was the British variety artist and actor Reg Varney. The first ATMs accepted only a single-use token or voucher, which was retained by the machine. These worked on various principles including radiation and low-coercivity magnetism that was wiped by the card reader to make fraud more difficult. The machine dispensed pre-packaged envelopes containing ten pounds sterling. The idea of a PIN stored on the card was developed by the British engineer James Goodfellow in 1965.

In 1968, the networked ATM was pioneered in Dallas, Texas, by Donald Wetzel who was a department head at an automated baggage-handling company called Docutel. In 1995, the Smithsonian's National Museum of American History recognised Docutel and Wetzel as the inventors of the networked ATM.

ATMs first came into wide UK use in 1973; the IBM 2984 was designed at the request of Lloyds Bank. The 2984 CIT (Cash Issuing

Terminal) was the first true Cashpoint, similar in function to today's machines; Cashpoint is still a registered trademark of Lloyds TSB in the UK. All were online and issued a variable amount which was immediately deducted from the account. A small number of 2984s were supplied to a USA bank. Notable historical models of ATMs include the IBM 3624 and 473x series, Diebold 10xx and TABS 9000 series, and NCR 5xxx series.

Location

ATMs are placed not only near or inside the premises of banks, but also in locations such as shopping centres/malls, airports, grocery stores, petrol/gas stations, restaurants, or any place large numbers of people may gather. These represent two types of ATM installations: on and off premise. On premise ATMs are typically more advanced, multifunction machines that complement an actual bank branch's capabilities and thus more expensive. Off premise machines are deployed by financial institutions and also ISOs (or Independent Sales Organisations) where there is usually just a straight need for cash, so they typically are the cheaper monofunction devices. In Canada, when an ATM is not operated by a financial institution it is known as a "White Label ATM".

In North America, banks often have drive-thru lanes providing access to ATMs.

Many ATMs have a sign above them indicating the name of the bank or organisation owning the ATM, and possibly including the list of ATM networks to which that machine is connected. This type of sign is called a topper.

Financial Networks

Most ATMs are connected to interbank networks, enabling people to withdraw and deposit money from machines not belonging to the bank where they have their account or in the country where their accounts are held (enabling cash withdrawals in local currency). Some examples of interbank networks include PULSE, PLUS, Cirrus, Interac and LINK.

ATMs rely on authorisation of a financial transaction by the card issuer or other authorising institution via the communications network. This is often performed through an ISO 8583 messaging system.

Many banks charge ATM usage fees. In some cases, these fees are charged solely to users who are not customers of the bank where the ATM is installed; in other cases, they apply to all users. Many people oppose these fees because ATMs are actually less costly for banks than withdrawals from human tellers.

In order to allow a more diverse range of devices to attach to their networks, some interbank networks have passed rules expanding the definition of an ATM to be a terminal that either has the vault within its footprint or utilises the vault or cash drawer within the merchant establishment, which allows for the use of a scrip cash dispenser.

ATMs typically connect directly to their ATM Controller via either a dial-up modem over a telephone line or directly via a leased line. Leased lines are preferable to POTS lines because they require less time to establish a connection. Leased lines may be comparatively expensive to operate versus a POTS line, meaning less-trafficked machines will usually rely on a dial-up modem. That dilemma may be solved as high-speed Internet VPN connections become more ubiquitous. Common lower-level layer communication protocols used by ATMs to communicate back to the bank include SNA over SDLC, TC500 over Async, X.25, and TCP/IP over Ethernet.

In addition to methods employed for transaction security and secrecy, all communications traffic between the ATM and the Transaction Processor may also be encrypted via methods such as SSL.

Global Use

There are no hard international or government-compiled numbers totalling the complete number of ATMs in use worldwide. Estimates developed by ATMIA place the number of ATMs in use at over 1.5 million as of August 2006.

For the purpose of analysing ATM usage around the world, financial institutions generally divide the world into seven regions, due to the penetration rates, usage statistics, and features deployed.

Four regions (USA, Canada, Europe, and Japan) have high numbers of ATMs per million people and generally slowing growth rates. Despite the large number of ATMs, there is additional demand for machines in the Asia/Pacific area as well as in Latin America. ATMs have yet to reach high numbers in the Near East/Africa.

The world's most northerly installed ATM is located at Longyearbyen, Svalbard, Norway.

The world's most southerly installed ATM is located at McMurdo Station, Antarctica.

While ATMs are ubiquitous on modern cruise ships, ATMs can also be found on some US Navy ships.

In the United Kingdom, an ATM may be colloquially referred to as a "Cashpoint", named after the Lloyds Bank ATM brand, or "hole-in-the-wall", after the equivalent Barclays brand. In Scotland the term Cashline has become a generic term for an ATM, based on the branding from the Royal Bank of Scotland.

Hardware

An ATM is typically made up of the following devices:

- CPU (to control the user interface and transaction sevices).
- Magnetic and/or Chip card reader (to identify the customer).
- PIN Pad (similar in layout to a Touch tone or Calculator keypad), often manufactured as part of a secure enclosure.
- Secure cryptoprocessor, generally within a secure enclosure.
- Display (used by the customer for performing the transaction).
- Function key buttons (usually close to the display) or a Touchscreen (used to select the various aspects of the transaction).
- Record Printer (to provide the customer with a record of their transaction).
- Vault (to store the parts of the machinery requiring restricted access).

Recently, due to heavier computing demands and the falling price of computer-like architectures, ATMs have moved away from custom hardware architectures using microcontrollers and/

or application-specific integrated circuits to adopting a hardware architecture that is very similar to a personal computer. Many ATMs are now able to use operating systems such as Microsoft Windows and Linux. Although it is undoubtedly cheaper to use commercial off-the-shelf hardware, it does make ATMs vulnerable to the same sort of problems exhibited by conventional computers.

Vaults

The vault of an ATM is within the footprint of the device itself and is where items of value are kept. Scrip cash dispensers do not incorporate a vault.

Mechanisms found inside the vault may include:

- Dispensing mechanism (to provide cash or other items of value).
- Deposit mechanism, including a Cheque Processing Module and Batch Note Acceptor (to allow the customer to make deposits).
- Security sensors (Magnetic, Thermal, Seismic).
- Locks: (to ensure controlled access to the contents of the vault).

ATM vaults are supplied by manufacturers in several grades. Factors influencing vault grade selection include cost, weight, regulatory requirements, ATM type, operator risk avoidance practices, and internal volume requirements.

Industry standard vault configurations include Underwriters Laboratories UL-291 "Business Hours" and Level 1 Safes, RAL TL-30 derivatives, and CEN EN 1143-1:2005 – CEN III/VdS and CEN IV/LGAI/VdS.

ATM manufacturers recommend that vaults be attached to the floor to prevent theft.

Software

With the migration to commodity PC hardware, standard commercial "off-the-shelf" operating systems and programming environments can be used inside of ATMs. Typical platforms used in ATM development include RMX, OS/2, and Microsoft operating systems (such as MS-DOS, PC-DOS, Windows NT, Windows 2000,

Windows XP Professional, or Windows XP Embedded). Java, Linux and Unix may also be used in these environments.

Linux is also finding some reception in the ATM marketplace. An example of this is Banrisul, the largest bank in the south of Brazil, which has replaced the MS-DOS operating systems in its ATMs with Linux. Banco do Brasil is also migrating ATMs to Linux.

Common application layer transaction protocols, such as Diebold 911 or 912, IBM PBM, and NCR NDC or NDC+ provide emulation of older generations of hardware on newer platforms with incremental extensions made over time to address new capabilities, although companies like NCR continuously improve these protocols issuing newer versions (latest NCR Aptra Advance NDC Version 3.x.y (Where x.y are subversions). Most major ATM manufacturers provide software packages that implement these protocols. Newer protocols such as IFX have yet to find wide acceptance by transaction processors.

With the move to a more standardised software base, financial institutions have been increasingly interested in the ability to pick and choose the application programmes that drive their equipment. WOSA/XFS, now known as CEN XFS (or simply XFS), provides a common API for accessing and manipulating the various devices of an ATM.

J/XFS is a Java implementation of the CEN XFS API.

While the perceived benefit of XFS is similar to the Java's "Write once, run anywhere" mantra, often different ATM hardware vendors have different interpretations of the XFS standard. The result of these differences in interpretation means that ATM applications typically use a middleware to even out the differences between various platforms.

Notable XFS middleware platforms include Triton PRISM, Diebold Agilis, CR2 Bank World, KAL Kalignite, NCR Corporation Aptra Edge, Phoenix Interactive VISTAatm, and Wincor Nixdorf Protopas.

With the move of ATMs to industry-standard computing environments, concern has risen about the integrity of the ATM's software stack.

Security

Security, as it relates to ATMs, has several dimensions. ATMs also provide a practical demonstration of a number of security systems and concepts operating together and how various security concerns are dealt with.

Physical

Early ATM security focused on making the ATMs invulnerable to physical attack; they were effectively safes with dispenser mechanisms. A number of attacks on ATMs resulted, with thieves attempting to steal entire ATMs by ram-raiding. Since late-1990s, criminal groups operating in Japan improved ram-raiding by stealing and using a truck loaded with a heavy construction machinery to effectively demolish or uproot an entire ATM and any housing to steal its cash.

Another attack method is to seal all openings of the ATM with silicone and fill the vault with a combustible gas or to place an explosive inside, attached, or near the ATM. This gas or explosive is ignited and the vault is opened or distorted by the force of the resulting explosion and the criminals can break in.

Modern ATM physical security, per other modern money-handling security, concentrates on denying the use of the money inside the machine to a thief, by means of techniques such as dye markers and smoke canisters.

Transactional Secrecy and Integrity

The security of ATM transactions relies mostly on the integrity of the secure cryptoprocessor: the ATM often uses commodity components that are not considered to be "trusted systems".

Encryption of personal information, required by law in many jurisdictions, is used to prevent fraud. Sensitive data in ATM transactions are usually encrypted with DES, but transaction processors now usually require the use of Triple DES. Remote Key Loading techniques may be used to ensure the secrecy of the initialisation of the encryption keys in the ATM. Message Authentication Code (MAC) or Partial MAC may also be used to ensure messages have not been tampered with while in transit between the ATM and the financial network.

Customer Identity Integrity

There have also been a number of incidents of fraud where criminals have attached fake keypads or card readers to existing machines. These have then been used to record customers' PINs and bank card information in order to gain unauthorised access to their accounts. Various ATM manufacturers have put in place countermeasures to protect the equipment they manufacture from these threats.

Alternate methods to verify cardholder identities have been tested and deployed in some countries, such as finger and palm vein patterns, iris, and facial recognition technologies. Cost of integrating and implementing these technologies along with concerns about consumer acceptance have limited their deployment so far.

Device Operation Integrity

Openings on the customer-side of ATMs are often covered by mechanical shutters to prevent tampering with the mechanisms when they are not in use. Alarm sensors are placed inside the ATM and in ATM servicing areas to alert their operators when doors have been opened by unauthorised personnel.

Rules are usually set by the government or ATM operating body that dictate what happens when integrity systems fail. Depending on the jurisdiction, a bank may or may not be liable when an attempt is made to dispense a customer's money from an ATM and the money either gets outside of the ATM's vault, or was exposed in a non-secure fashion, or they are unable to determine the state of the money after a failed transaction. Bank customers often complain that banks have made it difficult to recover money lost in this way, but this is often complicated by the bank's own internal policies regarding suspicious activities typical of the criminal element.

Customer Security

In some countries, multiple security cameras and security guards are a common feature. In the United States, The NY State Comptroller's Office has criticised the NY State Department of Banking for not following through on safety inspections of ATMs in high crime areas.

Critics of ATM operators assert that the issue of customer security appears to have been abandoned by the banking industry; it has been suggested that efforts are now more concentrated on deterrent legislation than on solving the problem of forced withdrawals.

At least as far back as July 30, 1986, critics of the industry have called for the adoption of an emergency PIN system for ATMs, where the user is able to send a silent alarm in response to a threat. Legislative efforts to require an emergency PIN system have appeared in Illinois, Kansas and Georgia, but none have succeeded as of yet.

Alternative Uses

Although ATMs were originally developed as just cash dispensers, they have evolved to include many other bank-related functions. In some countries, especially those which benefit from a fully integrated cross-bank ATM network (e.g.: Multibanco in Portugal), ATMs include many functions which are not directly related to the management of one's own bank account, such as:

- Deposit currency recognition, acceptance, and recycling;
- Paying routine bills, fees, and taxes (utilities, phone bills, social security, legal fees, taxes, etc.);
- Printing bank statements;
- Updating passbooks;
- Loading monetary value into stored value cards;
- Purchasing:
  - Postage stamps;
  - Lottery tickets;
  - Train tickets;
  - Concert tickets;
  - Shopping mall gift certificates.
- Games and promotional features;
- Donating to charities;
- Cheque Processing Module;
- Adding pre-paid cell phone credit.

Increasingly banks are seeking to use the ATM as a sales device to deliver pre-approved loans and targeted advertising using products such as ITM (the Intelligent Teller Machine) from CR2 or Aptra Relate from NCR. ATMs can also act as an advertising channel for companies to advertise their own products or third-party products and services.

In Canada, ATMs are called *guichets automatiques* in French and sometimes "Bank Machines" in English. The Interac shared cash network does not allow for the selling of goods from ATMs due to specific security requirements for PIN entry when buying goods. CIBC machines in Canada, are able to top-up the minutes on certain pay as you go phone's.

Manufactures have demonstrated and have deployed several different technologies on ATMs that have not yet reached worldwide acceptance, such as:

- Biometrics, where authorisation of transactions is based on the scanning of a customer's fingerprint, iris, face, etc. Biometrics on ATMs can be found in Asia.
- Cheque/Cash Acceptance, where the ATM accepts and recognise cheques and/or currency without using envelopes Expected to grow in importance in the US through Check 21 legislation.
- Bar code scanning.
- On-demand printing of "items of value" (such as movie tickets, traveller's cheques, etc.).
- Dispensing additional media (such as phone cards).
- Coordination of ATMs with mobile phones.
- Customer-specific advertising.
- Integration with non-banking equipment.

Reliability

Before an ATM is placed in a public place, it typically has undergone extensive testing with both test money and the backend computer systems that allow it to perform transactions. Banking customers also have come to expect high reliability in their ATMs, which provides incentives to ATM providers to minimise machine and network failures. Financial consequences of incorrect machine operation also provide high degrees of incentive to minimise malfunctions.

ATMs and the supporting electronic financial networks are generally very reliable, with industry benchmarks typically producing 98.25 per cent customer availability for ATMs and up to 99.999 per cent availability for host systems. If ATMs do go out of service, customers could be left without the ability to make transactions until the beginning of their bank's next time of opening hours.

Of course, not all errors are to the detriment of customers; there have been cases of machines giving out money without debiting the account, or giving out higher value notes as a result of incorrect denomination of banknote being loaded in the money cassettes. Errors that can occur may be mechanical (such as card transport mechanisms; keypads; hard disk failures); software (such as operating system; device driver; application); communications; or purely down to operator error.

To aid in reliability, some ATMs print each transaction to a roll paper journal that is stored inside the ATM, which allows both the users of the ATMs and the related financial institutions to settle things based on the records in the journal in case there is a dispute. In some cases, transactions are posted to an electronic journal to remove the cost of supplying journal paper to the ATM and for more convenient searching of data.

Improper money checking can cause the possibility of a customer receiving counterfeit banknotes from an ATM. While bank personnel are generally trained better at spotting and removing counterfeit cash, the resulting ATM money supplies used by banks provide no absolute guarantee for proper banknotes, as the Federal Criminal Police Office of Germany has confirmed that there are regularly incidents of false banknotes having been provided through bank ATMs. Some ATMs may be stocked and wholly owned by outside companies, which can further complicate this problem when it happens. Bill validation technology can be used by ATM providers to help ensure the authenticity of the cash before it is stocked in an ATM; ATMs that have cash recycling capabilities include this capability.

Fraud

As with any device containing objects of value, ATMs and the systems they depend on to function are the targets of fraud. Fraud against ATMs and people's attempts to use them takes several forms.

The first known instance of a fake ATM was installed at a shopping mall in Manchester, Connecticut in 1993. By modifying the inner workings of a Fujitsu model 7020 ATM, a criminal gang known as The Bucklands Boys were able to steal information from cards inserted into the machine by customers.

In some cases, bank fraud could occur at ATMs whereby the bank accidentally stocks the ATM with bills in the wrong denomination, therefore giving the customer more money than should be dispensed. The result of receiving too much money may be influenced on the card holder agreement in place between the customer and the bank.

In a variation of this, WAVY-TV reported an incident in Virginia Beach of September 2006 where a hacker who had probably obtained a factory-default administration password for a gas station's white label ATM caused the unit to assume it was loaded with $5 USD bills instead of $20s, enabling himself—and many subsequent customers—to walk away with four times the money they said they wanted to withdraw.

ATM behaviour can change during what is called "stand-in" time, where the bank's cash dispensing network is unable to access databases that contain account information (possibly for database maintenance). In order to give customers access to cash, customers may be allowed to withdraw cash up to a certain amount that may be less than their usual daily withdrawal limit, but may still exceed the amount of available money in their account, which could result in fraud.

Card Fraud

In an attempt to prevent criminals from shoulder surfing the customer's PINs, some banks draw privacy areas on the floor.

For a low-tech form of fraud, the easiest is to simply steal a customer's card. A later variant of this approach is to trap the card inside of the ATM's card reader with a device often referred to as a Lebanese loop. When the customer gets frustrated by not getting the card back and walks away from the machine, the criminal is able to remove the card and withdraw cash from the customer's account.

Another simple form of fraud involves attempting to get the customer's bank to issue a new card and stealing it from their mail.

The concept and various methods of copying the contents of an ATM card's magnetic stripe on to a duplicate card to access other people's financial information was well known in the hacking communities by late-1990.

In 1996, Andrew Stone, a computer security consultant from Hampshire in the UK, was convicted of stealing more than £1 million (at the time equivalent to US $1.6 million) by pointing high definition video cameras at ATMs from a considerable distance, and by recording the card numbers, expiry dates, etc. from the embossed detail on the ATM cards along with video footage of the PINs being entered.

After getting all the information from the videotapes, he was able to produce clone cards which not only allowed him to withdraw the full daily limit for each account, but also allowed him to sidestep withdrawal limits by using multiple copied cards. In court, it was shown that he could withdraw as much as £10,000 per hour by using this method. Stone was sentenced to five years and six months in prison.

By contrast, a newer high-tech *modus operandi* involves the installation of a magnetic card reader over the real ATM's card slot and the use of a wireless surveillance camera or a modified digital camera to observe the user's PIN. Card data is then cloned onto a second card and the criminal attempts a standard cash withdrawal. The availability of low-cost commodity wireless cameras and card readers has made it a relatively simple form of fraud, with comparatively low risk to the fraudsters.

In an attempt to stop these practices, countermeasures against card cloning have been developed by the banking industry, in particular by the use of smart cards which cannot easily be copied or spoofed by unauthenticated devices, and by attempting to make the outside of their ATMs tamper evident. Older chip-card security systems include the French Carte Bleue, Visa Cash, Mondex, Blue from American Express and EMV '96 or EMV 3.11. The most actively developed form of smart card security in the industry today is known as EMV 2000 or EMV 4.x.

EMV is widely used in the UK (Chip and PIN) and other parts of Europe, but when it is not available in a specific area, ATMs must fallback to using the easy to copy magnetic stripe to perform transactions. This fallback behaviour can be exploited. However, the fallback option has been removed by several UK banks, meaning if the chip is not read, the transaction will be declined.

Related Devices

A Talking ATM is a type of ATM that provides audible instructions so that persons who cannot read an ATM screen can independently use the machine. All audible information is delivered privately through a standard headphone jack on the face of the machine. Alternatively, some banks such as the Nordea and Swedbank use a built-in external speaker which may be invoked by pressing the talk button on the keypad. Information is delivered to the customer either through pre-recorded sound files or via text-to-speech speech synthesis.

A postal interactive kiosk may also share many of the same components as an ATM (including a vault), but only dispenses items relating to postage.

A scrip cash dispenser may share many of the same components as an ATM, but lacks the ability to dispense physical cash and consequently requires no vault. Instead, the customer requests a withdrawal transaction from the machine, which prints a receipt. The customer then takes this receipt to a nearby sales clerk, who then exchanges it for cash from the till.

A Teller Assist Unit may also share many of the same components as an ATM (including a vault), but they are distinct in that they are designed to be operated solely by trained personnel and not the general public, they do not integrate directly into interbank networks, and are usually controlled by a computer that is not directly integrated into the overall construction of the unit.

Bad Check Restitution Programme

A Bad Check Restitution Programme is an intermediate agency that works to retrieve funds from bad check writers in order to repay moneys owed to the recipients of the checks.

About half of all US states offer some type of Bad Check Restitution Programme, and these check recovery services vary in many ways. Some accept NSF, stop payment and closed account checks while others may only offer NSF check collection. You will also find that some have time limits (checks submitted for collection may need to be less than 90 or 180 days old). Some will not accept checks that were written under certain circumstances, including a post-dated check, one that the check writer asked the recipient to hold, or one that was written as an extension of credit.

Methods

A Bad Check Diversion Programme generally pursues the bad check writer by stating that the check writer has committed a criminal act, and is subject to prosecution. The check writer is told that s/he may avoid prosecution by meeting the guidelines of the programme, which generally include the payment of all monies owed to the recipient, a programme fee, and participation in a course designed to improve the check writer's habits.

Generally, enrolment in the programme is not an admission of guilt to a crime, and will not result in criminal charges being filed or a criminal record. The check writer is told that if s/he successfully completes all programme requirements, the case against him/her dismissed without any possibility of arrest, criminal charges or a record thereafter.

Those failing to complete programme requirements are threatened to have their case turned over to the district attorney to be prosecuted like any other criminal case. However, very few checks are ever forwarded to the district attorney, and the likelihood of actual prosecution is remote for most check writers.

Bad Check Restitution Programmes have an important place in recovering bad checks. They directly compete with private debt collectors, and have the advantage of being able to send threatening letters on official stationary, telling a check writer that s/he has committed a crime and will likely be prosecuted if s/he does not pay substantial fees and attend a class. They help business literally recover hundreds of thousands of dollars each year throughout the United States. Most Prosecutor offices try to make these programmes free to taxpayers (i.e. bad check collection is funded by fees paid by bad check writers). However, in many programmes, the check diversion company takes its fees out of the initial payments made by the check writer, so where a check writer only pays the check, and no additional fees, the diversion company ends up charging the merchant a 50 per cent commission.

Criticism of BCRPs

According to law enforcement agencies and district attorneys, BCRPs are diversion programmes operated by the county, state, or other jurisdiction that are responsible for collecting funds owed to victims. They claim the purpose is to recover the losses of the victims.

Many consumer advocates oppose the actions of BCRPs, particularly those operated by private, for-profit companies, stating that bad check writing is not a crime unless the check writer actually intended to defraud the recipient. The writer of the bad check is told that the use of the programme is optional, but is falsely threatened that the options are to participate, or risk going to jail. The writer is usually informed within the letter that entering the programme is not necessary, and it is permissible to stand trial, even though no charges have been, or are likely to be filed.

Sometimes the programme is handled internally by the law enforcement agency itself, which often generates a substantial portion of its overall budget from the check fees that it collects. In many cases, the law enforcement agency signs up with a private collection agency. The private company essentially pays the law enforcement agency a small portion of the fees it collect in exchange for permission to send demand letters on official law enforcement agency letterhead and to threaten to prosecute check writers who do not pay up to $200 in fees, plus the check itself. This is when, in most instances, there was no criminal case to dismiss, and no law enforcement official had reviewed the check writer's file to determine if there was evidence of a crime.

Lawsuits Against BCRPs

A number of lawsuits have been filed challenging the legality of these programmes. A Michigan federal court ruled that one programme violated federal fair debt collection practices laws. In an Iowa class action in federal court, the check restitution company, American Corrective Counselling Services, Inc., agreed to refund some fees to class members Template: Liles v. Am. Corrective Counselling Services, Inc., Case No. 00-10497, (USDC Iowa). In almost all states, it is not a crime to write a check that has not cleared, unless the check writer knew at the time the check was written that the check would not clear, and was intending to defraud the merchant. Check restitution programmes attempt to collect checks, without regard to criminal intent.

In several lawsuits in federal court in Michigan, California, Indiana, Florida, Iowa and other states, consumers have charged that the programme is rife with illegal and unfair collection practices, and is an abuse of government power. In a lawsuit in Iowa, Liles v. American Correcive Counselling, Inc., the check diversion company agreed to refund money to class members. In a lawsuit in Michigan, Gradisher v. Check Enforcement Unit, Inc., 210 F. Supp. 2d 907 (W.D. Mich. 2002), the court ruled that the collection practices violated the federal Fair Debt Collection Practices Act. On May 2, 2008, in Scharm v. Craighead, Civ. No. 05-1304 (E.D.Cal), the United States District Court ruled that the bad check restitution programme that was operated in two dozen California counties violated the Fair Debt Collection Practices Act in a variety of ways, including making false threats of prosecution, and charging illegal fees.

Balloon Payment

The phrase balloon payment or bullet payment refers to one of two ways for repaying a loan; the other type is called amortising payment or Amortisation (business).

With a balloon loan, a balloon payment is paid back when the loan comes to its contractual maturity, e.g. reaches the deadline set to repayment at the time the loan was granted, representing the full loan amount (also called principal). Periodic interest payments are generally made throughout the life of the loan.

In contrast, with amortisation, portions of the principal are periodically being repaid (along with the loan's interest payments) until the loan matures. With full amortisation, the amortisation schedule has been set so that the last periodical payment comprises the final portion of principal still due. With partial amortisation, a balloon payment will still be required at maturity, covering the part of the loan amount still outstanding.

Balloon payments or bullet payments are common for certain types of debt. Most bonds, for example, are non-amortising instruments where the coupon payments cover interest only, and the full amount of the bond's face value is paid at final maturity.

Bullet payments introduce a certain amount of risk for the borrower and the lender. In many cases, the intention of the borrower is to refinance the amount of the balloon payment at the final maturity date. Refinancing risk exists at this point, since it is possible that at the time of payment, the borrower may not be able to refinance the loan; the borrower faces the risk of having insufficient liquid funds, and the lender faces the risk that the payment may be delayed.

Bank Roll

A bank roll or roll is a paper (or sometimes plastic for numismatic purposes) container for a number of coins. In the United States, empty rolls are available for free at most banks and available in every denomination (though it is becoming increasingly difficult for half dollar and dollar to be readily made available). The rolls come flat and one side will have to be folded to allow for coins to be placed inside. When the roll is full, the top side will need to be folded. Typically, the full rolls are brought back to the banks in exchange for currency or to be deposited.

Searching Rolls

Often, coin collectors will ask for full rolls from the bank to search the contents in hopes of finding an interesting piece. Full rolls are also requested by vendors to make change.

Amount in a Roll in the United States

Each denomination has a different amount found in a roll and are colour coded by denomination:

- Cent: 50 coins, $0.50, red.
- Nickel: 40 coins, $2.00, blue *(in the past, sometimes found in 20 coin, $1.00, half-rolls).*
- Dime: 50 coins, $5.00, green.
- Quarter: 40 coins, $10.00, orange *(in the past, sometimes found in 20 coin, $5.00, half-rolls).*
- Half Dollar: 20 coins, $10.00, tan or brown *(in the past, sometimes found in 40 coin, $20.00, double-rolls).*
- Large Dollar: 20 coins, $20.00, white (obsolete) *(in the past, sometimes found in 10 coin, $10.00, half-rolls).*
- Small Dollar: 25 coins, $25.00, yellow.
- Quarter Eagle: 40 coins, $100.00 (obsolete).
- Half Eagle: 40 coins, $200.00 (obsolete).
- Eagle: 50 coins, $500.00 (obsolete).
- Double Eagle: 25 coins, $500.00 (obsolete).

Bank Run

A bank run (also known as a run on the bank) occurs when a large number of bank customers withdraw their deposits because they believe the bank is, or might become, insolvent. As a bank run progresses, it generates its own momentum, in a kind of self-fulfilling prophecy: as more people withdraw their deposits, the likelihood of default increases, and this encourages further withdrawals. This can destabilise the bank to the point where it faces bankruptcy.

A banking panic or bank panic is a financial crisis that occurs when many banks suffer runs at the same time. A systemic banking crisis is one where all or almost all of the banking capital in a country is wiped out. The resulting chain of bankruptcies can cause a long economic recession. Much of the Great Depression's economic damage was caused directly by bank runs. The cost of cleaning up a systemic banking crisis can be huge, with fiscal costs averaging 13 per cent of GDP and economic output losses averaging 20 per cent of GDP for important crises from 1970 to 2007.

Several techniques can help to prevent bank runs. They include temporary suspension of withdrawals, the organisation of central banks that act as a lender of last resort, the protection of deposit insurance systems such as the US Federal Deposit Insurance Corporation, and governmental bank regulation. These techniques do not always work: for example, even with deposit insurance, depositors may still be motivated by beliefs they may lack immediate access to deposits during a bank reorganisation.

Theory

Banks retain only a fraction of their deposits as cash. The remainder is invested in securities and loans. No bank has enough reserves on hand to cope with more than the fraction of deposits being taken out at once.

Diamond and Dybvig developed an influential model to explain why bank runs occur and why banks issue deposits that are more liquid than their assets. They view the bank as an intermediary between borrowers who prefer long-maturity loans and depositors who prefer liquid accounts.

In their model, business investment requires expenditures in the present to obtain returns that take time in coming, for example, spending on machines and buildings now for production in future years. A business or entrepreneur that needs to borrow to finance investment will want to give their investments a long time to generate returns before full repayment, and will prefer long maturity loans, which offer little liquidity to the lender. The households and firms who have the money to lend to these businesses may have sudden, unpredictable needs for cash, so they require fast access to their money in the form of liquid demand deposit accounts, that is, accounts with shortest possible maturity. Since borrowers need money and depositors fear to make these loans individually, banks provide a valuable service by aggregating funds from many individual deposits, portioning them into loans for borrowers, and spreading the risks both of default and sudden demands for cash.

If only a few depositors withdraw at any given time, this arrangement works well. Depositors' unpredictable needs for cash are unlikely to occur at the same time; that is, by the law of large numbers banks can expect only a small percentage of accounts withdrawn on any one day because individual expenditure needs are largely uncorrelated. A bank can make loans over a long horizon, while keeping only relatively small amounts of cash on hand to pay any depositors who may demand withdrawals.

However, if many depositors withdraw all at once, the bank itself (as opposed to individual investors) may run short of liquidity, and depositors will rush to withdraw their money, forcing the bank to liquidate many of its assets at a loss, and eventually to fail. If such a bank calls in its loans early, this may force businesses to disrupt their production, or individuals to sell their homes, causing further losses to the larger economy.

A bank run can occur even when started by a false story. Even depositors who know the story is false will have an incentive to withdraw, if they suspect other depositors will believe the story. The story becomes a self-fulfilling prophecy. Indeed, Robert K. Merton, who coined the term self-fulfilling prophecy, mentioned bank runs as a prime example of the concept in his book Social Theory and Social Structure.

The Diamond-Dybvig model provides an example of an economic game with more than one Nash equilibrium, where it is logical for individual depositors to engage in a bank run once they suspect one might start, even though that run will cause the bank to collapse.

Systemic Banking Crises

A bank run affects just one bank. A banking panic or bank panic is a financial crisis that occurs when many banks suffer runs at the same time. In a systemic banking crisis, all or almost all of the banking capital in a country is wiped out.

Systemic banking crises are associated with substantial fiscal costs and large output losses. Frequently, emergency liquidity support and blanket guarantees have been used to contain these crises, not always successfully. Although fiscal tightening may help contain market pressures if a crisis is triggered by unsustainable fiscal policies, expansionary fiscal policies are typically used. In crises of liquidity and solvency, central banks can provide liquidity to support illiquid banks. Depositor protection can help restore confidence, although it tends to be costly and does not necessarily speed up economic recovery. Intervention is often delayed in the hope that recovery will occur, and this delay increases the stress on the economy.

Some measures are more effective than others in containing economic fallout and restoring the banking system after a systemic crisis. These include establishing the scale of the problem, targeted debt relief programmes to distressed borrowers, corporate restructuring programmes, recognising bank losses, and adequately capitalising banks. Speedy intervention appears to substantially decrease stress on the economy. Programmes that are targeted, that specify clear quantifiable rules that limit access to preferred assistance, and that contain meaningful standards for capital regulation, appear to be more successful. Government-owned asset management companies are largely ineffective due to political constraints.

A silent run occurs when the implicit fiscal deficit from a government's unbooked loss exposure to zombie banks is large enough to deter depositors of those banks. As more depositors and investors begin to doubt whether a government can support a country's banking system, the silent run on the system can gather steam, causing the zombie banks' funding costs to increase.

If a zombie bank sells some assets at market value, its remaining assets contain a larger fraction of unbooked losses; if it rolls over its liabilities at increased interest rates, it squeezes its profits along with the profits of healthier competitors. The longer the silent run goes on, the more benefits are transferred from healthy banks and taxpayers to the zombie banks.

The cost of cleaning up after a crisis can be huge. In systemically important banking crises in the world from 1970 to 2007, the average net recapitalisation cost to the government was 6 per cent of GDP, fiscal costs associated with crisis management averaged 13 per cent of GDP (16 per cent of GDP if expense recoveries are ignored), and economic output losses averaged about 20 per cent of GDP during the first four years of the crisis.

Prevention

Several techniques can be used to help prevent bank runs.

Individual Banks

Some prevention techniques apply to individual banks, independently of the rest of the economy.

- A bank can take deposits from depositors who do not observe common information that might spark a run. For example, in the days before deposit insurance, it made sense for a bank to have a large lobby and fast service, to prevent a line of depositors from extending out into the street, causing passers-by to infer that a bank run is occurring.
- A bank can temporarily suspend withdrawals to stop a run. In many cases the threat of suspension prevents the run, which means the threat need not be carried out.
- Bank regulation or other constraints can impose a reserve ratio requirement, which limits the proportion of deposits which a bank can lend out, making it less likely for a bank run to start. This practice sets a limit on the fraction in fractional-reserve banking; in the extreme and hypothetical case, full-reserve banking requires a reserve ratio of 100 per cent.

Collective Prevention

Some prevention techniques apply across the whole economy, though they may still allow individual institutions to fail. These techniques create moral hazard, since they reduce incentives for banks to avoid making risky loans; the goal is for the benefits of collective prevention to outweigh the costs of excessive risk-taking.

- Central banks act as a lender of last resort. To prevent a bank run, the central bank guarantees that it will make short-term loans to banks, to ensure that, if they remain economically viable, they will always have enough liquidity to honour their deposits.
- Deposit insurance systems insure each depositor up to a certain amount, so that depositors' savings are protected even if the bank fails. This removes the incentive to withdraw one's deposits simply because others are withdrawing theirs. However, depositors may still be motivated by fears they may lack immediate access to deposits during a bank reorganisation.

History

Bank runs first appeared as part of cycles of credit expansion and its subsequent contraction. In the 16th century onwards, English goldsmiths issuing promissory notes suffered severe failures due to bad harvests plummeting parts of the country into famine and unrest. Other examples are the Dutch Tulip manias (1634-1637), the British South Sea Bubble (1717-1719), the French Mississippi Company (1717-1720), the "Post Napoleonic Depression" (1815-1830) and the Great Depression (1929-1939).

Bank runs have also been used to blackmail individuals or governments; for example in 1830 when the British Government under the Duke of Wellington overturned a majority government under the orders of the King, George IV, to prevent reform (the later 1832 Reform Act), he angered reformers and so a run on the banks was threatened under the rallying cry *"To stop the Duke go for gold!"*.

Many of the recessions in the United States were caused by banking panics. The Great Depression contained several banking crises consisting of runs on multiple banks from 1929 to 1933; some of these were specific to regions of the US. Much of the Depression's economic damage was caused directly by bank runs, and institutions put into place after the Depression have prevented runs on US commercial banks since the 1930s, even under conditions such as the US savings and loan crisis of the 1980s and 1990s. The Depression's bank runs left a lasting mark on the American psyche, exhibited in sometimes disturbing images such as the bleak scenes where the fictional hero George Bailey contemplates suicide in the movie *It's a Wonderful Life*.

Recent Incidents

- In 1999, a bank run happened in Malaysia where Bank Negara Malaysia (the Malaysian central bank) had to take control of MBf Finance Berhad, the biggest finance company in Malaysia during that time. Many of the finance company's 120 branches saw runs on their deposits, totalling about 17 billion Ringgit (US $4.49 billion).
- In 2001, during the Argentine economic crisis (1999-2002), a bank run and *corralito* was experienced in Argentina. There

are various theories into the cause. This contributed towards the bank runs in neighbouring Uruguay during the 2002 Uruguay banking crisis.

- In early August 2007, the American firm, Countrywide Financial suffered a bank run as a consequence of the subprime mortgage crisis.
- On 13 September 2007, the British bank Northern Rock arranged an emergency loan facility from the Bank of England, which it claimed was the result of short-term liquidity problems. The bank's defenders claimed its cash shortage was the result of overexposure to the failing US sub-prime mortgage market, while its critics argued that it was the result of Northern Rock's own careless lending practices. A run began the following day, Friday, with reports of its internet banking site being overloaded, and long queues outside branches that day, Saturday morning and the following Monday. News reports on 17 September stated that an estimated £2 billion GBP of retail deposits had been withdrawn by customers since the bank had applied for emergency funds.
- On Tuesday, 11 March 2008, a bank run began on the securities and banking firm Bear Stearns. While Bear Stearns was not an ordinary deposit-taking bank, it had financed huge long-term investments by selling short-maturity bonds (Asset Backed Commercial Paper), making it vulnerable to panic on the part of its bondholders. Credit officers of rival firms began to say that Bear Stearns would not be able to make good on its obligations. Within two days, Bear Stearns's capital base of $17 billion had dwindled to $2 billion in cash, and Bear Stearns told government officials that it saw little option other than to file for bankruptcy the next day. By 07:00 Friday, the Federal Reserve decided to lend Bear Stearns money, the first time since the Great Depression that it had lent to a non-bank. Stocks sank, and that day JP Morgan Chase began an effort to buy Bear Stearns as part of a government-sponsored bailout. The deal was arranged by Sunday in an effort to calm markets before overseas markets opened.

- On 11 July 2008, US mortgage lender Indy Mac Bank was seized by federal regulators. Indy Mac had been a stressed institution for months. The bank was capital-constrained and possibly heading for regulatory intervention. However, both regulators and the bank itself blamed its troubles on a letter from Sen. Charles E. Schumer questioning its viability. Following the public release of the letter on June 26, Indy Mac customers withdrew amounts averaging $100 million a day from the bank, or a total of $1.3 billion in cash. The run caused a liquidity crisis which forced Indy Mac to announce it was halting new loan submissions, closing its retail and wholesale lending divisions, and laying off 3,800 employees.
- On 25 September 2008, the Office of Thrift Supervision was forced to shut down Washington Mutual, the largest savings and loan in the United States and the sixth-largest overall financial institution, on a Thursday due to a massive run. Over the previous 10 days, customers had withdrawn $16.7 billion in deposits. This is currently the biggest bank failure in American financial history. Normally, banks are seized on Fridays to allow the FDIC the weekend to prepare the failed bank for takeover by another bank. However, Wa Mu's size led regulators to shut it down on a Thursday.
- On 6 October 2008, Landsbanki, Iceland's second largest bank, was put into government receivership. The Icelandic government used emergency powers to dismiss the board of directors of Landsbanki and took control of the failed institution. Prime Minister Geir Haarde also rushed measures through Parliament to give the country's largest bank, Kaupthing, a £400 m loan. In addition, Iceland pleaded with Russia to extend 3 bn in credit as western countries refused to help. With over 5 bn in savings held by Britons in Landsbanki, the Icelandic collapse threatens private citizens in the United Kingdom as well as companies in Iceland.

Bank Secrecy

Bank secrecy (or bank privacy) is a legal principle under which banks are allowed to protect personal information about their customers, through the use of numbered bank accounts or otherwise.

Effective bank secrecy is better achieved in certain countries, such as Switzerland or in tax havens, where offshore banks adhere to voluntary or statutory levels of privacy. Created by the Swiss Banking Act of 1934, which led to the famous Swiss Bank, the principle of bank secrecy is sometimes considered one of the main aspects of private banking.

It has also been accused by NGOs and governments of being one of the main instruments of underground economy and organised crime, in particular following the Class action suit against the Vatican Bank in the 1990s, the Clearstream scandal and September 11, 2001.

Advances in financial cryptography (e.g. public-key cryptography) could make it possible to use anonymous electronic money and anonymous digital bearer certificates to achieve financial privacy and anonymous internet banking, given enabling institutions (e.g. issuers of such certificates and digital cash) and computer systems that are secure against attackers.

Reasons for Bank Secrecy

There are a number of reasons to use banking privacy:

- To hide it from friends, spouse or other family members.
- To hide it from the employer. (Many employers restrict the ability of their staff to trade shares to prevent conflicts of interest).
- To store embezzled money.
- To launder money.
- To prevent confiscation of money, e.g., in the case of potential bankruptcy.
- Tax evasion (banking secrecy extends to tax agencies being refused permission to examine accounts).
- Tax resistance (by libertarians, or others, who oppose the institution collecting the tax).
- Protection from overbearing or corrupt local government agencies.
- Protection from litigation.
- For any other reason which requires no-one being able to identify the amount of money you have or have earned/ acquired.
- Privacy from press or publicity. Many newspapers annually publish "rich lists", which are list of the richest people in a country or an area. Many factors including the size of an individual's bank balance can be taken into account in drawing conclusions as to the size of his wealth.
- Protection from criminals. In some countries, criminal gangs can access information on bank customers. This might interest criminals, such as kidnappers, extortionists, or identity thieves.
- Protection from solicitation. This might include charities, venture capitalists seeking seed money, family members, beggars, or investment salesmen.
- Simply for privacy. The possession of liquid wealth attracts publicity, which is not always welcome.

Swiss Banking Act of 1934

Bank secrecy was invented by the 1934 Swiss Banking Act following a public scandal in France, when MP Fabien Alberty denounced tax evasion by eminent French personalities, including politicians, judges, industrialists, church dignitaries and directors of newspapers, who were hiding their money in Switzerland. He called these men of "a particularly ticklish patriotism", who "probably are unaware that the money they deposit abroad is lent by Switzerland to Germany".

The Peugeot brothers and Francois Coty, of the famous perfume family, were on his list. Since then, Swiss banks have acquired world-wide celebrity due to their numbered bank accounts, which critics such as ATTAC NGO alleged only help legalised tax evasion, money laundering and more generally the underground economy.

Under the principle of bank secrecy, privacy is statutorily enforced, with Swiss law strictly limiting any information shared with third parties, including tax authorities, foreign governments or even Swiss authorities, except when requested by a Swiss judge's subpoena.

However, *anonymous banking* is not strictly true as a term as all Swiss bank accounts, including numbered bank accounts, are linked to an identified individual under Swiss banking law. This law only permits a bank to share information with others in cases of severe criminal acts, such as identifying a terrorist's bank account. Any bank employee violating a client's privacy is punished quite severely by law. Many offshore banks, located in tax havens such as in the Cayman Islands and Panama, also have strict privacy laws.

US Bank Secrecy Act of 1970

The Bank Secrecy Act (or BSA) requires financial institutions to assist government agencies to detect and prevent money laundering. Specifically, the act requires financial institutions to keep records of cash purchases of negotiable instruments, file reports of cash transactions exceeding $10,000 (daily aggregate amount), and to report suspicious activity that might signify money laundering, tax evasion, or other criminal activities.

Criticisms

Numbered bank accounts, used by Swiss banks and other offshore banks located in tax havens, have been accused by NGOs such as ATTAC of being a major instrument of the underground economy, facilitating tax evasion and money laundering. After Al Capone's 1931 condemnation for tax evasion, "mobster Meyer Lansky took money from New Orleans slot machines and shifted it to accounts overseas. The Swiss secrecy law two years later assured him of a G-man-proof-banking. Later, he bought a Swiss bank and for years deposited his Havana casino take in Miami accounts, then wired the funds to Switzerland via a network of shell and holding companies and offshore accounts", according to journalist Lucy Komisar. Joseph Stiglitz, 2001 Nobel laureate for economics, told Komisar:

> "You ask why, if there's an important role for a regulated banking system, do you allow a non-regulated banking system to continue? It's in the interest of some of the moneyed interests to allow this to occur. It's not an accident; it could have been shut down at any time. If you said the US, the UK, the major G7 banks will not deal with offshore bank centres that don't comply with G7 banks regulations, these banks could not exist. They only exist because they engage in transactions with standard banks."

In 1999, a class action suit against the Vatican Bank criticised the role of Switzerland during World War II. Governments of developing countries accused Swiss banks of detaining most of the money stolen by corrupt dictators, which Oxfam International estimate to about $50 billion a year deposited in offshore tax havens, nearly the size of the $57 billion annual global aid budget.

Also in 1999, according to Lucy Komisar, banks "orchestrated a successful e-mail campaign to Congress" to "sink a 'know your customer' regulation proposed by the Federal Deposit Insurance Corporation".

In 2001, the United States learned that the Swiss had protected the bank that handled finances for Osama Bin Laden. One of them, the Bahrain International Bank, had funds transacting through non-published accounts of Clearstream, which has been qualified as a "bank of banks" and was involved in one of Luxembourg's major financial scandal.

The 2001 USA Patriot Act has created many new rules for US banks in an attempt to defeat bank secrecy. A list of such banks or shell banks are given to the US banks who are not allowed to wire money to them. All new customers to US banks must now be asked if they are US citizens. If not, they must state their occupation and whether they expect to be wired foreign moneys.

Banker's Dozen

A Banker's dozen is a play on the name Baker's dozen; it is one less than a dozen as compared to one more. It alludes to a method of lending where the interest is deducted beforehand, e.g., borrowing (owing) ten dollars but actually receiving only nine. One might relate it to the baker's dozen because it has a similar but opposite principle. Instead of adding one number, it subtracts one.

Banking Agent

A banking agent is a retail or postal outlet contracted by a financial institution or a mobile network operator to process clients' transactions. Rather than a branch teller, it is the owner or an employee of the retail outlet who conducts the transaction and lets clients deposit, withdraw, and transfer funds, pay their bills, enquire about an account balance, or receive government benefits or a direct deposit from their employer. Banking agents can be pharmacies, supermarkets, convenience stores, lottery outlets, post offices, and many more.

Globally, these retailers and post offices are increasingly utilised as important distribution channels for financial institutions. The points of service range from post offices in the Outback of Australia where clients from all banks can conduct their transactions, to rural France where the bank Credit Agricole uses corner stores to provide financial services, to small lottery outlets in Brazil at which clients can receive their social payments and access their bank accounts.

Banking agents are usually equipped with a combination of point-of-sale (POS) card reader, mobile phone, barcode scanner to scan bills for bill payment transactions, Personal Identification Number identification number (PIN) pads, and sometimes personal computers (PCs) that connect with the bank's server using a personal dial-up or other data connection. Clients that transact at the agent use a magstripe bank card or their mobile phone to access their bank account or e-wallet, respectively. Identification of customers is normally done through a PIN number, but could also involve biometrics. With regard to the transaction verification, authorisation, and settlement platform, banking agents are similar to any other remote bank channel.

Local regulation will determine if financial institutions are allowed to work through retail outlets. Regulators generally determine what kind of, if any, financial institutions are permitted to contract banking agents, what products can be offered at the retail outlets, how financial institutions have to handle cash transport, Know Your Customer requirements, consumer protection, and other operational areas.

Rationale for Banking Agents

Banking agents help financial institutions to divert existing customers from crowded branches providing a "complementary", often more convenient channel. Other financial institutions, especially in developing markets, use agents to reach an "additional" client segment or geography. Reaching poor clients in rural areas is often prohibitively expensive for financial institutions since transaction numbers and volumes do not cover the cost of a branch. In such environments banking agents that piggy bag on existing retail infrastructure – and lower set up and running cost – can play a vital role in offering many low-income people their first-time access to a range of financial services. Also, low-income clients often feel more comfortable banking at their local store than walking into a marble branch.

Banking agents are the backbone of mobile banking, i.e. performing transactions over a mobile device, most often a mobile phone. To enable clients to convert cash into electronic money and vice versa which can send be sent over their mobile phone, clients will have to visit a branch, automated teller machine (ATM), or banking agent. Especially in remote and rural locations, where cash is still the most important way to pay and transact, a mobile banking service is dependent on banking agents to enable clients to effectively use their service.

Transaction Process

For the client, there is no difference in accessing his or her bank account at the agent or in a branch or at an ATM. However, besides signing a contract with the financial institution it will be working for, the banking agent also has to open a bank account at the same. In addition, the store has to deposit a certain amount of cash into that account which will serve as the banking agent's "working capital." In many cases, rather than asking the agent to come up with the cash deposit, the financial institution will extend the store a credit line. The size of the credit line is normally not standardised, but adapted individually to each agent depending on its size, the expected volume of transactions and how long the agent has already been working with the bank. This is how the credit line will be used during each transaction:

- Client withdraws money ("cash-out" transaction): agent account is credited in same amount.
- Client deposits money ("cash-in" transaction): agent account is debited in same amount.

In case the agent's credit line had reached its limits, and the agent's bank account does not have sufficient funds, to cover the received funds, the POS will block and can only be deblocked if the funds have been deposited in the next bank account.

The transaction process for banking services using a bank card is simple:

1. An existing bank client presents his card at the agent and requests a specific transaction and the amount to be withdrawn, deposited, or transferred.
2. The agent selects the type of transaction on the POS device or personal computer, enters the amount, swipes the client's card through the device, and lets the client enter his PIN number.

3. A General Packet Radio Service (GPRS), dial up, or satellite communication connects with the bank's server to authorise the transaction.
4. Once the transaction has been authorised, the device prints the client's receipt.

Banking Agent Set-ups

There are principally three ways banks have used to set-up their equipment and marketing material within a store:

Cashier: This set-up is primarily being used for individual stores. Transaction volume should be relatively low and being processed by the store's staff in addition to their traditional sales. The technology equipment is located behind store's general cashier. Posters and marketing material will be limited to small section next to POS device and a small sign outside the store.

Stand: This set-up in which the bank sets up a little stand is used if transaction volume is larger and justify one staff member dedicated to man the POS device. Some financial institution prefer this set-up since clients do not feel as much as "banking" in a store and the bank's brand is much more visible.

Dedicated Store: This set-up is similar to a mini-branch, i.e. a small shop with around 1-3 tellers, but transactions are processed by non-bank staff.

Experience with Banking Agents

Pioneering banks, microfinance institutions, and mobile operators started to experiment with banking agent networks in various countries around the world such as Brazil, Peru, Colombia, Kenya, Mexico, Pakistan, the Philippines, and South Africa.

Latin America is the region with the strongest development towards banking agents. Here governments concerned about expanding financial sector infrastructure have adjusted regulation and are providing incentives for banks to reach new geographies and new client segments through banking agents.

Brazil is probably the most developed market where banking agents have significantly increased financial system infrastructure. Seventy-four institutions are currently managing around 90,000 points of sale in Brazil that reach all 5,561 municipalities. Within only 5 years, the banking agent network facilitated 12.4 m new bank accounts and today the network comprises 56 per cent of all points of sale in the Brazilian financial system. Financial institutions in other Latin-American markets such as Peru, Colombia, and Mexico have started to learn from the Brazilian experience, adjusted their regulation, and established their own banking agent networks. Pioneers in other regions can be found in Kenya, Mongolia, South Africa, and the Philippines.

Credit Union

A credit union is a cooperative financial institution that is owned and controlled by its members, and operated for the purpose of promoting thrift, providing credit at reasonable rates, and providing other financial services to its members. Many credit unions exist to further community development or sustainable international development on a local level. Worldwide, credit union systems vary significantly in terms of total system assets and average institution asset size since credit unions exist in a wide range of sizes, ranging from volunteer operations with a handful of members to institutions with several billion dollars in assets and hundreds of thousands of members. Yet credit unions are typically smaller than banks; for example, the average US credit union has $93 million in assets, while the average US bank has $1.53 billion, as of 2007.

The World Council of Credit Unions (WOCCU) defines credit unions as "not-for-profit cooperative institutions." In practice however, legal arrangements vary by jurisdiction. For example in Canada credit unions are regulated as for-profit institutions, and view their mandate as earning a reasonable profit to enhance services to members and ensure stable growth. This difference in viewpoints reflects credit unions' unusual organisational structure, which attempts to solve the principal-agent problem by ensuring that the owners and the users of the institution are the same people. In any case, credit unions generally cannot accept donations and must be able to prosper in a competitive market economy.

Credit unions differ from banks and other financial institutions in that the members who have accounts in the credit union are the owners of the credit union and they elect their board of directors in a democratic one person-one vote system regardless of the amount of money invested in the credit union. A credit union's policies governing interest rates and other matters are set by a volunteer Board of Directors elected by and from the membership itself. Credit unions offer many of the same financial services as banks, often using a different terminology; common services include: share accounts (savings accounts), share draft (checking) accounts, credit cards, share term certificates (certificates of deposit), and online banking.

Normally, only a member of a credit union may deposit money with the credit union, or borrow money from it. As such, credit unions have historically marketed themselves as providing superior member service and being committed to helping members improve their financial health. In the microfinance context, "credit unions provide a broader range of loan and savings products at a much cheaper cost (to their members) than do most microfinance institutions."

In some places, credit unions are called by other names; for example, in many African countries they are called *savings and credit cooperative organisations* (SACCOs), "to emphasise savings before credit." in Spanish-speaking countries, they are often called *cooperativas de ahorro y credito,* but in Mexico they are typically called a *caja popular*. French terms for "credit union" include *caisse populaire* and *banque populaire.* Afghani credit unions are called *Islamic investment and finance cooperatives* (IIFCs) to comply with Islamic lending practices.

Global Dispersion

Based on data from the World Council of Credit Unions, at the end of 2006 there were 46,377 credit unions in 97 countries around the world. Collectively they served 172 million retail members and oversaw US $1.1 trillion in assets. Note that the World Council does not include data from cooperative banks, so that, for example, some nations generally seen as the pioneers of credit unionism, such as Germany, France, Holland and Italy, are not included in their data. The European Association of Cooperative Banks reported 34 million members in those four countries at the end of 2005.

The nations with the most credit union activity are highly diverse. According to the World Council, nations with the greatest number of credit union members included the United States (87 million), India (20 million), Canada (11 million), South Korea (4.7 million), Japan (3.6 million), Mexico (3.6 million), Australia (3.5 million), Kenya (3.3 million), Ireland (3.0 million), Thailand and Brazil (2.6 million) each. Countries with the highest percentage of members in the economically active population were Dominica (147 per cent [numbers higher than 100 per cent are possible because the average person is a member of more than one credit union]), Ireland (110 %), Barbados (72%), Trinidad and Tobago (57%), Canada (48%), the United States (43%), Benin (27%), Australia (26%), Senegal and Mali (19%) each.

History

Modern credit union history dates to 1852, when Franz Hermann Schulze-Delitzsch consolidated the learning from two pilot projects, one in Eilenburg and the other in Delitzsch in Germany into what are generally recognised as the first credit unions in the world. He went on to develop a highly successful urban credit union system.

In 1864, Friedrich Wilhelm Raiffeisen founded the first rural credit union in Heddesdorf (now part of Neuwied) in Germany. Although Schulze-Delitzsch can claim chronological precedence, Raiffeisen is often viewed as more important today. Rural communities in Germany faced a far more severe shortage of financial institutions than the cities. They were viewed as unbankable because of very small, seasonal flows of cash and very limited human resources. The organisational methods Raiffeisen refined there, which levered what is today called *social capital*, have become a hallmark of the global credit union identity.

By the time of Raiffeisen's death in 1888 credit unions had spread to Italy, France, the Netherlands, England and Austria, among other nations. The Raiffeisen name is still used by Raiffeisenbank, the largest banking group in Austria (with subsidiaries throughout Central and Eastern Europe), Rabobank (Netherlands) and similarly-named agricultural credit unions in Germany.

The first credit union in North America, the Caisse populaire de Levis in Quebec, Canada, began operations on Jan. 23rd, 1901 with a ten cent deposit. Founder Alphonse Desjardins, a reporter in the Canadian Parliament, was moved to take up his mission in 1897 when he learned of a Montrealer who had been ordered by the court to pay nearly $5,000 in interest on a loan of $150 from a moneylender. Drawing extensively on European precedents, Desjardins developed a unique parish-based model for Quebec: the *caisse populaire.*

In the United States, St. Mary's Bank Credit Union of Manchester, New Hampshire holds the distinction as the first credit union. Assisted by a personal visit from Desjardins, St. Mary's was founded by French-speaking immigrants to Manchester from Quebec on November 24, 1908. America's Credit Union Museum now occupies the location of the home from which St. Mary's Bank Credit Union first operated.

Pierre Jay, then Massachusetts Commissioner of Banks and Edward Filene, a Bostonian merchant, were central in establishing enabling legislation in Massachusetts in 1909. The Woman's Educational and Industrial Union, credited with many social service initiatives, heard of this cooperative financial model and wrote to Des Jardins. He provided them with the data they needed and on November 23, 1910, the first non-faith-based or community credit union, established for all people in the greater Boston community, Industrial Credit Union, was chartered.

Filene also created the Credit Union National Extension Bureau, the forerunner of the Credit Union National Association, which was formed as a confederation of state leagues at a meeting in Estes Park, Colorado in 1934. Attendees at the meeting included Dora Maxwell who would go on to help establish hundreds of credit unions and programmes for the poor and Louise McCarren Herring, whose work to form credit unions and ensure their safe operation earned the title of "Mother of Credit Unions" in the United States.

In the same year, Congress passed the Federal Credit Union Act, which permitted credit unions to be organised anywhere in the United States. The legislation allowed credit unions to incorporate under either state or federal law, a system of dual chartering that persists today.

Not-for-profit Status and the Need for a Surplus

In the credit union context, the term "not-for-profit" should not be confused with "non-profit" charities or similar organisations. Credit unions are "not-for-profit" because they operate to serve their members rather than to maximise profits. Credit unions are not charities or similar organisations that rely on donations; to the contrary, credit unions are financial institutions that must turn what is, in economic terms, a small profit (i.e. surplus) to be able to continue to serve their members. According to WOCCU, a credit union's revenues (from loans and investments) do need to exceed its operating expenses and dividends (interest paid on deposits) in order to maintain capital and solvency and "credit unions use excess earnings to offer members more affordable loans, a higher return on savings, lower fees or new products and services."

Corporate Credit Unions

The majority of credit unions are known as *natural-person credit unions,* and provide service to individual consumers. Corporate credit unions (also known as *central credit unions* in Canada) also exist, but instead serve the needs of credit unions with operational support, funds clearing tasks as well as product and service delivery. In effect, they serve as a credit union's credit union. The largest corporate credit union in the United States is US Central Credit Union of Lenexa, Kansas, which serves as a central clearing house for corporate credit unions and holds approximately $49.1 billion in assets. The two largest corporate credit unions that serve only natural-person credit unions are Western Corporate Federal Credit Union (Wes Corp) in San Dimas, California and Southwest Corporate Federal Credit Union in Plano, Texas.

Credit Union Leagues and Associations

The World Council of Credit Unions is both a trade association for credit unions worldwide and a development agency. WOCCU's mission is to "assist its members and potential members to organise, expand, improve and integrate credit unions and related institutions as effective instruments for the economic and social development of all people."

Credit unions in the United States have traditionally employed a state/national trade association relationship that aligns credit unions with state "Credit Union Leagues" followed by national affiliation with the Credit Union National Association (CUNA) of Madison, Wisconsin. Federal credit unions may also be members of the National Association of Federal Credit Unions (NAFCU).

The Credit Union Executives Society (CUES), based in Madison, Wisconsin, provides professional development and resources to thousands of credit union executives and directors worldwide. It partners with world-renowned universities to offer graduate-level executive education specifically for credit union leaders.

The biggest UK credit union trade association is the Association of British Credit Unions Limited, more commonly known as *Association of British Credit Unions*, ABCUL. Some Scottish credit unions are represented by the much smaller Scottish League of Credit Unions (SLCU) which has headquarters in Glasgow; however, the overall majority of credit unions choose the main British Association.

Credit Union Central of Canada is the trade association for Canada's credit unions outside Quebec. The Desjardins Group represents Quebec's credit unions. Structurally, it blends the functions of a trade association and a more European-style cooperative bank.

Credit Unions often form cooperatives among themselves to provide services to members. A Credit Union Service Organisation (CUSO) is generally a for-profit subsidiary of one or more credit unions formed for this purpose. For example, CO-OP Financial Services, the largest credit union owned interbank network in the US, provides an ATM network and shared branching services to credit unions. Other examples of cooperatives among credit unions include credit counselling services as well as insurance and investment services.

United Kingdom

In the United Kingdom, credit unions are regulated by the FSA (Financial Services Authority). UK credit unions are classified under two types: type 1 are the smaller CUs while type 2 are larger. From November 2006 many type 2 CUs began offering their members debit card accounts which enabled CU members to obtain funds from any Link ATM. UK credit unions do not offer cheques as these are generally being phased out in UK financial transactions.

Credit unions in the UK now offer a wide range of services to their members; from direct debits to payroll deductions, from being able to send standing orders from their accounts to paying members bills to providing cheaper insurance facilities.

In the UK, one of the benefits of joining a credit union is the life insurance CU's provide their members free of charge. Also, if a member were to die then their loan value is wiped out with no further charge to the member's account or their family; further, in many cases their savings with the CU are doubled and passed to the next of kin. As recent history has shown, with the Christmas 'savings club' Farepak going bust in 2006 (very unfortunately unregulated, and not protected by UK law) and hundreds of Farepak customers losing all their savings, the real alternative of a regulated and protected CU is a able to provide both good savings rates and very affordable loans, in the safe knowledge that all CU customers savings are protected, if the worst happens.

Currently there is a government financial initiative mainly being operated by credit unions to bring financial services to the economically disadvantaged members of society. One aim is to significantly reduce the influence of door step lenders (and illegal "loan sharks") where a £300 loan over 30 weeks may involve paying back around £450; a credit union loan would typically require paying back around £325.

Canada

Canada has the highest per capita use of credit unions in North America, with more than a third of the population enrolled in one. They are concentrated in Quebec, where they are known as *caisses populaires* (people's banks), and in the Western provinces. As of Dec. 31, 2006 there were 549 member caisses and 5.8 million retail members in the Caisses Populaires Desjardins federation. According to data from Credit Union Central of Canada on the same date there were 10.8 million retail members controlling CAD $193 billion in assets across all of Canada. Aside from Desjardins, other major Canadian credit unions include Vancity, Coast Capital Savings, and Credit Union Atlantic.

United States

In the United States, credit unions have 86 million members, which is 43.47 per cent of the economically active population. US credit unions are not-for-profit, cooperative, tax-exempt organisations.

US credit unions can be chartered by either the federal government (federal credit unions) or by a state. All federal credit unions and 95 per cent of state-chartered credit unions have federal deposit insurance (called *share insurance*) through the National Credit Union Share Insurance Fund of at least $250,000 per member. This federal deposit insurance is backed by the full faith and credit of the United States government and is administered by the National Credit Union Administration. As of December 2006, the National Credit Union Share Insurance Fund had a higher insurance fund capital ratio than the FDIC Bank Insurance Fund. US credit unions also typically have higher equity capital ratios than US banks.

As of the end of 2007, the National Credit Union Share Insurance Fund insured more than $560 billion in deposits at 8,101 not-for-profit cooperative US credit unions. For comparison, the Federal Deposit Insurance Corporation insured more than $4,000 billion in deposits at 8,560 banks and thrift institutions. The NCUA and the FDIC are both independent federal agencies backed by the full faith and credit of the US government.

United States credit unions typically pay higher dividend (interest) rates on shares (deposits) and charge lower interest on loans than banks. Credit unions therefore often have a higher cost of assets (i.e. interest expense as a percentage of average assets) than commercial banks, with aggregate US credit union cost of assets being higher than the aggregate US bank cost of assets in eight of the thirteen years between 1995 and 2007. Credit union revenues (from loans and investments) do, however, need to exceed operating expenses and dividends (interest paid on deposits) in order to maintain capital and solvency.

Federal credit unions may apply to the National Credit Union Administration for Low-Income Credit Union or LICU status. To qualify for LICU status, the majority of the credit union's membership meet specific requirements in order to be considered "low-income". This LICU status allows the credit unions to benefit from certain NCUA programmes to enhance its capacity to serve underserved populations who may otherwise lack access to credit or other financial services. In addition, some state regulators also provide for similar low-income designations.

Unlike banks, which were caught redlining underserved areas in the 1970s, credit unions are not subject to federal "community reinvestment" requirements—essentially because credit unions, by their nature and mission of "people helping people," already meet the financial needs of a broad spectrum of people that fall within their fields of membership, and play an active role in community development and growth. Because of that, credit unions have successfully lobbied to exempt themselves from the (US federal) Community Reinvestment Act, the law that forces banks to provide services in low-income areas.

Home Mortgage Disclosure Act (2006) data shows that US credit unions approved 69 per cent of low and moderate-income borrowers' mortgage applications that they received, versus 47 per cent low/mod-income borrower approval rate for other US mortgage lenders, and also that US credit unions approved 62 per cent of minority members' mortgage applications, versus a 51 per cent minority approval rate for other US mortgage lenders. The 2006 Home Mortgage Disclosure Act data also shows that 25.2 per cent of all US credit union mortgage originations were mortgages for low or moderate-income borrowers, versus a 20.6 per cent low or moderate-income borrower mortgage origination percentage for other US mortgage lenders. The National Credit Union Administration, however, has long discouraged US credit unions from giving members loans that they may not be able to afford to repay and has forbidden other types of predatory lending and abusive credit practices. Federal credit unions are also forbidden from charging pre-payment penalties on loans.

Membership Restrictions: US governmental regulatory agencies require that credit unions restrict their membership to defined segments of the population, such as people who live, work, worship, or attend school in a well-defined geographic area; employees of specific companies or trades; members of specific non-profit groups (alumni associations, conservation or other advocacy organisations, lodges, churches, or the like); or a particular occupational group (teachers, doctors, etc.). In the US, this is referred to as a credit union's "field of membership." Internationally it is referred to as the 'common bond' or 'bond of association'.

Mergers of smaller credit unions with disparate membership bases often result in a credit union with a wide variety of ways to qualify to join; thus, a credit union may have a much broader "field of membership" than that credit union's name would imply.

Credit unions generally follow the principle of "once a member, always a member," which allows current credit union membership to continue even if the individual would no longer qualify to be a member (such as having changed professions or moved outside the area). However, many credit unions reserve the right of expulsion against a member who causes a financial loss. Some credit unions also have expelled members, including elected Board and Supervisory Committee volunteers, for making "whistleblower" complaints against credit union management.

If a member voluntarily terminates their membership, they may or may not be eligible to rejoin, depending on the credit union's policies and government regulations.

Credit unions may typically be chartered to serve a specific employee or associational group or groups (often called a *Select Employee Group* or "SEG Charter"), all members of a trade, industry, or profession (a "TIP Charter"), or have a "Community Charter" (typically a field of membership of anyone who lives, works, goes to school, or attends religious services in a particular city, county, or counties). In the United States, when a credit union converts to a Community Charter from a SEG Charter or TIP Charter, it can continue to serve its existing members as well as anyone who lives, works, worships, or attends school within its new geographical field of membership, but cannot admit new members from its former SEG(s) or TIP (unless the group in question is located within "the new community credit union's boundaries"). Similarly, a credit union that converts to a TIP or SEG charter from a different charter type can no longer admit new members from its old field of membership.

Typically, members' families – such as immediate family or household members – can also join the credit union. In the United States, the National Credit Union Administration or a state regulator – depending upon whether or not the credit union is chartered by the federal government or by a state – decides whether or not to approve or deny proposed field of membership expansions or charter conversions to other credit union charters, and similar procedures are typically used in other countries.

Credit Unions and Banks in the United States: Tension has always existed between member-owned cooperative credit unions and for-profit banks in the US. When credit unions were first organising in the United States in the early-twentieth century, the banking industry was opposed, remaining so ever since. Despite the fact that credit unions continue to hold a very small share of the financial services market, banks and bank trade associations consistently put anti-credit union legislation at the top of their agendas.

Due to their status as not-for-profit, member-owned financial institutions with no source of secondary investment capital, credit unions in the United States are exempt from federal and state income taxes (but, not from employment or property taxes). Additionally, credit union members pay income tax on dividends earned through financial participation in the credit union; this is similar to the taxation structure enjoyed by many banks incorporated under the Internal Revenue Code.

Bank holding companies and their affiliates aggressively compete to provide services to credit unions through their ATM networks, corporate checking accounts, and certificate of deposit programmes. In 2007, the American Bankers Association barred credit union employees from attending ABA sponsored educational seminars. This includes online classes that require registration. Based upon the pre-text that the ABA only wants to serve its members, the American Bankers Association continues to attempt to weaken credit unions and take back the 6 per cent market share that credit unions currently hold.

Credit unions maintain that no matter their size or field of membership, the fact that they are owned by their members and not shareholders makes them fundamentally different from banks.

Credit Union-to-Bank Conversions: Since 1995, over thirty US credit unions have converted from credit union charters to bank charters. These conversions are generally initiated by a credit union's leadership team, rather than from the rank-and-file membership, and have created sharp controversy within the credit union industry. Some have questioned whether these conversions are in the best interests of the credit union members, and have compared them to the mutual savings bank conversion raids of the 1980s.

Like the mutual savings raids, credit union conversions have been very lucrative for executives and directors of converting credit unions. CU Financial, a consulting firm that helps credit union management execute these conversions, has explained in marketing materials that if a credit union with $50 million in capital converts to a stock bank, under certain conditions a pay-off in the "$1.2 million range for each director is not out of the question," while executives might also expect additional stock compensation that "could lead to a $10 million plus ownership stake for a capable CEO".

Members of at least six credit unions have organised to oppose their management's conversion proposals, objecting that this insider enrichment comes at the detriment of credit union members. They point out that while insiders have made windfall profits, most members have lost their ownership stake without compensation, and face worse rates and fees after the conversion. Comparisons of interest rates show that credit unions that have converted to banks now charge their members more for loans, and pay less for savings. Member groups have included Save Columbia Credit Union, Save First Basin Credit Union, and DFCU Owners United.

The National Centre for Member Trust is a consumer protection non-profit "formed to support the member-owners of credit unions that are attempting to convert to banks." The Coalition for Credit Union Charter Options is an advocacy group for converting credit unions. UC Berkeley Professor of Financial Institutions James Wilcox is an expert who has released a number of studies on the issue. His findings are summarised in Credit Union Conversions: Ripe for Abuse ... and Reforms, published in the Credit Union Times July of 2006.

Savings and Loan Association

Savings and loan association, also known as a thrift, is a financial institution that specialises in accepting savings deposits and making mortgage loans. The term is mainly used in the United States; similar institutions in the United Kingdom, Ireland and some Commonwealth countries include building societies and trustee savings banks.

They are often mutually held (often called *mutual savings banks*), meaning that the depositors and borrowers are members with voting rights, and have the ability to direct the financial and managerial goals of the organisation. It is possible for a savings and loan to be a joint stock company and even publicly traded. This means, however, that it truly no longer is an association and depositors and borrowers no longer have any managerial control.

Early History

At the beginning of the 19th century, banking was still something only done by those who had assets or wealth that needed safekeeping. The first savings bank in the United States, the Philadelphia Savings Fund Society, was established on December 20, 1816, and by the 1830s such institutions had become widespread. Savings and loans accepted deposits and used those deposits, along with other capital that was in their possession, to make loans. What was revolutionary was that the management of the savings and loan was determined by those that held deposits and in some instances had loans. The amount of influence in the management of the organisation was determined based on the amount on deposit with the institution.

The overriding goal of the savings and loan association was to encourage savings and investment by common people and to give them access to a financial intermediary that otherwise had not been open to them in the past. The savings and loan was also there to provide loans for the purchase of large ticket items, usually homes, for worthy and responsible borrowers. The early savings and loans were in the business of "neighbours helping neighbours".

In the United Kingdom, the first savings bank was founded in 1810 by the Reverend Henry Duncan, Doctor of Divinity, the minister of Ruthwell Church in Dumfriesshire, Scotland. It is home to the Savings Bank Museum, in which there are records relating to the history of the savings bank movement in Great Britain, as well as family memorabilia relating to Henry Duncan and other prominent people of the surrounding area. However, the main type of institution similar to US savings and loan associations in the United Kingdom is not the savings bank, but the building society and had existed since the 1770s.

The Savings and Loan in the 20th Century (in the US)

The savings and loan association became a strong force in the early-20th century through assisting people with home ownership, through mortgage lending, and further assisting their members with basic saving and investing outlets, typically through passbook savings accounts and term certificates of deposit.

The savings and loan associations of this era were famously portrayed in the 1946 film *It's a Wonderful Life*.

Mortgage Lending: The earliest of mortgages were not offered by banks, but by insurance companies, and they differed greatly from the mortgage or home loan that is familiar today. Most early mortgages were short term with some kind of balloon payment at the end of the term, or they were interest-only loans which did not pay anything towards the principal of the loan with each payment. As such, many people were either perpetually in debt in a continuous cycle of refinancing their home purchase, or they lost their home through foreclosure when they were unable to make the balloon payment at the end of the term of that loan.

The US Congress passed the Federal Home Loan Bank Act in 1932, during the Great Depression. It established the Federal Home Loan Bank and associated Federal Home Loan Bank Board to assist other banks in providing funding to offer long term, amortised loans for home purchases. The idea was to get banks involved in lending, not insurance companies, and to provide realistic loans which people could repay and gain full ownership of their homes.

Savings and loan associations sprung up all across the United States because there was low-cost funding available through the Federal Home Loan Bank for the purposes of mortgage lending.

Further Advantages: Savings and loans were given a certain amount of preferential treatment by the Federal Reserve inasmuch as they were given the ability to pay higher interest rates on savings deposits compared to a regular commercial bank. The idea was that with marginally higher savings rates, savings and loans would attract more deposits that would allow them to continue to write more mortgage loans, which would keep the mortgage market liquid, and funds would always be available to potential borrowers.

However, savings and loans were not allowed to offer checking accounts until the late-1970s. This reduced the attractiveness of savings and loans to consumers, since it required consumers to hold accounts across multiple institutions in order to have access to both checking privileges and competitive savings rates.

In the 1980s, the situation changed. The United States Congress granted all thrifts in 1980, including savings and loan associations, the power to make consumer and commercial loans and to issue transaction accounts. Designed to help the thrift industry retain its deposit base and to improve its profitability, the Depository Institutions Deregulation and Monetary Control Act (DIDMCA) of 1980 allowed thrifts to make consumer loans up to 20 per cent of their assets, issue credit cards, accept negotiable order of withdrawal (NOW) accounts from individuals and non-profit organisations, and invest up to 20 per cent of their assets in commercial real estate loans.

In 1982, the Garn-St. Germain Depository Institutions Act was passed and increased the proportion of assets that thrifts could hold in consumer and commercial real estate loans and allowed thrifts to invest 5 per cent of their assets in commercial loans until January 1, 1984, when this percentage increased to 10 per cent.

Decline: During the Savings and Loan Crisis, from 1986 to 1995, the number of US federally insured savings and loans in the

United States declined from 3,234 to 1,645. This was primarily, but not exclusively, due to unsound real estate lending. The market share of S&Ls for single family mortgage loans went from 53 per cent in 1975 to 30 per cent in 1990.

The following is a detailed summary of the major causes for losses that hurt the savings and loan business in the 1980s according to the United States League of Savings:

1. Lack of net worth for many institutions as they entered the 1980s, and a wholly inadequate net worth regulation.
2. Decline in the effectiveness of Regulation Q in preserving the spread between the cost of money and the rate of return on assets, basically stemming from inflation and the accompanying increase in market interest rates.
3. Absence of an ability to vary the return on assets with increases in the rate of interest required to be paid for deposits.
4. Increased competition on the deposit gathering and mortgage origination sides of the business, with a sudden burst of new technology making possible a whole new way of conducting financial institutions generally and the mortgage business specifically.
5. A rapid increase in investment powers of associations with passage of the Depository Institutions Deregulation and Monetary Control Act (the Garn-St. Germain Act), and, more important, through state legislative enactments in a number of important and rapidly growing states. These introduced new risks and speculative opportunities which were difficult to administer. In many instances, management lacked the ability or experience to evaluate them, or to administer large volumes of non-residential construction loans.
6. Elimination of regulations initially designed to prevent lending excesses and minimise failures. Regulatory relaxation permitted lending, directly and through participations, in distant loan markets on the promise of high returns. Lenders, however, were not familiar with these distant markets. It also permitted associations to participate extensively in speculative construction activities with builders and developers who had little or no financial stake in the projects.

7. Fraud and insider transaction abuses were the principal cause for some 20 per cent of savings and loan failures the past three years and a greater percentage of the dollar losses borne by the FSLIC.
8. A new type and generation of opportunistic savings and loan executives and owners – some of whom operated in a fraudulent manner – whose takeover of many institutions was facilitated by a change in FSLIC rules reducing the minimum number of stockholders of an insured association from 400 to one.
9. Dereliction of duty on the part of the board of directors of some savings associations. This permitted management to make uncontrolled use of some new operating authority, while directors failed to control expenses and prohibit obvious conflict of interest situations.
10. A virtual end of inflation in the American economy, together with overbuilding in multifamily, condominium type residences and in commercial real estate in many cities. In addition, real estate values collapsed in the energy states – Texas, Louisiana, Oklahoma particularly due to falling oil prices – and weakness occurred in the mining and agricultural sectors of the economy.
11. Pressures felt by the management of many associations to restore net worth ratios. Anxious to improve earnings, they departed from their traditional lending practices into credits and markets involving higher risks, but with which they had little experience.
12. The lack of appropriate, accurate, and effective evaluations of the savings and loan business by public accounting firms, security analysts, and the financial community.
13. Organisational structure and supervisory laws, adequate for policing and controlling the business in the protected environment of the 1960s and 1970s, resulted in fatal delays and indecision in the examination/supervision process in the 1980s.
14. Federal and state examination and supervisory staffs insufficient in number, experience, or ability to deal with the new world of savings and loan operations.

15. The inability or unwillingness of the Bank Board and its legal and supervisory staff to deal with problem institutions in a timely manner. Many institutions, which ultimately closed with big losses, were known problem cases for a year or more. Often, it appeared, political considerations delayed necessary supervisory action.

The Consequences of Governmental Acts and Reforms: As a result, the Financial Institutions Reform, Recovery and Enforcement Act of 1989 (FIRREA) dramatically changed the savings and loan industry and its federal regulation. Here are the highlights of this legislation, signed into law August 9, 1989:

1. The Federal Home Loan Bank Board (FHLBB) and the Federal Savings and Loan Insurance Corporation (FSLIC) were abolished.
2. The Office of Thrift Supervision (OTS), a bureau of the Treasury Department, was created to charter, regulate, examine, and supervise savings institutions.
3. The Federal Housing Finance Board (FHFB) was created as an independent agency to oversee the 12 federal home loan banks (also called *district banks*).
4. The Savings Association Insurance Fund (SAIF) replaced the FSLIC as an ongoing insurance fund for thrift institutions (like the FDIC, the FSLIC was a permanent corporation that insured savings and loan accounts up to $100,000). SAIF is administered by the Federal Deposit Insurance Corp.
5. The Resolution Trust Corporation (RTC) was established to dispose of failed thrift institutions taken over by regulators after January 1, 1989. The RTC will make insured deposits at those institutions available to their customers.
6. FIRREA gives both Freddie Mac and Fannie Mae additional responsibility to support mortgages for low and moderate-income families.

The Characteristics of Savings and Loan Associations

The most important purpose of these institutions is to make mortgage loans on residential property. These organisations, which also are known as *savings associations, building and loan associations, cooperative banks* (in New England), and *homestead associations* (in Louisiana), are the primary source of financial assistance to a large segment of American homeowners. As home-financing institutions, they give primary attention to single-family residences and are equipped to make loans in this area.

Some of the most important characteristics of a savings and loan association are:

1. It is generally a locally owned and privately managed home financing institution.
2. It receives individuals' savings and uses these funds to make long-term amortised loans to home purchasers.
3. It makes loans for the construction, purchase, repair, or refinancing of houses.
4. It is state or federally chartered.

Non-banking Financial Companies

Non-Bank Financial Companies (NBFCs) are financial institutions that provide banking services without meeting the legal definition of a bank, i.e., one that does not hold a banking licence. Operations are, regardless of this, still exercised under bank regulation. However, this depends on the jurisdiction, as in some jurisdictions, such as New Zealand, any company can do the business of banking, and there are no banking licences issued.

Services Provided

Non-bank institutions frequently acts as:

- Suppliers of loans and credit facilities,
- Supporting investments in property,
- Trading money market instruments,
- Funding private education,
- Wealth management such as Managing portfolios of stocks and shares,
- Underwrite stock and shares, TFCs and other obligations,
- Retirement planning,
- Advise companies in merger and acquisition,

- Prepare feasibility, market or industry studies for companies,
- Discounting services, e.g., discounting of instruments.

However, they are typically not allowed to take deposits from the general public and have to find other means of funding their operations such as issuing debt instruments.

Regulation

For European NBFCs the Payment Services Directive (PSD) is a regulatory initiative from the European Commission to regulate payment services and payment service providers throughout the European Union (EU) and European Economic Area (EEA). The PSD describes which type of organisations can provide payment services in Europe (credit institutions, i.e., banks) and certain authorities (e.g. Central Banks, government bodies), Electronic Money Institutions (EMI), and also creates the new category of Payment Institutions). Organisations that are not credit institutions or EMI, can apply for an authorisation as Payment Institution in any EU country of their choice (where they are established) and then passport their payment services into other Member States across the EU.

Classification

Depending upon their nature of activities, non-banking finance companies can be classified into the following categories:

1. Development finance institutions.
2. Leasing companies.
3. Investment companies.
4. Modaraba companies.
5. House finance companies.
6. Venture capital companies.
7. Discount and guarantee houses.

Insurance

Insurance, in law and economics, is a form of risk management primarily used to hedge against the risk of a contingent loss. Insurance is defined as the equitable transfer of the risk of a loss, from one entity to another, in exchange for a premium, and can be thought of a guaranteed small loss to prevent a large, possibly devastating large loss. An insurer is a company selling the insurance. The insurance rate is a factor used to determine the amount, called the *premium*, to be charged for a certain amount of insurance coverage. Risk management, the practice of appraising and controlling risk, has evolved as a discrete field of study and practice.

Principles of Insurance

Commercially insurable risks typically share seven common characteristics:

1. *A Large Number of Homogeneous Exposure Units:* The vast majority of insurance policies are provided for individual members of very large classes. Automobile insurance, for example, covered about 175 million automobiles in the United States in 2004. The existence of a large number of homogeneous exposure units allows insurers to benefit from the so-called "law of large numbers," which in effect states that as the number of exposure units increases, the actual results are increasingly likely to become close to expected results. There are exceptions to this criterion. Lloyd's of London is famous for insuring the life or health of actors, actresses and sports figures. Satellite Launch insurance covers events that are infrequent. Large commercial property policies may insure exceptional properties for which there are no 'homogeneous' exposure units. Despite failing on this criterion, many exposures like these are generally considered to be insurable.
2. *Definite Loss:* The event that gives rise to the loss that is subject to insurance should, at least in principle, take place at a known time, in a known place, and from a known cause. The classic example is death of an insured person on a life insurance policy. Fire, automobile accidents, and worker injuries may all easily meet this criterion. Other types of losses may only be definite in theory. Occupational disease, for instance, may involve prolonged exposure to injurious conditions where no specific time, place or cause is identifiable. Ideally, the time, place and cause of a loss should

be clear enough that a reasonable person, with sufficient information, could objectively verify all three elements.

3. *Accidental Loss:* The event that constitutes the trigger of a claim should be fortuitous, or at least outside the control of the beneficiary of the insurance. The loss should be 'pure,' in the sense that it results from an event for which there is only the opportunity for cost. Events that contain speculative elements, such as ordinary business risks, are generally not considered insurable.
4. *Large Loss:* The size of the loss must be meaningful from the perspective of the insured. Insurance premiums need to cover both the expected cost of losses, plus the cost of issuing and administering the policy, adjusting losses, and supplying the capital needed to reasonably assure that the insurer will be able to pay claims. For small losses these latter costs may be several times the size of the expected cost of losses. There is little point in paying such costs unless the protection offered has real value to a buyer.
5. *Affordable Premium:* If the likelihood of an insured event is so high, or the cost of the event so large, that the resulting premium is large relative to the amount of protection offered, it is not likely that anyone will buy insurance, even if on offer. Further, as the accounting profession formally recognises in financial accounting standards, the premium cannot be so large that there is not a reasonable chance of a significant loss to the insurer. If there is no such chance of loss, the transaction may have the form of insurance, but not the substance.
6. *Calculable Loss:* There are two elements that must be at least estimable, if not formally calculable: the probability of loss, and the attendant cost. Probability of loss is generally an empirical exercise, while cost has more to do with the ability of a reasonable person in possession of a copy of the insurance policy and a proof of loss associated with a claim presented under that policy to make a reasonably definite and objective evaluation of the amount of the loss recoverable as a result of the claim.

7. *Limited Risk of Catastrophically Large Losses:* The essential risk is often aggregation. If the same event can cause losses to numerous policyholders of the same insurer, the ability of that insurer to issue policies becomes constrained, not by factors surrounding the individual characteristics of a given policyholder, but by the factors surrounding the sum of all policyholders so exposed. Typically, insurers prefer to limit their exposure to a loss from a single event to some small portion of their capital base, on the order of 5 per cent. Where the loss can be aggregated, or an individual policy could produce exceptionally large claims, the capital constraint will restrict an insurer's appetite for additional policyholders. The classic example is earthquake insurance, where the ability of an underwriter to issue a new policy depends on the number and size of the policies that it has already underwritten. Wind insurance in hurricane zones, particularly along coast lines, is another example of this phenomenon. In extreme cases, the aggregation can affect the entire industry, since the combined capital of insurers and reinsurers can be small compared to the needs of potential policyholders in areas exposed to aggregation risk. In commercial fire insurance it is possible to find single properties whose total exposed value is well in excess of any individual insurer's capital constraint. Such properties are generally shared among several insurers, or are insured by a single insurer who syndicates the risk into the reinsurance market.

Indemnification

The technical definition of "indemnity" means to make whole again. There are two types of insurance contracts: 1) an "indemnity" policy; and 2) a "pay on behalf" or "on behalf of" policy. The difference is significant on paper, but rarely material in practice.

An "indemnity" policy will never pay claims until the insured has paid out of pocket to some third party; for example, a visitor to your home slips on a floor that you left wet and sues you for $10,000 and wins. Under an "indemnity" policy the homeowner would have to come up with the $10,000 to pay for the visitor's fall and then would be "indemnified" by the insurance carrier for the out of pocket costs (the $10,000).

Under the same situation, a "pay on behalf" policy, the insurance carrier would pay the claim and the insured (the homeowner) would not be out of pocket for anything. Most modern liability insurance is written on the basis of "pay on behalf" language.

An entity seeking to transfer risk (an individual, corporation, or association of any type, etc.) becomes the 'insured' party once risk is assumed by an 'insurer', the insuring party, by means of a contract, called an *insurance policy*. Generally, an insurance contract includes, at a minimum, the following elements: the parties (the insurer, the insured, the beneficiaries), the premium, the period of coverage, the particular loss event covered, the amount of coverage (i.e. the amount to be paid to the insured or beneficiary in the event of a loss), and exclusions (events not covered). An insured is thus said to be "indemnified" against the loss events covered in the policy.

When insured parties experience a loss for a specified peril, the coverage entitles the policyholder to make a 'claim' against the insurer for the covered amount of loss as specified by the policy. The fee paid by the insured to the insurer for assuming the risk is called the *premium*. Insurance premiums from many insureds are used to fund accounts reserved for later payment of claims—in theory for a relatively few claimants—and for overhead costs. So long as an insurer maintains adequate funds set aside for anticipated losses (i.e. reserves), the remaining margin is an insurer's profit.

Insurers' Business Model

Insurers make money in two ways: 1) through underwriting, the process by which insurers select the risks to insure and decide how much in premiums to charge for accepting those risks, and 2) by investing the premiums they collect from insured parties.

The most complicated aspect of the insurance business is the underwriting of policies. Using a wide assortment of data, insurers predict the likelihood that a claim will be made against their policies and price products accordingly. To this end, insurers use actuarial science to quantify the risks they are willing to assume and the premium they will charge to assume them. Data is analysed to fairly accurately project the rate of future claims based on a given risk. Actuarial science uses statistics and probability to analyse the risks associated with the range of perils covered, and these scientific principles are used to determine an insurer's overall exposure. Upon termination of a given policy, the amount of premium collected and the investment gains thereon minus the amount paid out in claims is the insurer's underwriting profit on that policy. Of course, from the insurer's perspective, some policies are winners (i.e. the insurer pays out less in claims and expenses than it receives in premiums and investment income) and some are losers (i.e. the insurer pays out more in claims and expenses than it receives in premiums and investment income).

An insurer's underwriting performance is measured in its combined ratio. The loss ratio (incurred losses and loss-adjustment expenses divided by net earned premium) is added to the expense ratio (underwriting expenses divided by net premium written) to determine the company's combined ratio. The combined ratio is a reflection of the company's overall underwriting profitability. A combined ratio of less than 100 per cent indicates underwriting profitability, while anything over 100 indicates an underwriting loss.

Insurance companies also earn investment profits on "float". "Float" or available reserve is the amount of money, at hand at any given moment, that an insurer has collected in insurance premiums but has not been paid out in claims. Insurers start investing insurance premiums as soon as they are collected and continue to earn interest on them until claims are paid out.

In the United States, the underwriting loss of property and casualty insurance companies was $142.3 billion in the five years ending 2003. But overall profit for the same period was $68.4 billion, as the result of float. Some insurance industry insiders, most notably Hank Greenberg, do not believe that it is forever possible to sustain a profit from float without an underwriting profit as well, but this opinion is not universally held. Naturally, the "float" method is difficult to carry out in an economically depressed period. Bear markets do cause insurers to shift away from investments and to toughen up their underwriting standards. So a poor economy generally means high insurance premiums. This tendency to swing between profitable and unprofitable periods over time is commonly known as the *underwriting* or *insurance cycle*.

Property and casualty insurers currently make the most money from their auto insurance line of business. Generally better statistics are available on auto losses and underwriting on this line of business has benefited greatly from advances in computing. Additionally, property losses in the US, due to natural catastrophes, have exacerbated this trend.

Finally, claims and loss handling is the materialised utility of insurance. In managing the claims-handling function, insurers seek to balance the elements of customer satisfaction, administrative handling expenses, and claims overpayment leakages. As part of this balancing act, fraudulent insurance practices are a major business risk that must be managed and overcome.

History of Insurance

In some sense we can say that insurance appears simultaneously with the appearance of human society. We know of two types of economies in human societies: money economies (with markets, money, financial instruments and so on) and non-money or natural economies (without money, markets, financial instruments and so on). The second type is a more ancient form than the first. In such an economy and community, we can see insurance in the form of people helping each other. For example, if a house burns down, the members of the community help build a new one. Should the same thing happen to one's neighbour, the other neighbours must help. Otherwise, neighbours will not receive help in the future. This type of insurance has survived to the present day in some countries where modern money economy with its financial instruments is not widespread (for example countries in the territory of the former Soviet Union).

Turning to insurance in the modern sense (i.e. insurance in a modern money economy, in which insurance is part of the financial sphere), early methods of transferring or distributing risk were practised by Chinese and Babylonian traders as long ago as the 3rd and 2nd millennia BC, respectively. Chinese merchants travelling treacherous river rapids would redistribute their wares across many vessels to limit the loss due to any single vessel's capsising. The Babylonians developed a system which was recorded in the famous Code of Hammurabi, c. 1750 BC, and practised by early Mediterranean sailing merchants. If a merchant received a loan to fund his shipment, he would pay the lender an additional sum in exchange for the lender's guarantee to cancel the loan should the shipment be stolen.

Achaemenian monarchs of Iran were the first to insure their people and made it official by registering the insuring process in governmental notary offices. The insurance tradition was performed each year in Norouz (beginning of the Iranian New Year); the heads of different ethnic groups as well as others willing to take part, presented gifts to the monarch. The most important gift was presented during a special ceremony. When a gift was worth more than 10,000 Derrik (Achaemenian gold coin) the issue was registered in a special office. This was advantageous to those who presented such special gifts. For others, the presents were fairly assessed by the confidants of the court. Then the assessment was registered in special offices.

The purpose of registering was that whenever the person who presented the gift registered by the court was in trouble, the monarch and the court would help him. Jahez, a historian and writer, writes in one of his books on ancient Iran: "Whenever the owner of the present is in trouble or wants to construct a building, set up a feast, have his children married, etc. the one in charge of this in the court would check the registration. If the registered amount exceeded 10,000 Derrik, he or she would receive an amount of twice as much."

A thousand years later, the inhabitants of Rhodes invented the concept of the 'general average'. Merchants whose goods were being shipped together would pay a proportionally divided premium which would be used to reimburse any merchant whose goods were jettisoned during storm or sinkage.

The Greeks and Romans introduced the origins of health and life insurance c. 600 AD when they organised guilds called *benevolent societies* which cared for the families and paid funeral expenses of members upon death. Guilds in the Middle Ages served a similar purpose. The Talmud deals with several aspects of insuring goods. Before insurance was established in the late-17th century, "friendly societies" existed in England, in which people donated amounts of money to a general sum that could be used for emergencies.

Separate insurance contracts (i.e. insurance policies not bundled with loans or other kinds of contracts) were invented in Genoa in the 14th century, as were insurance pools backed by pledges of landed estates. These new insurance contracts allowed insurance to be separated from investment, a separation of roles that first proved useful in marine insurance. Insurance became far more sophisticated in post-Renaissance Europe, and specialised varieties developed.

Towards the end of the seventeenth century, London's growing importance as a centre for trade increased demand for marine insurance. In the late-1680s, Edward Lloyd opened a coffee house that became a popular haunt of ship owners, merchants, and ships' captains, and thereby a reliable source of the latest shipping news. It became the meeting place for parties wishing to insure cargoes and ships, and those willing to underwrite such ventures. Today, Lloyd's of London remains the leading market (note that it is not an insurance company) for marine and other specialist types of insurance, but it works rather differently than the more familiar kinds of insurance.

Insurance as we know it today can be traced to the Great Fire of London, which in 1666 devoured 13,200 houses. In the aftermath of this disaster, Nicholas Barbon opened an office to insure buildings. In 1680, he established England's first fire insurance company, "The Fire Office," to insure brick and frame homes.

The first insurance company in the United States underwrote fire insurance and was formed in Charles Town (modern-day Charleston), South Carolina, in 1732. Benjamin Franklin helped to popularise and make standard the practice of insurance, particularly against fire in the form of perpetual insurance. In 1752, he founded the Philadelphia Contributionship for the Insurance of Houses from Loss by Fire. Franklin's company was the first to make contributions towards fire prevention. Not only did his company warn against certain fire hazards, it refused to insure certain buildings where the risk of fire was too great, such as all wooden houses. In the United States, regulation of the insurance industry is highly Balkanised, with primary responsibility assumed by individual state insurance departments. Whereas insurance markets have become centralised nationally and internationally, state insurance commissioners operate individually, though at times in concert through a national insurance commissioners' organisation. In recent years, some have called for a dual state and federal regulatory system [commonly referred to as the Optional Federal Charter (OFC)] for insurance similar to that which oversees state banks and national banks.

Types of Insurance

Any risk that can be quantified can potentially be insured. Specific kinds of risk that may give rise to claims are known as *perils*. An insurance policy will set out in detail which perils are covered by the policy and which are not. For example, auto insurance would typically cover both property risk (covering the risk of theft or damage to the car) and liability risk (covering legal claims from causing an accident). A homeowner's insurance policy in the US typically includes property insurance covering damage to the home and the owner's belongings, liability insurance covering certain legal claims against the owner, and even a small amount of coverage for medical expenses of guests who are injured on the owner's property.

Business insurance can be any kind of insurance that protects businesses against risks. Some principal subtypes of business insurance are: a) the various kinds of professional liability insurance, also called *professional indemnity insurance*, which are discussed below under that name; and b) the business owner's policy (BOP), which bundles into one policy many of the kinds of coverage that a business owner needs, in a way analogous to how homeowners insurance bundles the coverages that a homeowner needs.

Health: Health insurance policies by the National Health Service in the United Kingdom (NHS) or other publicly-funded health programmes will cover the cost of medical treatments. Dental insurance, like medical insurance, is coverage for individuals to protect them against dental costs. In the US, dental insurance is often part of an employer's benefits package, along with health insurance. Most countries rely on public funding to ensure that all citizens have universal access to health care.

Disability:

- Disability insurance policies provide financial support in the event the policyholder is unable to work because of disabling illness or injury. It provides monthly support to help pay such obligations as mortgages and credit cards.
- Total permanent disability insurance provides benefits when a person is permanently disabled and can no longer work in their profession, often taken as an adjunct to life insurance.
- Disability overhead insurance allows business owners to cover the overhead expenses of their business while they are unable to work.
- Workers' compensation insurance replaces all or part of a worker's wages lost and accompanying medical expenses incurred because of a job-related injury.

Casualty: Casualty insurance insures against accidents, not necessarily tied to any specific property.

- Crime insurance is a form of casualty insurance that covers the policyholder against losses arising from the criminal acts of third parties. For example, a company can obtain crime insurance to cover losses arising from theft or embezzlement.
- Political risk insurance is a form of casualty insurance that can be taken out by businesses with operations in countries in which there is a risk that revolution or other political conditions will result in a loss.

Life: Life insurance provides a monetary benefit to a descedent's family or other designated beneficiary, and may specifically provide for income to an insured person's family, burial, funeral and other final expenses. Life insurance policies often allow the option of having the proceeds paid to the beneficiary either in a lump sum cash payment or an annuity.

Annuities provide a stream of payments and are generally classified as insurance because they are issued by insurance companies and regulated as insurance and require the same kinds of actuarial and investment management expertise that life insurance requires. Annuities and pensions that pay a benefit for life are sometimes regarded as insurance against the possibility that a retiree will outlive his or her financial resources. In that sense, they are the complement of life insurance and, from an underwriting perspective, are the mirror image of life insurance.

Certain life insurance contracts accumulate cash values, which may be taken by the insured if the policy is surrendered or which may be borrowed against. Some policies, such as annuities and endowment policies, are financial instruments to accumulate or liquidate wealth when it is needed.

In many countries, such as the US and the UK, the tax law provides that the interest on this cash value is not taxable under certain circumstances. This leads to widespread use of life insurance as a tax-efficient method of saving as well as protection in the event of early death.

In US, the tax on interest income on life insurance policies and annuities is generally deferred. However, in some cases the benefit derived from tax deferral may be offset by a low return. This depends upon the insuring company, the type of policy and other variables (mortality, market return, etc.). Moreover, other income tax saving vehicles [e.g. IRAs, 401(k) plans, Roth IRAs] may be better alternatives for value accumulation. A combination of low-cost term life insurance and a higher-return tax-efficient retirement account may achieve better investment return.

Property: Property insurance provides protection against risks to property, such as fire, theft or weather damage. This includes specialised forms of insurance such as fire insurance, flood insurance, earthquake insurance, home insurance, inland marine insurance or boiler insurance.

- Automobile insurance, known in the UK as *motor insurance,* is probably the most common form of insurance and may cover both legal liability claims against the driver and loss of or damage to the insured's vehicle itself. Throughout the United States an auto insurance policy is required to legally operate a motor vehicle on public roads. In some jurisdictions, bodily injury compensation for automobile accident victims has been changed to a no-fault system, which reduces or eliminates the ability to sue for compensation but provides automatic eligibility for benefits. Credit card companies insure against damage on rented cars.

  - Driving School Insurance provides cover for any authorised driver whilst undergoing tuition, cover also unlike other motor policies provides cover for instructor liability where both the pupil and driving instructor are equally liable in the event of a claim.

- Aviation insurance insures against hull, spares, deductibles, hull wear and liability risks.
- Boiler insurance (also known as *boiler* and *machinery insurance* or *equipment breakdown insurance*) insures against accidental physical damage to equipment or machinery.
- Builder's risk insurance insures against the risk of physical loss or damage to property during construction. Builder's risk insurance is typically written on an "all risk" basis covering damage due to any cause (including the negligence of the insured) not otherwise expressly excluded.
- Crop insurance "Farmers use crop insurance to reduce or manage various risks associated with growing crops. Such risks include crop loss or damage caused by weather, hail, drought, frost damage, insects, or disease, for instance."
- Earthquake insurance is a form of property insurance that pays the policyholder in the event of an earthquake that causes damage to the property. Most ordinary homeowners insurance policies do not cover earthquake damage. Most earthquake insurance policies feature a high deductible. Rates depend on location and the probability of an earthquake, as well as the construction of the home.
- A fidelity bond is a form of casualty insurance that covers policyholders for losses that they incur as a result of fraudulent acts by specified individuals. It usually insures a business for losses caused by the dishonest acts of its employees.
- Flood insurance protects against property loss due to flooding. Many insurers in the US do not provide flood insurance in

some portions of the country. In response to this, the federal government created the National Flood Insurance Programme which serves as the insurer of last resort.

- Home insurance or homeowners' insurance.
- Marine insurance and marine cargo insurance cover the loss or damage of ships at sea or on inland waterways, and of the cargo that may be on them. When the owner of the cargo and the carrier are separate corporations, marine cargo insurance typically compensates the owner of cargo for losses sustained from fire, shipwreck, etc., but excludes losses that can be recovered from the carrier or the carrier's insurance. Many marine insurance underwriters will include "time element" coverage in such policies, which extends the indemnity to cover loss of profit and other business expenses attributable to the delay caused by a covered loss.
- Surety bond insurance is a three party insurance guaranteeing the performance of the principal.
- Terrorism insurance provides protection against any loss or damage caused by terrorist activities.
- Volcano insurance is an insurance that covers volcano damage in Hawaii.
- Windstorm insurance is an insurance covering the damage that can be caused by hurricanes and tropical cyclones.

Liability: Liability insurance is a very broad superset that covers legal claims against the insured. Many types of insurance include an aspect of liability coverage. For example, a homeowner's insurance policy will normally include liability coverage which protects the insured in the event of a claim brought by someone who slips and falls on the property; automobile insurance also includes an aspect of liability insurance that indemnifies against the harm that a crashing car can cause to others' lives, health, or property. The protection offered by a liability insurance policy is twofold: a legal defence in the event of a lawsuit commenced against the policyholder and indemnification (payment on behalf of the insured) with respect to a settlement or court verdict. Liability policies typically cover only the negligence of the insured, and will not apply to results of wilful or intentional acts by the insured.

- Environmental liability insurance protects the insured from bodily injury, property damage and cleanup costs as a result of the dispersal, release or escape of pollutants.
- Errors and omissions insurance.
- Professional liability insurance, also called *professional indemnity insurance,* protects insured professionals such as architectural corporation and medical practice against potential negligence claims made by their patients/clients. Professional liability insurance may take on different names depending on the profession. For example, professional liability insurance in reference to the medical profession may be called *malpractice insurance.* Notaries public may take out errors and omissions insurance *(E&O).* Other potential E&O policyholders include, for example, real estate brokers, home inspectors, appraisers, and website developers.
- Directors and officers liability insurance protects an organisation (usually a corporation) from costs associated with litigation resulting from mistakes made by directors and officers for which they are liable. In the industry, it is usually called "D&O" for short.
- Prize indemnity insurance protects the insured from giving away a large prize at a specific event. Examples would include offering prizes to contestants who can make a half-court shot at a basketball game, or a hole-in-one at a golf tournament.

Credit: Credit insurance repays some or all of a loan when certain things happen to the borrower such as unemployment, disability, or death.

- Mortgage insurance insures the lender against default by the borrower. Mortgage insurance is a form of credit insurance, although the name credit insurance more often is used to refer to policies that cover other kinds of debt.

Other Types:

- Collateral protection insurance or CPI, insures property (primarily vehicles) held as collateral for loans made by lending institutions.
- Defence Base Act Workers' compensation or DBA Insurance provides coverage for civilian workers hired by the

government to perform contracts outside the US and Canada. DBA is required for all US citizens, US residents, US Green Card holders, and all employees or subcontractors hired on overseas government contracts. Depending on the country, Foreign Nationals must also be covered under DBA. This coverage typically includes expenses related to medical treatment and loss of wages, as well as disability and death benefits.

- Expatriate insurance provides individuals and organisations operating outside of their home country with protection for automobiles, property, health, liability and business pursuits.
- Financial loss insurance protects individuals and companies against various financial risks. For example, a business might purchase coverage to protect it from loss of sales if a fire in a factory prevented it from carrying out its business for a time. Insurance might also cover the failure of a creditor to pay money it owes to the insured. This type of insurance is frequently referred to as "business interruption insurance." Fidelity bonds and surety bonds are included in this category, although these products provide a benefit to a third party (the "obligee") in the event the insured party (usually referred to as the "obligor") fails to perform its obligations under a contract with the obligee.
- Kidnap and ransom insurance.
- Locked funds insurance is a little-known hybrid insurance policy jointly issued by governments and banks. It is used to protect public funds from tamper by unauthorised parties. In special cases, a government may authorise its use in protecting semi-private funds which are liable to tamper. The terms of this type of insurance are usually very strict. Therefore, it is used only in extreme cases where maximum security of funds is required.
- Nuclear incident insurance covers damages resulting from an incident involving radioactive materials and is generally arranged at the national level.
- Pet insurance insures pets against accidents and illnesses — some companies cover routine/wellness care and burial, as well.

- Pollution Insurance, which consists of first-party coverage for contamination of insured property either by external or on-site sources. Coverage for liability to third parties arising from contamination of air, water, or land due to the sudden and accidental release of hazardous materials from the insured site. The policy usually covers the costs of cleanup and may include coverage for releases from underground storage tanks. Intentional acts are specifically excluded.
- Purchase insurance is aimed at providing protection on the products people purchase. Purchase insurance can cover individual purchase protection, warranties, guarantees, care plans and even mobile phone insurance. Such insurance is normally very limited in the scope of problems that are covered by the policy.
- Title insurance provides a guarantee that title to real property is vested in the purchaser and/or mortgagee, free and clear of liens or encumbrances. It is usually issued in conjunction with a search of the public records performed at the time of a real estate transaction.
- Travel insurance is an insurance cover taken by those who travel abroad, which covers certain losses such as medical expenses, loss of personal belongings, travel delay, personal liabilities, etc.

Insurance Financing Vehicles:

- Protected Self-insurance is an alternative risk financing mechanism in which an organisation retains the mathematically calculated cost of risk within the organisation and transfers the catastrophic risk with specific and aggregate limits to an insurer so the maximum total cost of the programme is known. A properly designed and underwritten Protected Self-insurance Programme reduces and stabilises the cost of insurance and provides valuable risk management information.
- Retrospectively Rated Insurance is a method of establishing a premium on large commercial accounts. The final premium is based on the insured's actual loss experience during the policy term, sometimes subject to a minimum and maximum

premium, with the final premium determined by a formula. Under this plan, the current year's premium is based partially (or wholly) on the current year's losses, although the premium adjustments may take months or years beyond the current year's expiration date. The rating formula is guaranteed in the insurance contract. Formula: retrospective premium = converted loss + basic premium × tax multiplier. Numerous variations of this formula have been developed and are in use.

- Fraternal insurance is provided on a cooperative basis by fraternal benefit societies or other social organisations.
- Formal self insurance is the deliberate decision to pay for otherwise insurable losses out of one's own money. This can be done on a formal basis by establishing a separate fund into which funds are deposited on a periodic basis, or by simply forgoing the purchase of available insurance and paying out-of-pocket. Self insurance is usually used to pay for high-frequency, low-severity losses. Such losses, if covered by conventional insurance, mean having to pay a premium that includes loadings for the company's general expenses, cost of putting the policy on the books, acquisition expenses, premium taxes, and contingencies. While this is true for all insurance, for small, frequent losses the transaction costs may exceed the benefit of volatility reduction that insurance otherwise affords.
- No-fault insurance is a type of insurance policy (typically automobile insurance) where insureds are indemnified by their own insurer regardless of fault in the incident.
- Reinsurance is a type of insurance purchased by insurance companies or self-insured employers to protect against unexpected losses. Financial reinsurance is a form of reinsurance that is primarily used for capital management rather than to transfer insurance risk.
- Stop-loss insurance provides protection against catastrophic or unpredictable losses. It is purchased by organisations who do not want to assume 100 per cent of the liability for losses arising from the plans. Under a stop-loss policy, the insurance

company becomes liable for losses that exceed certain limits called *deductibles*.

- Social insurance can be many things to many people in many countries. But a summary of its essence is that it is a collection of insurance coverages (including components of life insurance, disability income insurance, unemployment insurance, health insurance, and others), plus retirement savings, that requires participation by all citizens. By forcing everyone in society to be a policyholder and pay premiums, it ensures that everyone can become a claimant when or if he/she needs to. Along the way this inevitably becomes related to other concepts such as the justice system and the welfare state.

Closed Community Self-insurance: Some communities prefer to create virtual insurance amongst themselves by other means than contractual risk transfer, which assigns explicit numerical values to risk. A number of religious groups, including the Amish and some Muslim groups, depend on support provided by their communities when disasters strike.

The risk presented by any given person is assumed collectively by the community who all bear the cost of rebuilding lost property and supporting people whose needs are suddenly greater after a loss of some kind. In supportive communities where others can be trusted to follow community leaders, this tacit form of insurance can work. In this manner the community can even out the extreme differences in insurability that exist among its members. Some further justification is also provided by invoking the moral hazard of explicit insurance contracts.

In the United Kingdom, The Crown (which, for practical purposes, meant the Civil service) did not insure property such as government buildings. If a government building was damaged, the cost of repair would be met from public funds because, in the long run, this was cheaper than paying insurance premiums. Since many UK government buildings have been sold to property companies, and rented back, this arrangement is now less common and may have disappeared altogether.

Insurance Companies

Insurance companies may be classified into two groups:

- Life insurance companies, which sell life insurance, annuities and pensions products.
- Non-life, General, or Property/Casualty insurance companies, which sell other types of insurance.

General insurance companies can be further divided into these subcategories.

- Standard Lines.
- Excess Lines.

In most countries, life and non-life insurers are subject to different regulatory regimes and different tax and accounting rules. The main reason for the distinction between the two types of company is that life, annuity, and pension business is very long-term in nature – coverage for life assurance or a pension can cover risks over many decades. By contrast, non-life insurance cover usually covers a shorter period, such as one year.

In the United States, standard line insurance companies are "main stream" insurers. These are the companies that typically insure autos, homes or businesses. They use pattern or "cookie-cutter" policies without variation from one person to the next. They usually have lower premiums than excess lines and can sell directly to individuals. They are regulated by state laws that can restrict the amount they can charge for insurance policies.

Excess line insurance companies (aka Excess and Surplus) typically insure risks not covered by the standard lines market. They are broadly referred as being all insurance placed with non-admitted insurers. Non-admitted insurers are not licensed in the states where the risks are located. These companies have more flexibility and can react faster than standard insurance companies because they are not required to file rates and forms as the "admitted" carriers do. However, they still have substantial regulatory requirements placed upon them. State laws generally require insurance placed with surplus line agents and brokers not to be available through standard licensed insurers.

Insurance companies are generally classified as either mutual or stock companies. This is more of a traditional distinction as true mutual companies are becoming rare. Mutual companies are owned by the policyholders, while stockholders (who may or may not own policies) own stock insurance companies. Other possible forms for an insurance company include reciprocals, in which policyholders 'reciprocate' in sharing risks, and Lloyds organisations.

Insurance companies are rated by various agencies such as A. M. Best. The ratings include the company's financial strength, which measures its ability to pay claims. It also rates financial instruments issued by the insurance company, such as bonds, notes, and securitisation products.

Reinsurance companies are insurance companies that sell policies to other insurance companies, allowing them to reduce their risks and protect themselves from very large losses. The reinsurance market is dominated by a few very large companies, with huge reserves. A reinsurer may also be a direct writer of insurance risks as well.

Captive insurance companies may be defined as limited-purpose insurance companies established with the specific objective of financing risks emanating from their parent group or groups. This definition can sometimes be extended to include some of the risks of the parent company's customers. In short, it is an in-house self-insurance vehicle. Captives may take the form of a "pure" entity (which is a 100 per cent subsidiary of the self-insured parent company); of a "mutual" captive (which insures the collective risks of members of an industry); and of an "association" captive (which self-insures individual risks of the members of a professional, commercial or industrial association). Captives represent commercial, economic and tax advantages to their sponsors because of the reductions in costs they help to create and for the ease of insurance risk management and the flexibility for cash flows they generate. Additionally, they may provide coverage of risks which is neither available nor offered in the traditional insurance market at reasonable prices.

The types of risk that a captive can underwrite for their parents include property damage, public and product liability, professional indemnity, employee benefits, employers' liability, motor and medical aid expenses. The captive's exposure to such risks may be limited by the use of reinsurance.

Captives are becoming an increasingly important component of the risk management and risk financing strategy of their parent. This can be understood against the following background:

- Heavy and increasing premium costs in almost every line of coverage.
- Difficulties in insuring certain types of fortuitous risk.
- Differential coverage standards in various parts of the world.
- Rating structures which reflect market trends rather than individual loss experience.
- Insufficient credit for deductibles and/or loss control efforts.

There are also companies known as *insurance consultants*. Like a mortgage broker, these companies are paid a fee by the customer to shop around for the best insurance policy amongst many companies. Similar to an insurance consultant, an 'insurance broker' also shops around for the best insurance policy amongst many companies. However, with insurance brokers, the fee is usually paid in the form of commission from the insurer that is selected rather than directly from the client.

Neither insurance consultants nor insurance brokers are insurance companies and no risks are transferred to them in insurance transactions. Third party administrators are companies that perform underwriting and sometimes claims handling services for insurance companies. These companies often have special expertise that the insurance companies do not have.

The financial stability and strength of an insurance company should be a major consideration when buying an insurance contract. An insurance premium paid currently provides coverage for losses that might arise many years in the future. For that reason, the viability of the insurance carrier is very important. In recent years, a number of insurance companies have become insolvent, leaving their policyholders with no coverage (or coverage only from a government-backed insurance pool or other arrangement with less attractive payouts for losses). A number of independent rating agencies, such as Best's, Fitch, Standard and Poor's, and Moody's Investors Service, provide information and rate the financial viability of insurance companies.

Global Insurance Industry

Global insurance premiums grew by 8.0 per cent in 2006 (or 5 per cent in real terms) to reach $3.7 trillion due to improved profitability and a benign economic environment characterised by solid economic growth, moderate inflation and strong equity markets. Profitability improved in both life and non-life insurance in 2006 compared to the previous year. Life insurance premiums grew by 10.2 per cent in 2006 as demand for annuity and pension products rose. Non-life insurance premiums grew by 5 per cent due to growth in premium rates. Over the past decade, global insurance premiums rose by more than a half as annual growth fluctuated between 2 per cent and 11 per cent.

Advanced economies account for the bulk of global insurance. With premium income of $1,485 bn, Europe was the most important region, followed by North America ($1,258 bn) and Asia ($801 bn). The top four countries accounted for nearly two-thirds of premiums in 2006. The US and Japan alone accounted for 43 per cent of world insurance, much higher than their 7 per cent share of the global population. Emerging markets accounted for over 85 per cent of the world's population but generated only around 10 per cent of premiums. The volume of UK insurance business totalled $418 bn in 2006 or 11.2 per cent of global premiums.

Controversies

Insurance Insulates Too Much: By creating a "security blanket" for its insureds, an insurance company may inadvertently find that its insureds may not be as risk-averse as they might otherwise be (since, by definition, the insured has transferred the risk to the insurer). This problem is known to the insurance industry as moral hazard. To reduce their own financial exposure, insurance companies have contractual clauses that mitigate their obligation to provide coverage if the insured engages in behaviour that grossly magnifies their risk of loss or liability.

For example, life insurance companies may require higher premiums or deny coverage altogether to people who work in hazardous occupations or engage in dangerous sports. Liability insurance providers do not provide coverage for liability arising from intentional torts committed by the insured. Even if a provider were so irrational as to want to provide such coverage, it is against the public policy of most countries to allow such insurance to exist, and thus it is usually illegal.

Complexity of Insurance Policy Contracts: Insurance policies can be complex and some policyholders may not understand all the fees and coverages included in a policy. As a result, people may buy policies on unfavourable terms. In response to these issues, many countries have enacted detailed statutory and regulatory regimes governing every aspect of the insurance business, including minimum standards for policies and the ways in which they may be advertised and sold.

Many institutional insurance purchasers buy insurance through an insurance broker. Brokers represent the buyer (not the insurance company), and typically counsel the buyer on appropriate coverage and policy limitations. A broker generally holds contracts with many insurers, thereby allowing the broker to "shop" the market for the best rates and coverage possible.

Insurance may also be purchased through an agent. Unlike a broker, who represents the policyholder, an agent represents the insurance company from whom the policyholder buys. An agent can represent more than one company.

Redlining: Redlining is the practice of denying insurance coverage in specific geographic areas, supposedly because of a high likelihood of loss, while the alleged motivation is unlawful discrimination. Racial profiling or redlining has a long history in the property insurance industry in the United States. From a review of industry underwriting and marketing materials, court documents, and research by government agencies, industry and community groups, and academics, it is clear that race has long affected and continues to affect the policies and practices of the insurance industry.

In determining premiums and premium rate structures, insurers consider quantifiable factors, including location, credit scores, gender, occupation, marital status, and education level.

However, the use of such factors is often considered to be unfair or unlawfully discriminatory, and the reaction against this practice has in some instances led to political disputes about the ways in which insurers determine premiums and regulatory intervention to limit the factors used.

An insurance underwriter's job is to evaluate a given risk as to the likelihood that a loss will occur. Any factor that causes a greater likelihood of loss should theoretically be charged a higher rate. This basic principle of insurance must be followed if insurance companies are to remain solvent. Thus, "discrimination" against (i.e. negative differential treatment of) potential insureds in the risk evaluation and premium-setting process is a necessary by-product of the fundamentals of insurance underwriting. For instance, insurers charge older people significantly higher premiums than they charge younger people for term life insurance. Older people are thus treated differently than younger people (i.e. a distinction is made, discrimination occurs). The rationale for the differential treatment goes to the heart of the risk a life insurer takes: Old people are likely to die sooner than young people, so the risk of loss (the insured's death) is greater in any given period of time and therefore the risk premium must be higher to cover the greater risk. However, treating insureds differently when there is no actuarially sound reason for doing so is unlawful discrimination.

What is often missing from the debate is that prohibiting the use of legitimate, actuarially sound factors means that an insufficient amount is being charged for a given risk, and there is thus a deficit in the system. The failure to address the deficit may mean insolvency and hardship for all of a company's insureds.

Insurance Patents: New insurance products can now be protected from copying with a business method patent in the United States.

A recent example of a new insurance product that is patented is Usage Based auto insurance. Early versions were independently invented and patented by a major US auto insurance company, Progressive Auto Insurance and a Spanish independent inventor, Salvador Minguijon Perez.

Many independent inventors are in favour of patenting new insurance products since it gives them protection from big companies when they bring their new insurance products to market. Independent inventors account for 70 per cent of the new US patent applications in this area.

Many insurance executives are opposed to patenting insurance products because it creates a new risk for them. The Hartford insurance company, for example, recently had to pay $80 million to an independent inventor, Bancorp Services, in order to settle a patent infringement and theft of trade secret lawsuit for a type of corporate owned life insurance product invented and patented by Bancorp.

Inventors can now have their insurance US patent applications reviewed by the public in the Peer to Patent programme.

The Insurance Industry and Rent Seeking: Certain insurance products and practices have been described as rent seeking by critics. That is, some insurance products or practices are useful primarily because of legal benefits, such as reducing taxes, as opposed to providing protection against risks of adverse events. Under United States tax law, for example, most owners of variable annuities and variable life insurance can invest their premium payments in the stock market and defer or eliminate paying any taxes on their investments until withdrawals are made. Sometimes this tax deferral is the only reason people use these products. Another example is the legal infrastructure which allows life insurance to be held in an irrevocable trust which is used to pay an estate tax while the proceeds themselves are immune from the estate tax.

Criticism of Insurance Companies: Some people believe that modern insurance companies are money-making businesses which have little interest in insurance. They argue that the purpose of insurance is to spread risk so the reluctance of insurance companies to take on high-risk cases (e.g. houses in areas subject to flooding, or young drivers) runs counter to the principle of insurance.

Other criticisms include:

- Insurance policies contain too many exclusion clauses. For example, some house insurance policies do not cover damage to garden walls.

- Many insurance companies now use call centres and staff attempt to answer questions by reading from a script. It is difficult to speak to anybody with expert knowledge. While policyholders find their premium payments decrease when dealing with companies who sacrifice the use of trained insurance agents, they also risk greater financial loss due to inadequate coverage protection. Those companies who invest in educated insurance agents provide a valued service to the community. Policyholders who work with knowledgeable insurance agents are more likely to identify needs, evaluate options, purchase sufficient insurance protection, and minimise the risk of heavy financial loss for themselves and their family.

Organisation for Economic Cooperation and Development

The Organisation for Economic Cooperation and Development (OECD) (in French: *Organisation de cooperation et de developpement economiques, OCDE*) is an international organisation of thirty countries that accept the principles of representative democracy and free-market economy. It originated in 1948 as the Organisation for European Economic Cooperation (OEEC), led by Robert Marjolin of France, to help administer the Marshall Plan for the reconstruction of Europe after World War II. Later, its membership was extended to non-European states. In 1961, it was reformed into the Organisation for Economic Cooperation and Development by the Convention on the Organisation for Economic Cooperation and Development.

The OECD's headquarters are at the Chateau de la Muette in Paris.

Objectives and Action: The OECD provides a setting in which governments can compare policy experiences, seek answers to common problems, identify good practices, and coordinate domestic and international policies. The mandate of the OECD is broad, covering economic, environmental, and social issues. It is a forum where peer pressure can act as a powerful incentive to improve policy and implement "soft law" – non-binding instruments that can occasionally lead to binding treaties.

Exchanges between OECD governments flow from information and analysis provided by a secretariat in Paris. The secretariat collects data, monitors trends, and analyses and forecasts economic developments. It also researches social changes or evolving patterns in trade, environment, agriculture, technology, taxation and other areas. The OECD is also known as a *premium statistical agency*, as it publishes highly-comparable statistics on a very wide number of subjects.

Over the past several decades, the OECD has tackled a range of economic, social, and environmental issues while further deepening its engagement with business, trade unions and other representatives of civil society. Collaboration at the OECD regarding taxation, for example, have fostered the growth of a global web of bilateral tax treaties.

OECD Meetings: Every year, more than 40,000 delegates visit the OECD to attend committees' and other meetings, principally organised by the OECD Secretariat. Former Deputy-Secretary General Pierre Vinde estimated in 1997 that the cost born by the member countries, such as sending their officials to OECD meetings and maintaining permanent delegations, is equivalent to the cost of running the secretariat. This ratio is unique among inter-governmental organisations. In other words, the OECD is more a persistent forum or network of officials and experts than an administration.

Noteworthy meetings include:

- The yearly Ministerial Council Meeting, with the Ministers of Economy of all member countries and the candidates for enhanced engagement countries.
- The yearly OECD Forum, which brings together leaders from business, government, labour, civil society and international organisations. This takes the form of conferences and discussions and is open to the public.
- Thematic Ministerial Meetings, held between Ministers of a given domain (i.e. all Ministers of Labour, all Ministers of Environment, etc.).
- The biannual World Forum on Statistics, Knowledge and Policies, which doesn't usually take place in the OECD. This

series of meetings has the ambition to measure and foster progress in societies.

Statistics: All OECD activities are backed-up by statistics, and given the variety of OECD activities, it is a very good source of comparable statistics.

OECD statistics are available in several forms:

- As interactive databases on Source OECD.
- As static files or dynamic database views on the OECD Statistics portal.
- And as Stat Links (in most OECD books, there is a URL which links to the underlying data).

Reference Works: The OECD is responsible for the OECD Guidelines for the Testing of Chemicals, a continually-updated document which is a *de facto* standard (i.e. soft law).

In addition, the OECD publishes and continually updates a model tax convention which serves as a template for bilateral negotiations regarding tax coordination and cooperation. This model is accompanied by a set of commentaries which reflect OECD-level interpretation of the content of the model convention provisions. This model generally allocates the primary right to tax to the country from which capital investment originates (i.e. the home, or resident country) rather than the country in which the investment is made (the host, or source country).

As a result, it is most effective as between two countries with reciprocal investment flows (such as among the OECD member countries), but can be very unbalanced when one of the signatory countries is economically weaker than the other (such as between OECD and non-OECD pairings).

Structure

Financing: The OECD's annual budget, currently around US $510 million (EUR 342.9 million), is funded by the member countries based on a formula related to the size of each member's gross national product. The largest contributor is the United States, which contributes about one quarter of the budget, followed by Japan with 16 per cent, Germany with 9 per cent and the UK and

France with 7 per cent. The OECD governing council sets the budget and scope of work on a two-yearly basis.

Bodies: The OECD's structure revolves around 3 major bodies:

- The OECD member countries, each represented by a delegation led by an ambassador. Together, they form the council.
- The OECD Secretariat, led by the Secretary-General. The Secretariat is organised in directorates. There are some 2,500 agents in the OECD Secretariat.
- The OECD committees, one for each work area of the OECD. Committee members are typically subject-matter experts from member and non-member countries. The committees commission all the work on each theme (publications, task forces, conferences, and so on). The committee members then relay the conclusions to their capitals.

Secretariat: The OECD Secretariat is organised in Directorates:

- Centre for Entrepreneurship, SMEs and Local Development.
- Centre for Tax Policy and Administration.
- Development Cooperation Directorate.
- Directorate for Education.
- Directorate for Employment, Labour and Social Affairs.
- Directorate for Financial and Enterprise Affairs.
- Directorate for Science, Technology and Industry.
- Economics Department.
- Environment Directorate.
- Public Governance and Territorial Development Directorate.
- Statistics Directorate.
- Trade and Agriculture Directorate.
- General Secretariat.
- Executive Directorate.
- Public Affairs and Communication Directorate.

Linked Autonomous Entities:

- Business and Industry Advisory Committee (BIAC).
- Development Centre.

- International Transport Forum – formally known as the European Conference of Ministers of Transport.
- International Energy Agency.
- Nuclear Energy Agency.
- Sahel and West Africa Club.
- Trade Union Advisory Committee (TUAC).

Committees: Representatives of the 30 OECD member countries meet in specialised committees to advance ideas and review progress in specific policy areas, such as economics, trade, science, employment, education or financial markets.

There are about 200 committees, working groups and expert groups. Some 40,000 senior officials from national administrations go to OECD committee meetings each year to request, review and contribute to work undertaken by the OECD secretariat. At home, they have online access to documents and can exchange information through a special network.

Relations with Non-members and Enlargement

Currently, 25 non-members participate as regular observers or full participants in OECD Committees. About 50 non-members are engaged in OECD working parties, schemes or programmes. The OECD conducts a policy dialogue and capacity building activities with non-members (Country Programmes, Regional Approaches and Global Forums) to share their views on best policy practices and to bear on OECD's policy debate. The Centre for Cooperation with Non-Members (CCNM) develops and oversees the strategic orientations of the OECD's global relations with non-members.

On 16 May 2007, the OECD Ministerial Council decided to open accession discussions with Chile, Estonia, Israel, the Russian Federation and Slovenia. It was also decided to strengthen OECD's cooperation with Brazil, China, India, Indonesia and South Africa, through a process of enhanced engagement or as full members. The OECD will also explore the possibilities for enhanced cooperation with selected countries and regions of strategic interest to the OECD, giving priority to South East Asia with a view to identifying countries for possible membership.

History

The Organisation for European Economic Cooperation (OEEC) was founded in 1948 to help administer the Marshall Plan for the reconstruction of Europe after World War II. The headquarters was in the Chateau de la Muette in Paris, France. As the Marshall Plan faded, the OEEC focused on economic questions.

In the 1950s, the OEEC provided the framework for negotiations aimed at determining conditions for setting up a European Free Trade Area, to bring the Common Market of the Six and the other OEEC members together on a multilateral basis. In 1958, a European Nuclear Energy Agency was set up under the OEEC.

Following the 1957 Rome Treaties to launch Europe's Common Market, the Convention on the Organisation for Economic Cooperation and Development was drawn up to reform the OEEC. The Convention was signed in December 1960 and the OECD officially superseded the OEEC in September 1961. It consisted of the European founder countries of the OEEC plus the United States and Canada, with Japan joining three years later.

More than just increasing its internal structure, OECD progressively created agencies: the Development Centre (1961), International Energy Agency (IEA, 1974), Financial Action Task Force on Money Laundering and terrorist financing (1989).

Personnel Policy

As an international organisation the terms of employment of OECD staff are not governed by the laws of the country in which their offices are located. Agreements with the host country safeguard the organisation's impartiality with regard to the host and member countries. Hiring and firing practices, working hours and environment, holiday time, pension plans, health insurance and life insurance, salaries, expatriation benefits and general conditions of employment are managed according to rules and regulations proper to the OECD. In order to maintain similar working conditions to similarly-structured organisations, the OECD participates as an independent organisation in the system of coordinated European organisations, whose other members include NATO, the Western European Union and the European Patent Organisation.

Special Programmes and Actions

Between 1995 and 1997, the OECD designed the much disputed Multilateral Agreement on Investment (MAI), which was rejected. A Swedish journalist discovered the agreement, which was until then clandestinely negotiated. It would have disburdened foreign investments of any claims on the part of the concerned regions and countries (also of social, environmental standards). In 1976, the OECD adopted the Declaration on International Investment and Multinational Enterprises, which was rewritten and annexed by the OECD Guidelines for Multinational Enterprises in 2000.

Among other areas, the OECD has taken a role in coordinating international action on corruption and bribery, creating the OECD Anti-bribery Convention, which came into effect in February 1999. It has been ratified by thirty-seven countries.

The OECD has also constituted a anti-spam task force, which submitted a detailed report, with several quite useful background papers on spam problems in developing countries, best practices for ISPs, e-mail marketers, etc., appended. It works on the information economy and the future of the internet economy.

It has published the *OECD Environmental Outlook to 2030*, which shows that tackling the key environmental problems we face today – including climate change, biodiversity loss, water scarcity, and the health impacts of pollution – is both achievable and affordable.

PISA: OECD publish the Programme for International Student Assessment (PISA) which allow to compare education performances between countries.

Action against Tax Havens: Since 1998, the OECD has led a charge against what it deems "harmful" tax practices, principally targeting the activities of tax havens (while principally accepting the policies of its member countries which would tend to encourage tax competition). These efforts have been met with mixed reaction, with the primary objection apparently linked to ideas about the sanctity of tax policy as a matter of sovereign entitlement. Liechtenstein's recent skirmish with German and US tax authorities is a vivid illustration of what the OECD is encountering in this area.

Nevertheless, the OECD maintains a 'blacklist' of countries it considers uncooperative in the drive for transparency of tax affairs and the effective exchange of information, officially called "The *List of Uncooperative Tax Havens*".

International Monetary Fund

The International Monetary Fund (IMF) is an international organisation that oversees the global financial system by following the macroeconomic policies of its member countries, in particular those with an impact on exchange rates and the balance of payments. It also offers financial and technical assistance to its members, making it an international lender of last resort. Its headquarters are located in Washington, D.C., USA.

Organisation and Purpose

The International Monetary Fund was created in 1944, with a goal to stabilise exchange rates and supervise the reconstruction of the world's international payment system. Countries contributed to a pool which could be borrowed from, on a temporary basis, by countries with payment imbalances.

The IMF describes itself as "an organisation of 185 countries (Montenegro being the 185th, as of January 18, 2007), working to foster global monetary cooperation, secure financial stability, facilitate international trade, promote high employment and sustainable economic growth, and reduce poverty". With the exception of North Korea, Cuba, Andorra, Monaco, Liechtenstein, Tuvalu, and Nauru, all UN member states participate directly in the IMF. Most are represented by other member states on a 24-member Executive Board but all member countries belong to the IMF's Board of Governors.

History: The International Monetary Fund was formally created in July 1944 during the United Nations Monetary and Financial Conference. The representatives of 45 governments met in the Mount Washington Hotel in the area of Bretton Woods, New Hampshire, United States of America, with the delegates to the conference agreeing on a framework for international economic cooperation. The IMF was formally organised on December 27, 1945, when the first 29 countries signed its Articles of Agreement.

The statutory purposes of the IMF today are the same as when they were formulated in 1944.

Today: The IMF's influence in the global economy steadily increased as it accumulated more members. The number of IMF member countries has more than quadrupled from the 44 states involved in its establishment, reflecting in particular the attainment of political independence by many developing countries and more recently the collapse of the Soviet bloc. The expansion of the IMF's membership, together with the changes in the world economy, have required the IMF to adapt in a variety of ways to continue serving its purposes effectively.

In an apparent move to curb the sudden rise of gold prices, and to shore up the falling value of the US Dollar, the International Monetary Fund's executive board approved a broad financial overhaul plan that could lead to the eventual sale of a little over 400 tons of its substantial gold supplies. IMF Managing Director Dominique Strauss-Kahn welcomed the board's decision April 7, 2008 to propose a new framework for the fund, designed to close a projected $400 million budget deficit over the next few years. The budget proposal includes sharp spending cuts of $100 million until 2011 that will include up to 380 staff dismissals.

Data Dissemination Systems

In 1995, the International Monetary Fund began work on data dissemination standards with the view of guiding IMF member countries to disseminate their economic and financial data to the public. The International Monetary and Financial Committee (IMFC) endorsed the guidelines for the dissemination standards and they were split into two tiers: The General Data Dissemination System (GDDS) and the Special Data Dissemination Standard (SDDS).

The International Monetary Fund executive board approved the SDDS and GDDS in 1996 and 1997, respectively and subsequent amendments were published in a revised "Guide to the General Data Dissemination System". The system is aimed primarily at statisticians and aims to improve many aspects of statistical systems in a country. It is also part of the World Bank Millennium Development Goals and Poverty Reduction Strategic Papers.

The IMF established a system and standard to guide members in the dissemination to the public of their economic and financial data. Currently there are two such systems: General Data Dissemination System (GDDS) and its superset Special Data Dissemination System (SDDS), for those member countries having or seeking access to international capital markets.

The primary objective of the GDDS is to encourage IMF member countries to build a framework to improve data quality and increase statistical capacity building. This will involve the preparation of metadata describing current statistical collection practices and setting improvement plans. Upon building a framework, a country can evaluate statistical needs, set priorities in improving the timeliness, transparency, reliability and accessibility of financial and economic data.

Some countries initially used the GDDS, but lately upgraded to SDDS.

Some entities that are not themselves IMF members also contribute statistical data to the systems:

- Palestinian Authority - GDDS.
- Hong Kong - SDDS.
- European Union institutions:
  - The European Central Bank for the Eurozone - SDDS.
  - Eurostat for the whole EU - SDDS, thus providing data from Cyprus (not using any DD System on its own) and Malta (using only GDDS on its own).

Membership Qualifications

Any country may apply for membership to the IMF. The application will be considered first by the IMF's Executive Board. After its consideration, the Executive Board will submit a report to the Board of Governors of the IMF with recommendations in the form of a "Membership Resolution." These recommendations cover the amount of quota in the IMF, the form of payment of the subscription, and other customary terms and conditions of membership. After the Board of Governors has adopted the "Membership Resolution," the applicant state needs to take the legal steps required under its own law to enable it to sign the IMF's

Articles of Agreement and to fulfil the obligations of IMF membership. Similarly, any member country can withdraw from the Fund, although that is rare. For example, in April 2007, the President of Ecuador Rafael Correa announced the expulsion of the World Bank representative in the country. A few days later, at the end of April, Venezuelan President Hugo Chavez announced that the country would withdraw from the IMF and the World Bank. Chavez dubbed both organisations as "the tools of the empire" that "serve the interests of the North". As of April 2008, both countries remain as members of both organisations. Venezuela was forced to back down because a withdrawal would have triggered default clauses in the country's sovereign bonds.

A member's quota in the IMF determines the amount of its subscription, its voting weight, its access to IMF financing, and its allocation of Special Drawing Rights (SDRs). A member state cannot unilaterally increase its quota – increases must be approved by the Executive Board and are linked to formulas that include many variables such as the size of a country in the world economy. For example, in 2001, China was prevented from increasing its quota as high as it wished, ensuring it remained at the level of the smallest G7 economy (Canada). In September 2005, the IMF's member countries agreed to the first round of *ad hoc* quota increases for four countries, including China.

On March 28, 2008, the IMF's Executive Board ended a period of extensive discussion and negotiation over a major package of reforms to enhance the institution's governance that would shift quota and voting shares from advanced to emerging markets and developing countries. The Fund's Board of Governors must vote on these reforms by April 28, 2008.

Assistance and Reforms

The primary mission of the IMF is to provide financial assistance to countries that experience serious financial and economic difficulties using funds deposited with the IMF from the institution's 185 member countries. Member states with balance of payments problems, which often arise from these difficulties, may request loans to help fill gaps between what countries earn and/or are able to borrow from other official lenders and what countries must spend to operate, including to cover the cost of importing basic goods and services. In return, countries are usually required to launch certain reforms, which have often been dubbed the "Washington Consensus". These reforms are generally required because countries with fixed exchange rate policies can engage in fiscal, monetary, and political practices which may lead to the crisis itself.

For example, nations with severe budget deficits, rampant inflation, strict price controls, or significantly over-valued or under-valued currencies run the risk of facing balance of payment crises. Thus, the structural adjustment programmes are at least ostensibly intended to ensure that the IMF is actually helping to prevent financial crises rather than merely funding financial recklessness.

IMF/World Bank Support of Military Dictatorships

The role of the Bretton Woods institutions has been controversial since the late Cold War period, as the IMF policy-makers supported military dictatorships friendly to American and European corporations. Critics also claim that the IMF is generally apathetic or hostile to their views of democracy, human rights, and labour rights. The controversy has helped spark the anti-globalisation movement. Arguments in favour of the IMF say that economic stability is a precursor to democracy, however critics highlight various examples in which democratised countries fell after receiving IMF loans.

Criticism

Two criticisms from economists have been that financial aid is always bound to so-called "Conditionalities", including Structural Adjustment Programmes. Conditionalities, which are the economic performance targets established as a pre-condition for IMF loans, it is claimed, retard social stability and hence inhibit the stated goals of the IMF, while Structural Adjustment Programmes lead to an increase in poverty in recipient countries.

Typically the IMF and its supporters advocate a Keynesian approach. As such, adherents of supply-side economics generally find themselves in open disagreement with the IMF. The IMF frequently advocates currency devaluation, criticised by proponents of supply-side economics as inflationary. Secondly, they link higher taxes under "austerity programmes" with economic contraction.

Currency devaluation is recommended by the IMF to the governments of poor nations with struggling economies. Supply-side economists claim these Keynesian IMF policies are destructive to economic prosperity.

That said, the IMF sometimes advocates "austerity programmes," increasing taxes even when the economy is weak, in order to generate government revenue and balance budget deficits, which is the opposite of Keynesian policy. These policies were criticised by Joseph E. Stiglitz, former chief economist and senior vice president at the World Bank, in his book *Globalisation and Its Discontents*. He argued that by converting to a more Monetarist approach, the fund no longer had a valid purpose, as it was designed to provide funds for countries to carry out Keynesian reflations, and that the IMF "was not participating in a conspiracy, but it was reflecting the interests and ideology of the Western financial community."

Complaints are also directed towards International Monetary Fund gold reserve being undervalued. At its inception in 1945, the IMF pegged gold at US $35 per troy ounce of gold. In 1973, the Nixon administration lifted the fixed asset value of gold in favour of a world market price. Hence, the fixed exchange rates of currencies tied to gold were switched to a floating rate, also based on market price and exchange. This largely came about because *Petrodollars* outside the United States were more than could be backed by the gold at Fort Knox under the fixed exchange rate system. The fixed rate system only served to limit the amount of assistance the organisation could use to help debt-ridden countries. Current IMF rules prohibit members from linking their currencies to gold.

Argentina, which had been considered by the IMF to be a model country in its compliance to policy proposals by the Bretton Woods institutions, experienced a catastrophic economic crisis in 2001, which some believe to have been caused by IMF-induced budget restrictions — which undercut the government's ability to sustain national infrastructure even in crucial areas such as health, education, and security – and privatisation of strategically vital national resources. Others attribute the crisis to Argentina's maldesigned fiscal federalism, which caused subnational spending to increase rapidly. The crisis added to widespread hatred of this institution in Argentina and other South American countries, with many blaming the IMF for the region's economic problems. The current – as of early-2006 – trend towards moderate left-wing governments in the region and a growing concern with the development of a regional economic policy largely independent of big business pressures has been ascribed to this crisis.

Another example of where IMF Structural Adjustment Programmes aggravated the problem was in Kenya. Before the IMF got involved in the country, the Kenyan central bank oversaw all currency movements in and out of the country. The IMF mandated that the Kenyan central bank had to allow easier currency movement. However, the adjustment resulted in very little foreign investment, but allowed Kamlesh Manusuklal Damji Pattni, with the help of corrupt government officials, to siphon off billions of Kenyan shillings in what came to be known as the *Goldenberg scandal*, leaving the country worse off than it was before the IMF reforms were implemented. In a recent interview, the Prime Minister of Romania stated that "Since 2005, IMF is constantly making mistakes when it appreciates the country's economic performances".

Overall the IMF success record is perceived as limited. While it was created to help stabilise the global economy, since 1980 critics claim over 100 countries (or reputedly most of the Fund's membership) have experienced a banking collapse that they claim have reduced GDP by four per cent or more, far more than at any time in Post-Depression history. The considerable delay in the IMF's response to any crisis, and the fact that it tends to only respond to them or even create them rather than prevent them, has led many economists to argue for reform. In 2006, an IMF reform agenda called the *Medium Term Strategy* was widely endorsed by the institution's member countries. The agenda includes changes in IMF governance to enhance the role of developing countries in the institution's decision-making process and steps to deepen the effectiveness of its core mandate, which is known as *economic surveillance* or helping member countries adopt macroeconomic policies that will sustain global growth and reduce poverty. On June 15, 2007, the Executive Board of the IMF adopted the 2007 Decision on Bilateral Surveillance, a landmark measure that replaced a 30-year-old decision of the Fund's member countries on how the IMF should analyse economic outcomes at the country level.

Whatever the feelings people in the Western world have for the IMF, research by the Pew Research Centre shows that more than 60 per cent of Asians and 70 per cent of Africans feel that the IMF and the World Bank have a positive effect on their country. However, it is pertinent to note that the survey aggregated international organisations including the World Trade Organisation. Also, a similar percentage of people in the Western world believed that these international organisations had a positive effect on their countries. In 2005, the IMF was the first multilateral financial institution to implement a sweeping debt-relief programme for the world's poorest countries known as the *Multilateral Debt Relief Initiative*. By year-end 2006, 23 countries mostly in sub-Saharan Africa and Central America had received total relief of debts owed the IMF.

In 2008, a study by analysts from Cambridge and Yale universities published on the open-access Public Library of Science concluded that strict conditions on the international loans by the IMF resulted in hundreds of thousands of deaths in Eastern Europe by tuberculosis as public health care had to be weakened. In the 21 countries which the IMF had given loans, tuberculosis deaths rose by 16.6 per cent.

Past Managing Directors

Historically the IMF's managing director has been European and the president of the World Bank has been from the United States. However, this standard is increasingly being questioned and competition for these two posts may soon open up to include other qualified candidates from any part of the world. Executive Directors, who confirm the managing director, are voted in by Finance Ministers from countries they represent. The First Deputy

Managing Director of the IMF, the second-in-command, has traditionally been (and is today) an American.

The IMF is for the most part controlled by the major Western Powers, with voting rights on the Executive board based on a quota derived from the relative size of a country in the global economy. Critics claim that the board rarely votes and passes issues contradicting the will of the US or Europeans, which combined represent the largest bloc of shareholders in the Fund. On the other hand, Executive Directors that represent emerging and developing countries have many times strongly defended the group of nations in their constituency. Alexandre Kafka, who represented several Latin American countries for 32 years as Executive Director (including 21 as the dean of the Board), is a prime example. Mohamed Finaish from Libya, the Executive Director representing the majority of the Arab World and Pakistan, was a tireless defender of the developing nations' rights at the IMF until the 1992 elections. Rodrigo Rato became the ninth Managing Director of the IMF on June 7, 2004 and resigned his post at the end of October 2007.

Media Representation of the IMF

Life and Debt a documentary film, deals with the IMF's policies' influence on Jamaica and its economy from a critical point of view. In 1978, one year after Jamaica first entered a borrowing relationship with the IMF, the Jamaican dollar was still worth more on the open exchange than the US dollar; by 1995, when Jamaica terminated that relationship, the Jamaican dollar had eroded to less than 2 cents US. Such observations lead to skepticism that IMF involvement is necessarily helpful to a third world economy.

The Debt of Dictators explores the lending of billions of dollars by the IMF, World Bank multinational banks and other international financial institutions to brutal dictators throughout the world.

Global Banking

World Bank

The World Bank is an internationally supported bank that provides financial and technical assistance to developing countries for development programmes (e.g. bridges, roads, schools, etc.) with the stated goal of reducing poverty. The differs from the World Bank Group in that the former comprises only the International Bank for Reconstruction and Development and the International Development Association, while the latter incorporates these entities in addition to three others. The World Bank was formally established on December 27, 1945, following the ratification of the Bretton Woods agreement.

The concept was originally conceived in July 1944 at the United Nations Monetary and Financial Conference. Two years later, the Bank issued its first loan: $250 million to France for post-war reconstruction, the main focus of the Bank's work in the early post-World War II years. Over time, the "development" side of the Bank's work has assumed a larger share of its lending, although it is still involved in post-conflict reconstruction, together with reconstruction after natural disasters, response to humanitarian emergencies and post-conflict rehabilitation needs affecting developing and transition economies. There are some criticisms of the results of the World Bank's "development schemes" leading to corruption and widespread exploitation of the corporations who are given monopolies of developing nations' resources.

The World Bank is one of the two Bretton Woods Institutions which were created in 1944 to rebuild a war-torn Europe after World War II. Later, largely due to the contributions of the Marshall Plan, the World Bank was forced to find a new area in which to focus its efforts. Subsequently, it began attempting to rebuild the infrastructure of Europe's former colonies. Since then it has made a variety of changes regarding its focus and goals. From 1968-1981 it focused largely on poverty alleviation. From the 1980s and into the 1990s its main focus was both debt management and structural adjustment.

Activities

The World Bank's current focus is on the achievement of the Millennium Development Goals (MDGs), goals calling for the elimination of poverty and the implementation of sustainable development. Of the two constituent parts of the Bank, the IBRD lends primarily to "middle-income countries" at interest rates which reflect a small mark-up over its own (AAA-rated) borrowings from capital markets; while the IDA provides low or no interest loans and grants to low income countries with little or no access to international credit markets. The IBRD is a market based non-profit organisation, using its high credit rating to make up for the relatively low interest rate on its loans, while the IDA is funded primarily by periodic "replenishments" (grants) voted to the institution by its more affluent member countries.

The Bank's mission is to aid developing countries and their inhabitants achieve development and the reduction of poverty, including achievement of the MDGs, by helping countries develop an environment for investment, jobs and sustainable growth, thus promoting economic growth through investment and enabling the poor to share the fruits of economic growth. The World Bank sees the five key factors necessary for economic growth and the creation of an enabling business environment as:

1. *Build Capacity:* Strengthening governments and educating government officials

2. *Infrastructure Creation:* Implementation of legal and judicial systems for the encouragement of business, the protection of individual and property rights and the honouring of contracts
3. *Development of Financial Systems:* The establishment of strong systems capable of supporting endeavours from micro credit to the financing of larger corporate ventures
4. *Combating Corruption:* Support for countries' efforts at eradicating corruption
5. *Research, Consultancy and Training:* The World Bank provides platform for research on development issues, consultancy and conduct training programmes (web based, on line, video/ tele conferencing and class room based) open for those who are interested from academia, students, government and non-governmental organisation (NGO) officers, etc.

The Bank obtains funding for its operations primarily through the IBRD's sale of AAA-rated bonds in the world's financial markets. The IBRD's income is generated from its lending activities, with its borrowings leveraging its own paid-in capital, plus the investment of its "float". The IDA obtains the majority of its funds from forty donor countries who replenish the bank's funds every three years, and from loan repayments, which then become available for relending.

The Bank offers two basic types of loans: investment loans and development policy loans. The former are made for the support of economic and social development projects, whereas the latter provide quick disbursing finance to support countries' policy and institutional reforms. While the IBRD provides loans with a relatively low interest rate, the IDA's "credits" are interest free. The project proposals of borrowers are evaluated for their economical, financial, social and environmental aspects prior to their approval.

The Bank also distributes grants for the facilitation of development projects through the encouragement of innovation, cooperation between organisations and the participation of local stakeholders in projects. IDA grants are predominantly used for:

- Debt burden relief in the most indebted and poverty struck countries;

- Amelioration of sanitation and water supply;
- Support of vaccination and immunisation programmes for the reduction of communicable diseases such as malaria;
- Combating the HIV/AIDS pandemic;
- Support civil society organisations;
- Creating initiatives for the reduction of greenhouse gases.

The Bank not only provides financial support to its member states, but also analytical and advisory services to facilitate the implementation of the lasting economic and social improvements that are needed in many underdeveloped countries, as well as educating members with the knowledge necessary to resolve their development problems while promoting economic growth.

Leadership

The president of the World Bank is responsible for chairing the meetings of the Boards of Directors and for overall management of the World Bank. The Executive Directors make up the Board of Directors, usually meeting twice a week to oversee activities such as the approval of loans and guarantees, new policies, the administrative budget, country assistance strategies and borrowing and financing decisions. The vice presidents of the World Bank are its principal managers, in charge of regions, sectors, networks and functions. There are 24 vice presidents, 3 senior vice presidents and 2 executive vice presidents.

Areas of Operation

The World Bank is active in the following areas:

- Agriculture and Rural Development.
- Conflict and Development.
- Development Operations and Activities.
- Economic Policy.
- Education.
- Energy.
- Environment.
- Financial Sector.
- Gender.

- Governance.
- Health, Nutrition and Population.
- Industry.
- Information and Communication Technologies.
- Information, Computing and Telecommunications.
- International Economics and Trade.
- Labour and Social Protections.
- Law and Justice.
- Macroeconomic and Economic Growth.
- Mining.
- Poverty Reduction.
- Poverty.
- Private Sector.
- Public Sector Governance.
- Rural Development.
- Social Development.
- Social Protection.
- Trade.
- Transport.
- Urban Development.
- Water Resources.
- Water Supply and Sanitation.

Comprehensive Development Framework

According to the World Bank, in virtually all successful assistance projects the country itself was the driving factor. The Bank therefore strives to help governments lead and implement their own development strategies and thus take a stronger hand in their own future development. The strategy was initiated by the former president of the bank, James Wolfensohn. Since 1999, it has followed a set of philosophies known as the *Comprehensive Development Framework*. These philosophies state that:

- Development strategies should be comprehensive and shaped by a long-term vision;

- Development goals and strategies should be "owned" by the country, based on local stakeholder participation in shaping them;
- Countries receiving assistance should lead the management and coordination of aid programmes through stakeholder partnerships;
- Development performance should be evaluated through measurable results on the ground in order to adjust the strategy to outcomes and a changing world.

Poverty Reduction Strategies

For the poorest developing countries in the world the World Bank's assistance plans are based on Poverty Reduction Strategies; by combining a cross-section of local groups with an extensive analysis of the country's financial and economical situation the World Bank develops a strategy pertaining uniquely to the country in question. The government then identifies the country's priorities and targets for the reduction of poverty, and the World Bank aligns its aid efforts correspondingly.

The Bank supports certain kinds of poor people's organisations such as the Self-employed Women's Union and Shack/Slum Dwellers International.

Forty-five countries pledged US $25.1 billion in "aid for the world's poorest countries", aid that goes to the World Bank International Development Association (IDA) which distributes the gifts to eighty poorer countries. While wealthier nations sometimes fund their own aid projects, including those for diseases recently, and although IDA is the recipient of criticism, Robert B. Zoellick, the president of the World Bank, said when the gifts were announced on December 15, 2007, that IDA money "is the core funding that the poorest developing countries rely on".

Clean Technology Fund Management

The World Bank has been assigned temporary management responsibility of the Clean Technology Fund (CTF), focused on making renewable energy cost-competitive with coal-fired power as quickly as possible, but this may not continue after UN's Copenhagen climate change conference in December, 2009, because its continued investment in huge coal-fired power plants.

Training Wing

World Bank Institute: The World Bank Institute (WBI) creates learning opportunities for countries, World Bank staff and clients, and people committed to poverty reduction and sustainable development. WBI's work programme includes training, policy consultations, and the creation and support of knowledge networks related to international economic and social development.

Global Development Learning Network: The Global Development Learning Network (GDLN) is a partnership of over 120 learning centres (GDLN Affiliates) in nearly 80 countries around the world. GDLN Affiliates collaborate in holding events that connect people across countries and regions for learning and dialogue on development issues. Offering a combination of distance learning tools such as interactive videoconferencing and the internet, and expert facilitation and learning techniques, GDLN Affiliates enable individuals, teams, and organisations working in development around the world to communicate, share knowledge, and learn from each others' experiences in a timely and cost-effective manner.

GDLN clients are typically NGOs, government, private sector and development agencies who find that they work better together on subregional, regional or global development issues and challenges using the facilities and tools offered by GDLN Affiliates. Clients also benefit from the ability of Affiliates to help them choose and apply these tools effectively, and to tap development practitioners and experts worldwide. GDLN Affiliates facilitate around 1,000 videoconference-based activities a year on behalf of their clients, reaching some 90,000 people worldwide. Most of these activities bring together participants in two or more countries over a series of session. A majority of GDLN activities are organised by small government agencies and NGOs.

GDLN Asia Pacific: The GDLN in the East Asia and Pacific region has experienced rapid growth and Distance Learning Centres now operate, or are planned in 20 countries: Australia, Mongolia, Cambodia, China, Indonesia, Singapore, Philippines, Sri Lanka, Japan, Papua New Guinea, South Korea, Thailand, Laos, Timor Leste, Fiji, Afghanistan, Bangladesh, India, Nepal and New Zealand. With over 180 Distance Learning Centres, it is the largest development learning network in the Asia and Pacific region. The Secretariat Office of GDLN Asia Pacific is located in the Centre of Academic Resources of Chulalongkorn University, Bangkok, Thailand.

GDLN Asia Pacific was launched at the GDLN's East Asia and Pacific regional meeting held in Bangkok from 22 to 24 May 2006. Its vision is to become "the premier network exchanging ideas, experience and know-how across the Asia Pacific Region". GDLN Asia Pacific is a separate entity to The World Bank. It has endorsed its own Charter and Business Plan and, in accordance with the Charter, a GDLN Asia Pacific Governing Committee has been appointed.

The Governing Committee has determined that the most appropriate legal status for the GDLN AP in Thailand is a "Foundation". The World Bank is currently engaging a solicitor in Thailand to process all documentation in order to obtain this legal status.

GDLN Asia Pacific is built on the principle of shared resources among partners engaged in a common task, and this is visible in the organisational structures that exist, as the network evolves. Physical space for its headquarters is provided by the host of the GDLN Centre in Thailand - Chulalongkorn University; Technical expertise and some infrastructure is provided by the Tokyo Development Learning Centre (TDLC); Fiduciary services are provided by Australian National University (ANU) Until the GDLN Asia Pacific is established as a legal entity tin Thailand, ANU, has offered to assist the governing committee, by providing a means of managing the inflow and outflow of funds and of reporting on them. This admittedly results in some complexity in contracting arrangements, which need to be worked out on a case by case basis and depends to some extent on the legal requirements of the countries involved.

Country Assistance Strategies

As a guideline to the World Bank's operations in any particular country, a Country Assistance Strategy is produced, in cooperation with the local government and any interested stakeholders and may rely on analytical work performed by the World Bank or other parties. In the case of low income countries, the Country Assistance Strategy is derived from the country's Poverty Reduction.

Criticism

Some critics of the World Bank believe that the institution was not started in order to reduce poverty but rather to support United States' business interests, and argue that the bank has actually increased poverty and been detrimental to the environment, public health, and cultural diversity. Some critics also claim that the World Bank has consistently pushed a "neo-liberal" agenda, imposing policies on developing countries which have been damaging, destructive and anti-developmental. Some intellectuals in developing countries have argued that the World Bank is deeply implicated in contemporary modes of donor and NGO driven imperialism and that its intellectual output functions to blame the poor for their condition.

It has also been suggested that the World Bank is an instrument for the promotion of US or Western interests in certain regions of the world. Consequently, seven South American nations have established the Bank of the South in order to minimise US influence in the region. Criticisms of the structure of the World Bank refer to the fact that the president of the World Bank is always a citizen of the United States, nominated by the President of the United States (though subject to the approval of the other member countries).

There have been accusations that the decision-making structure is undemocratic, as the US effectively has a veto on some constitutional decisions with just over 16 per cent of the shares in the bank; moreover, decisions can only be passed with votes from countries whose shares total more than 85 per cent of the bank's shares. A further criticism concerns internal governance and the manner in which the World Bank is alleged to lack transparency to external publics.

Members

The International Bank for Reconstruction and Development (IBRD) has 185 member countries, while the International Development Association (IDA) has 167 members. Each member state of IBRD should be also a member of the International Monetary Fund (IMF) and only members of IBRD are allowed to join other institutions within the Bank (such as IDA).

Universal Bank

A universal bank is a bank that participate in all kinds of banking activities. It is a bank that is both a Commercial bank and an Investment bank.

Unlike the UK and the United States most Germanic countries do not distinguish between the two. In the United States, the Glass-Steagall Act of 1933 historically prevented commercial and investment banks from operating as a single institution, but this situation may be flux due to the Economic crisis of 2008. Deutsche Bank of Germany is one of the world's largest universal banks.

Bank Regulations in United States

Bank regulation in the United States is highly fragmented compared to other G-10 countries where most countries have only one bank regulator. In the US, banking is regulated at both the federal and state level. Depending on a banking organisation's charter-type and organisational structure, it may be subject to numerous federal and state banking regulators. Unlike Japan and the United Kingdom, where regulatory authority over the banking, securities and insurance industries is combined into one single financial services agency, the US maintains separate securities, commodities, and insurance regulatory agencies (which are separate from the bank regulatory agencies) at the federal and state level as well.

The US also has one of the most highly regulated banking environments in the world; however, many of the regulations are not safety and soundness related, but are instead focused on privacy, disclosure, fraud prevention, anti-money laundering, anti-terrorism, anti-usury lending, and promoting lending to lower-income segments. Even individual cities enact their own financial regulation laws (for example, for usury lending).

Federal Regulatory Agencies

A bank's primary federal regulator could be the Federal Deposit Insurance Corporation, the Federal Reserve Board, the Office of the Comptroller of the Currency, or the Office of Thrift Supervision. And within the Federal Reserve Board, there are 12 districts centred around 12 regional Federal Reserve Banks, each of which carries out the Federal Reserve Board's bank regulatory responsibilities in its respective district. Credit Unions in the United States are subject to certain similar bank-like regulations and are supervised by the National Credit Union Administration.

State Regulatory Agencies

State-chartered banks are also subject to the regulation and supervision of the state regulatory agency of the state in which they were chartered. State regulation of state-chartered banks applies in addition to federal regulation. For example, a California state bank that is not a member of the Federal Reserve System would be regulated by both the California Department of Financial Institutions and the FDIC. Likewise, a Nevada state bank that is a member of the Federal Reserve System would be jointly regulated by the Nevada Division of Financial Institutions and the Federal Reserve.

Federal Laws and Regulations

State banking laws also apply to state-chartered banks and certain non-bank affiliates of federally-chartered banks.

Fair Credit Reporting Act (FCRA): The Fair Credit Reporting Act (or FCRA) regulates the collection, sharing, and use of customer credit information. The act allows consumers to obtain a copy of their credit report records from Credit bureaus that hold information on them, provides for consumers to dispute negative information held, and sets time limits after which negative information is suppressed. It requires that consumers be informed when negative information is added to their credit records, and when adverse action is taken based on a credit report.

Lending Limits: Lending limit regulations restrict the total amount of loans and credits that a bank may extend to a single borrower. This restriction is usually stated as a percentage of the bank's capital or assets. For example, a national bank generally must limit its total outstanding loans and credits to any single borrower to no more than 15 per cent of the bank's total capital and surplus. Some state banking regulations also contain similar lending limits applicable to state-chartered banks. Both federal and state laws generally allow for a higher lending limit, up to 25 per cent of capital and surplus for national banks, when the portion of the credit that exceed the initial lending limit is fully secured.

Federal Reserve Regulations

Regulation A – Extensions of Credit by Federal Reserve Banks: This regulation establishes rules regarding extensions of credit made by a Federal Reserve Bank to banks and other institutions (i.e. discount window lending). The Federal Reserve Board made significant amendments to Regulation A in 2003 including amendments to price certain discount window lending at above-market rates and to restrict borrowing to banks in generally sound condition.

In amending the regulation, the Federal Reserve Board noted that many banks had expressed their unwillingness to use discount window borrowing because their use of such a funding source was interpreted as sign of the bank's financial weakness or distress. The Federal Reserve Board indicated its hope that the 2003 amendments would make discount window lending a more attractive funding option to banks.

Regulation B – Equal Credit Opportunity: The Equal Credit Opportunity Act (ECOA) states that creditors which regularly extend credit to customers, which includes banks, retailers, finance companies, and bankcard companies, should evaluate candidates on credit worthiness alone, rather than other factors – race, colour, religion, national origin or sex. Discrimination on marital status, welfare recipience, and age is generally prohibited with exceptions, as is discrimination based on a consumer's good faith exercise of their credit protection rights.

Regulation C – Home Mortgage Disclosure Act (HMDA): The HMDA requires financial institutions to maintain and annually disclose data about home purchases, home purchase pre-approvals, home improvement, and refinance applications involving 1 to 4 unit and multifamily dwellings. It also requires branches and loan centres to display an HMDA poster.

Regulation D — Reserve Requirements for Depository Institutions:

- Establishes reserve requirement guidelines.
- Regulates certain early withdrawals from certificate of deposit accounts.
- Defines what qualifies as DDA/NOW accounts.
- Defines limitations on certain withdrawals on savings and money market accounts.
  - Unlimited transfers or withdrawals if made in person, by ATM, by mail, or by messenger.
  - In all other instances, there is a limit of six transfers or withdrawals. No more than three of these transactions may be made payable to a third party (by check, draft, point-of-sale, etc.).
  - Some banks will charge a fee with each excess transaction.
  - Bank must close accounts where this transaction limit is constantly exceeded.

Regulation O – Loans to Insiders: Regulation O establishes varying quantitative and qualitative limits and reporting requirements on extensions of credit made by a bank to its "insiders" or the insiders of the bank's affiliates. The term "insiders" includes executive officers, directors, principal shareholders and the related interests of such parties.

Regulation Q – Prohibition Against Payment of Interest on Certain Deposit Account Types: Regulation Q prohibits banks from paying interest on demand deposit accounts. A "demand deposit" account includes many, but not all checking accounts. Banks, however, may pay interest on Negotiable Order of Withdrawal accounts (NOW accounts) offered to consumers and certain entities (but not commercial enterprises other than sole-proprietors).

Regulation W – Transactions Between Member Banks and their Affiliates: Regulation W establishes quantitative and qualitative requirements for loans, purchases of assets, and other transactions between banks and their affiliates. The term "affiliate" is broadly defined and includes parent companies, companies that share a parent company with the bank, companies that are under other types of common control with the bank (e.g. by a trust), companies with interlocking directors (a majority of directors, trustees, etc. are the same as a majority of the bank's), subsidiaries, and certain other types of companies.

Regulation BB — Community Reinvestment Act (CRA):

- Insured depository institutions are required to reinvest in the communities they serve. There should be an emphasis on low- and moderate- income (LMI) census tracts and individuals.
- Insured depository institutions must display a CRA notice.
- Each branch must have a current CRA public file or access to it via the company's internet. The bank has 10 days to provide the information to you in person or via mail.

Regulation CC — Expedited Funds Availability Act:

- Defines when standard holds and exception holds can be placed on check deposits, and defines the maximum length of time the money can be held.
- Regulation CC only applies to transaction accounts, which does not include savings accounts, money market accounts, or time deposit accounts.
- Regulation CC does not apply to frequently overdrawn accounts or to deposits involving suspect checks.
- Regulation CC does not apply to new accounts (open 30 days or less). For a new account, your financial institution may place a hold on your deposits for longer than their normal policy. This protects financial institutions from check fraud. Next day availability is still required for deposits of cash and for electronic payments.
- Regulation CC provides an exception for emergency conditions such as adverse weather conditions, war, or a computer breakdown.
- Regulation CC provides an exception for suspect checks.
  - Funds from electronic direct deposits are available the same day.

- Funds from cash deposits must be available at the beginning of the following business day.
- Deposits made in person and meeting certain requirements must be made available by the next business day.
- ATMs must have a posting explaining when the effective date of deposit is. Typically, it will take longer to have access to funds when using an ATM that is not at a branch location to make a deposit.
- Funds from local checks must be available two business days after the effective date of deposit. Non-local checks take longer to process and can be held up to 5 business days from the effective date of deposit (with the exception of the $100 which must be received the following business day).
- $100 of the total deposits from a customer on the same day is available at the beginning of the following business day (business days exclude Saturdays, Sundays, and legal holidays). This is known as the $100 Rule.

  [Note – The $100 Rule does not apply to new accounts (defined as accounts open for 30 days or less)].

• There is an exception to Regulation CC for large dollar amounts.
  - Standard holds:
    - § The first $4,900: 2 business days;
    - § The remaining amount over $5,000: 7 business days.
  - Exception Holds:
    - § The first $4,900: 5 business days;
    - § The remaining amount over $5,000: 11 business days.
  - Special Check Deposits, including guaranteed items such as cashiers checks:
    - § The first $5,000 must be made available immediately.

• A bank's hold policy can be less stringent than the guidelines outlined in Reg. CC, but it cannot exceed the guidelines.

Regulation DD – Truth in Savings Act: The purpose of this part is to enable consumers to make informed decisions about accounts at depository institutions. This part requires depository institutions to provide disclosures so that consumers can make meaningful comparisons among depository institutions. This regulation is not applicable to credit unions.

- Part 230 – Truth in Savings.

Pre-emption of State Banking Laws

By statute and judicial interpretation of statutes and the United States Constitution, federal banking statutes and the regulations and other guidance issued by federal banking regulatory agencies often pre-empt state laws that would regulate certain activities of nationally chartered banking institutions and their subsidiaries. Specific exceptions to the general rule of federal pre-emption exist, e.g. some contract law, escheat law, and insurance law.

Fiduciary Activities of Savings and Loans, or Thrifts

One example of OTS Pre-emption begins with Section 550.136(a) of the OTS Regulations, providing that "... OTS occupies the field of the regulation of the fiduciary activities of Federal savings associations. ... Accordingly, Federal savings associations may exercise fiduciary powers as authorised under Federal law, including this part, without regard to State laws that purport to regulate or otherwise affect their fiduciary activities, except to the extent provided in 12 U.S.C. § 1464(n) . . . or in paragraph (c) of this section." 12 U.S.C. § 1464(n), authorises fiduciary activities for federal savings associations, and specifies certain state law requirements that are applicable to federal savings associations. Section 550.136(c) lists six types of state laws that in certain specified circumstances are not pre-empted with respect to Federal savings associations.

Advanced Bank of Asia

Advanced Bank of Asia Ltd. is one of commercial banks in Kingdom of Cambodia (as per National Bank of Cambodia).

Banking in China

China's banking system has undergone significant changes in the last two decades: banks are now functioning more like banks than before. Nevertheless, China's banking industry has remained in the government's hands even though banks have gained more autonomy. China's accession to WTO will lead to a significant opening of this industry to foreign participation.

The central bank of the People's Republic of China is the People's Bank of China.

The "big four" state-owned commercial banks are the Bank of China, the China Construction Bank, the Industrial and Commercial Bank of China and the Agricultural Bank of China.

Supervisory Bodies

The People's Bank of China (PBOC) is China's central bank, which formulates and implements monetary policy. The PBOC maintains the banking sector's payment, clearing and settlement systems, and manages official foreign exchange and gold reserves. It oversees the State Administration of Foreign Exchange (SAFE) for setting foreign-exchange policies.

According to the 1995 Central Bank law, PBOC has full autonomy in applying the monetary instruments, including setting interest rate for commercial banks and trading in government bonds. The State Council maintains oversight of PBOC policies.

China Banking Regulatory Commission (CBRC) was officially launched on April 28, 2003, to take over the supervisory role of the PBOC. The goal of the landmark reform is to improve the efficiency of bank supervision and to help the PBOC to further focus on the macro economy and currency policy.

According to the official announcement by CBRC posted on its website, the CBRC is responsible for "the regulation and supervision of banks, asset management companies, trust and investment companies as well as other deposit-taking financial institutions. Its mission is to maintain a safe and sound banking system in China."

Domestic Key Players

State-owned Commercial Banks – The 'Big Four': In 1995, the Chinese Government introduced the Commercial Bank Law to commercialise the operations of the four state-owned banks, the Bank of China (BOC), the China Construction Bank (CCB), the Agricultural Bank of China (ABC), and the Industrial and Commercial Bank of China (ICBC).

The Industrial and Commerce Bank of China (ICBC) is the largest bank in China by total assets, total employees and total customers. ICBC differentiates itself from the other State Owned Commercial Banks by being second in foreign exchange business and 1st in RMB clearing business. It used to be the major supplier of funds to China's urban areas and manufacturing sector.

The Bank of China (BOC) specialises in foreign-exchange transactions and trade finance. In 2002, BOC Hong Kong (Holdings) was successfully listed on the Hong Kong Stock Exchange. The US $2.8 billion offering was over-subscribed by 7.5 times. The deal was a significant move in the reform of China's banking industry.

The China Construction Bank (CCB) specialises in medium to long-term credit for long-term specialised projects, such as infrastructure projects and urban housing development.

The Agriculture Bank of China (ABC) specialises in providing financing to China's agricultural sector and offers wholesale and retail banking services to farmers, township and village enterprises (TVEs) and other rural institutions.

Policy Banks: Three new "policy" banks, the Agricultural Development Bank of China (ADBC), China Development Bank (CDB), and the Export-Import Bank of China (Chexim), were established in 1994 to take over the government-directed spending functions of the four state-owned commercial banks. These banks are responsible for financing economic and trade development and state-invested projects.

ADBC provides funds for agricultural development projects in rural areas; the CDB specialises in infrastructure financing, and Chexim specialises in trade financing.

Second Tier Commercial Banks: In addition to the big four state-owned commercial banks, there are smaller commercial banks. The largest ones in this group include the Bank of Communications, CITIC Industrial Bank, China Everbright Bank, Hua Xia Bank, China Minsheng Bank, Guangdong Development Bank, Shenzhen Development Bank, China Merchants Bank, Shanghai Pudong Development Bank and Fujian Industrial Bank. The second tier banks are generally healthier in terms of asset quality and profitability and have much lower non-performing loan ratios than the big four..

Trust and Investment Corporations: In the midst of the reforms of the 1980s, the government established some new investment banks that engaged in various forms of merchant and investment banking activities. However, many of the 240 or so international trust and investment corporations (ITICs) established by government agencies and provincial authorities experienced severe liquidity problems after the bankruptcy of the Guangdong International Trust and Investment Corporation (GITIC) in late-1998. The largest surviving ITIC is China International Trust and Investment Corporation (CITIC), which has a banking subsidiary known as CITIC Industrial Bank.

Reforms in the Banking Industry: Years of government-directed lending has presented Chinese banks with large amounts of non-performing loans. According to the Central Bank's report, non-performing loans account for 21.4 per cent to 26.1 per cent of total lending of China's four big banks in 2002. In 1999, four asset management companies (AMC) were established to transfer the non-performing assets from the banks. The AMCs plan to repackage the non-performing loans into viable assets and sell them off to the investors.

PBOC has encouraged banks to diversify their portfolios by increasing their services to the private sector and individual consumers. In July 2000, a personal credit rating system was launched in Shanghai to be used to assess consumer credit risk and set ratings standards. This is an important move in developing China's consumer credit industry, and increase bank loans to individuals.

The central government has allowed several small banks to raise capital through bonds or stock issues. Followed the listing of Shenzhen Development Bank and Pudong Development Bank, China Minsheng Bank, the only private bank in China, was listed on the Shanghai Stock Exchange (A-Share) in December 2000. More Chinese banks are expected to list in the next two years in order to raise capital.

The reform of the banking system has been accompanied by PBOC's decision to decontrol interest rates. Market-based interest rate reform is intended to establish the pricing mechanism of the deposit and lending rates based on market supply and demand.

The central bank would continue to adjust and guide the interest rate development, which allows the market mechanism to play a dominant role in financial resource allocation.

The sequence of the reform is to liberalise the interest rate of foreign currency before that of domestic currency, lending before deposit, large amount and long term before small amount and short term. As a first step, the PBOC liberalised the interest rates for foreign currency loans and large deposits (US $3 million and over) in September 2000. Rate for deposits below US $3 million remain subject to PBOC control. In March 2002, the PBOC unified foreign currency interest rate policies for Chinese and foreign financial institutions in China. Small foreign exchange deposits of Chinese residents with foreign banks in China were included in the PBOC interest rate administration of small foreign exchange deposits, so that domestic and foreign financial institutions are treated fairly with regard to the interest rate policy of foreign exchange deposits.

As interest rate liberalisation progressed, the PPOC liberalised, simplified or abandoned 114 categories of interest rates initially under control since 1996. At present, 34 categories of interest rates remain subject to PBOC control. The full liberalisation of interest rates on other deposit accounts, including checking and saving accounts, is expected to take much longer. On the lending side, market-determined interest rates on loans will first be introduced in rural areas and then followed by rate liberalisation in cities.

Credit Cards

Between 1985 and 2006, China has issued 714 million banking cards, of which almost 96 per cent are debit cards. Only 29.13 million of the banking cards are credit cards, and 4 million of these carry the China Union Pay logo. There are over 110 banking card issuers in China, which include the 'big four' banks (Industrial and Commercial Bank of China, the Bank of China, China Construction Bank, and the Agricultural Bank of China), as well as fast-growing second tier banks and city commercial banks.

As of June 2004, China had approximately 476,000 POS machines and 64,000 ATMs. About 300,000 merchants in China accept banking cards.

China's state-owned commercial banks recently began to issue a dual-currency card, allowing cardholders to purchase goods within China in RMB and overseas in US dollars.

According to a 2003 research study by VISA, the average per transaction purchase with a card was US $253. Consumers used their credit cards mainly to purchase houses, vehicles, and home appliances, as well as to pay utility bills.

One major issue is the lack of a national credit bureau to provide credit information for banks to evaluate individual loan applicants. In 2002, the Shanghai Information Office and the People's Bank of China Shanghai branch established the first personal credit data organisation involving 15 commercial banks. The Chinese Government, aiming to promote a nationwide credit system, has also set up a credit system research group. At present, large cities, such as Beijing, Guangzhou, Shenzhen, Chongqing, and Chengdu, are calling for a reliable credit data system. The PBOC is currently evaluating the feasibility of establishing a nationwide credit bureau.

Other obstacles include lack of merchant acceptance and a weak infrastructure for card processing. At present, only 2 per cent of merchants in China are equipped to handle card transactions, although in some major cities like Shanghai the percentage is over 30 per cent. China Union Pay was established to set-up a national processing network connecting merchants and banks. China Union Pay has set-up bankcard network service centres in 18 cities in addition to a national bankcard information switch centre.

Products and services in the credit card system that the Chinese government wants to develop are credit card-related hardware, including POS and ATMs, credit card-related software for banks and merchants; and Credit and risk management training programmes.

Foreign Banks

China's entry into the WTO is expected to create opportunities for foreign banks. As a milestone move to honour its WTO commitments, China released the *Rules for Implementing the Regulations Governing Foreign Financial Institutions in the People's*

Republic of China in January 2002. The rules provide detailed regulations for implementing the administration of the establishment, registration, scope of business, qualification, supervision, dissolution and liquidation of foreign financial institutions.

They also stipulate that foreign bank branches conducting full aspects of foreign-currency business and full aspects of RMB business to all categories of clients are required to have operating capital of at least 600 million RMB (US $72.3 million), of which at least 400 million RMB (US $48.2 million) must be held in RMB and at least 200 million RMB (US $24.1 million) in freely convertible currency.

Client restriction on foreign currency business was lifted immediately after China's entry into the WTO on December 11, 2001. Since then, foreign financial institutions have been permitted to provide foreign currency services to Chinese enterprises and individuals, and have been permitted to provide local currency business to all Chinese clients by the end of 2006.

Furthermore, when China entered the WTO, geographic restrictions placed on RMB-denominated business was phased out in four major cities—Shanghai, Shenzhen, Tianjin and Dalian. Then, on December 1, 2002, foreign-funded banks were allowed to commence RMB-denominated business in Guangzhou, Zhuhai, Qingdao, Nanjing and Wuhan.

Electronic Banking

In 1994, China started the "Golden Card Project," enabling cards issued by banks to be used all over the country through a network. The establishment of the China Association of Banks rapidly promoted the inter-bank card network and by the end of 2004, the inter-region-inter-bank network had reached 600 cities, including all prefecture-level cities and more than 300 economically developed county-level cities.

Securities and Futures Commission, Hong Kong

The Securities and Futures Commission of Hong Kong is the independent statutory body charged with regulating the securities and futures markets in Hong Kong. It is the main authority and supervision board for the security market in Hong Kong. Even though it is consider to be a branch of the government body, it run separate to the government itself. It consist of a CEO.

Banking in India

Banking in India originated in the first decade of 18th century. The first banks were The General Bank of India, which started in 1786, and Bank of Hindustan, both of which are now defunct. The oldest bank in existence in India is the State Bank of India, which originated in the "The Bank of Bengal" in Calcutta in June 1806. This was one of the three presidency banks, the other two being the Bank of Bombay and the Bank of Madras. The presidency banks were established under charters from the British East India Company. They merged in 1925 to form the Imperial Bank of India, which, upon India's independence, became the State Bank of India. For many years the Presidency banks acted as quasi-central banks, as did their successors. The Reserve Bank of India formally took on the responsibility of regulating the Indian banking sector from 1935. After India's independence in 1947, the Reserve Bank was nationalised and given broader powers.

Early History

The first fully Indian owned bank was the Allahabad Bank, established in 1865. However, at the end of late-18th century, there were hardly any banks in India in the modern sense of the term. The American Civil War stopped the supply of cotton to Lancashire from the Confederate States. Promoters opened banks to finance trading in Indian cotton. With large exposure to speculative ventures, most of the banks opened in India during that period failed. The depositors lost money and lost interest in keeping deposits with banks. Subsequently, banking in India remained the exclusive domain of Europeans for next several decades until the beginning of the 20th century.

Foreign banks too started to arrive, particularly in Calcutta, in the 1860s. The Comptoire d'Escompte de Paris opened a branch in Calcutta in 1860, and another in Bombay in 1862; branches in Madras and Pondichery, then a French colony, followed. Calcutta was the most active trading port in India, mainly due to the trade of the British Empire, and so became a banking centre.

Around the turn of the 20th century, the Indian economy was passing through a relative period of stability. Around five decades had elapsed since the Indian Mutiny, and the social, industrial and other infrastructure had improved. Indians had established small banks, most of which served particular ethnic and religious communities.

The presidency banks dominated banking in India. There were also some exchange banks and a number of Indian joint stock banks. All these banks operated in different segments of the economy. The exchange banks, mostly owned by Europeans, concentrated on financing foreign trade. Indian joint stock banks were generally under capitalised and lacked the experience and maturity to compete with the presidency and exchange banks. This segmentation let Lord Curzon to observe, *"In respect of banking it seems we are behind the times. We are like some old fashioned sailing ship, divided by solid wooden bulkheads into separate and cumbersome compartments."*

By the 1900s, the market expanded with the establishment of banks such as Punjab National Bank, in 1895 in Lahore and Bank of India, in 1906, in Mumbai – both of which were founded under private ownership. Punjab National Bank is the first Swadeshi Bank founded by the leaders like Lala Lajpat Rai, Sardar Dyal Singh Majithia. The Swadeshi movement in particular inspired local businessmen and political figures to found banks of and for the Indian community. A number of banks established then have survived to the present such as Bank of India, Corporation Bank, Indian Bank, Bank of Baroda, Canara Bank and Central Bank of India.

From World War I to Independence

The period during the First World War (1914-1918) through the end of the Second World War (1939-1945), and two years thereafter until the independence of India were challenging for Indian banking. The years of the First World War were turbulent, and it took its toll with banks simply collapsing despite the Indian economy gaining indirect boost due to war-related economic activities. At least 94 banks in India failed between 1913 and 1918 as indicated in the following table:

Years	*Number of banks that failed*	*Authorised capital (Rs. Lakhs)*	*Paid-up Capital (Rs. Lakhs)*
1913	12	274	35
1914	42	710	109
1915	11	56	5
1916	13	231	4
1917	9	76	25
1918	7	209	1

Post-independence

The partition of India in 1947 adversely impacted the economies of Punjab and West Bengal, paralysing banking activities for months. India's independence marked the end of a regime of the Laissez-faire for the Indian banking. The Government of India initiated measures to play an active role in the economic life of the nation, and the Industrial Policy Resolution adopted by the government in 1948 envisaged a mixed economy. This resulted into greater involvement of the state in different segments of the economy including banking and finance. The major steps to regulate banking included:

- In 1948, the Reserve Bank of India, India's central banking authority, was nationalised, and it became an institution owned by the Government of India.
- In 1949, the Banking Regulation Act was enacted which empowered the Reserve Bank of India (RBI) "to regulate, control, and inspect the banks in India."
- The Banking Regulation Act also provided that no new bank or branch of an existing bank may be opened without a licence from the RBI, and no two banks could have common directors.

However, despite these provisions, control and regulations, banks in India except the State Bank of India, continued to be owned and operated by private persons. This changed with the nationalisation of major banks in India on 19th July, 1969.

Nationalisation

By the 1960s, the Indian banking industry has become an important tool to facilitate the development of the Indian economy. At the same time, it has emerged as a large employer, and a debate has ensued about the possibility to nationalise the banking industry. Indira Gandhi, the then Prime Minister of India expressed the intention of the GOI in the annual conference of the All India Congress Meeting in a paper entitled *"Stray thoughts on Bank Nationalisation."* The paper was received with positive enthusiasm. Thereafter, her move was swift and sudden, and the GOI issued an ordinance and nationalised the 14 largest commercial banks with effect from the midnight of July 19, 1969. Jayaprakash Narayan, a national leader of India, described the step as a *"masterstroke of political sagacity."* Within two weeks of the issue of the ordinance, the Parliament passed the Banking Companies (Acquisition and Transfer of Undertaking) Bill, and it received the presidential approval on 9th August, 1969.

A second dose of nationalisation of 6 more commercial banks followed in 1980. The stated reason for the nationalisation was to give the government more control of credit delivery. With the second dose of nationalisation, the GOI controlled around 91 per cent of the banking business of India. Later on, in the year 1993, the government merged New Bank of India with Punjab National Bank. It was the first and only merger between nationalised banks and resulted in the reduction of the number of nationalised banks from 20 to 19. After this, until the 1990s, the nationalised banks grew at a pace of around 4 per cent, closer to the average growth rate of the Indian economy.

Liberalisation

In the early-1990s, the then Narsimha Rao government embarked on a policy of liberalisation, licensing a small number of private banks. These came to be known as *New Generation tech-savvy banks,* and included Global Trust Bank (the first of such new generation banks to be set up), which later amalgamated with Oriental Bank of Commerce, UTI Bank (now renamed as Axis Bank), ICICI Bank and HDFC Bank. This move, along with the rapid growth in the economy of India, revitalised the banking sector in India, which has seen rapid growth with strong contribution from all the three sectors of banks, namely, government banks, private banks and foreign banks.

The next stage for the Indian banking has been set up with the proposed relaxation in the norms for Foreign Direct Investment, where all Foreign Investors in banks may be given voting rights which could exceed the present cap of 10 per cent, at present it has gone up to 49 per cent with some restrictions.

The new policy shook the Banking sector in India completely. Bankers, till this time, were used to the 4-6-4 method (Borrow at 4 per cent; Lend at 6 per cent; Go home at 4) of functioning. The new wave ushered in a modern outlook and *tech-savvy* methods of working for traditional banks. All this led to the retail boom in India. People not just demanded more from their banks but also received more.

Current Situation

Currently (2007), banking in India is generally fairly mature in terms of supply, product range and reach – even though reach in rural India still remains a challenge for the private sector and foreign banks. In terms of quality of assets and capital adequacy, Indian banks are considered to have clean, strong and transparent balance sheets relative to other banks in comparable economies in its region. The Reserve Bank of India is an autonomous body, with minimal pressure from the government. The stated policy of the Bank on the Indian Rupee is to manage volatility but without any fixed exchange rate – and this has mostly been true.

With the growth in the Indian economy expected to be strong for quite sometime – especially in its services sector – the demand for banking services, especially retail banking, mortgages and investment services are expected to be strong. One may also expect M&As, takeovers, and asset sales.

In March 2006, the Reserve Bank of India allowed Warburg Pincus to increase its stake in Kotak Mahindra Bank (a private sector bank) to 10 per cent. This is the first time an investor has been allowed to hold more than 5 per cent in a private sector bank since the RBI announced norms in 2005 that any stake exceeding 5 per cent in the private sector banks would need to be vetted by them.

Currently, India has 88 scheduled commercial banks (SCBs) – 27 public sector banks (that is with the Government of India holding a stake) after merger of New Bank of India in Punjab National Bank in 1993, 29 private banks (these do not have government stake; they may be publicly listed and traded on stock exchanges) and 31 foreign banks. They have a combined network of over 53,000 branches and 17,000 ATMs. According to a report by ICRA Limited, a rating agency, the public sector banks hold over 75 per cent of total assets of the banking industry, with the private and foreign banks holding 18.2 per cent and 6.5 per cent respectively.

Reserve Bank of India

The Reserve Bank of India is the central bank of India, and was established on April 1, 1935 in accordance with the provisions of the Reserve Bank of India Act, 1934. The Central Office of the Reserve Bank was initially established in Calcutta but was permanently moved to Mumbai in 1937. Though originally privately owned, RBI has been fully owned by the Government of India since nationalisation in 1949.

Duvvuri Subbarao who succeeded Y. Venugopal Reddy on September 2, 2008 is the current Governor of RBI.

The Reserve Bank of India was set up on the recommendations of the Hilton Young Commission. The commission submitted its report in the year 1926, though the bank was not set up for nine years.

The Preamble of the Reserve Bank of India describes the basic functions of the Reserve Bank as to regulate the issue of Bank Notes and keeping of reserves with a view to securing monetary stability in India and generally to operate the currency and credit system of the country to its advantage.

It has 22 regional offices, most of them in state capitals.

Policy Rate (2008)

Bank Rate 6.00 per cent. Repo Rate 9.00 per cent. Reverse Repo Rate 6.00.

Reserve Ratios (2008)

Cash Reserve Ratio 7.5 per cent. (effective October 12th, 2008) Statutory Liquidity Ratio 25.0 per cent.

Lending or Deposit Rates (2008)

Prime Lending Rate 12.75 per cent-13.25 per cent. Saving Bank Rate 3.5 per cent Deposit Rate 7.50 per cent-10.75.

Board of Directors

The Reserve Bank's affairs are governed by a central board of directors. The board is appointed by the Government of India in keeping with the Reserve Bank of India Act.

On June 27, 2006, the Union Government of India reconstituted the Central Board of Directors of the Reserve Bank of India (RBI) with 13 members, including Azim Premji and Kumar Mangalam Birla.

On 1 July, 2006, in an attempt to enhance the quality of customer service and strengthen the grievance redressal mechanism, the Reserve Bank of India constituted a new department – Customer Service Department (CSD).

Monetary Authority

- Formulates, implements and monitors the Monetary Policy, announced twice a year.
- Announces the Credit Policy, announced twice a year – in April it announces new policy initiatives, the October pronouncement is a review of the April policy.
- Objective: Maintaining price stability and ensuring adequate flow of credit to productive sectors.
- Maintain optimum Liquidity in the economy.

System of Note Issue

- RBI Maintains *Minimum Reserve System* for Note issue.

This means that RBI can issue any amount of currency notes provided it keeps the minimum statutory limit of Rs. 200 crores worth Gold and Securities.

Regulator and Supervisor of the Financial System

- Prescribes broad parameters of banking operations within which the country's banking and financial system functions.
- Objective: maintain public confidence in the system, protect depositors' interest and provide cost-effective banking

services to the public. The Banking Ombudsman Scheme has been formulated by the Reserve Bank of India (RBI) for effective redressal of complaints by bank customers.

Manager of Exchange Control

- Manages the Foreign Exchange Management Act, 1999.
- Objective: To facilitate external trade and payment and promote orderly development and maintenance of foreign exchange market in India.

Issuer of Currency

- Issues and exchanges or destroys currency and coins not fit for circulation.
- Objective: The main objective is to give the public adequate supply of currency of good quality and to provide loans to commercial banks to maintain or improve the GDP.

The basic objectives of RBI are to issue bank notes, to maintain the currency and credit system of the country to utilise it in its best advantage, and to maintain the reserves. RBI maintains the economic structure of the country so that it can achieve the objective of price stability as well as economic development, because both objectives are diverse in themselves.

Developmental Role

- Performs a wide range of promotional functions to support national objectives.
- To incubate or establish financial institutions of national importance, for, e.g.: NABARD, IDBI.

Related Functions

- *Banker to the Government:* Performs merchant banking function for the central and the state governments; also acts as their banker.
- *Banker to banks:* Maintains banking accounts of all scheduled banks.
- Owner and operator of the depository (SGL) and exchange (NDS) for government bonds.

There is now an international consensus about the need to focus the tasks of a central bank upon central banking. RBI is far out of touch with such a principle, owing to the sprawling mandate.

Major Liabilities of Commercial Banks

Figures below are in millions of Indian Rupees:

Year	Deposits and other Accounts	Bills Payable
1950	9,983	173
1955	11,592	262
1960	20,218	317
1965	32,897	446
1970	64,793	923
1975	156,665	2,254
1980	439,869	10,995
1985	1,032,134	24,556
1990	1,820,468	38,656
1995	3,984,352	116,622

Major Assets of Commercial Banks

Figures below are in millions of Indian Rupees:

Year	Investments	Advances
1950	4,330	5,353
1955	4,600	7,037
1960	7,241	12,458
1965	9,884	21,954
1970	18,148	46,850
1975	45,999	106,167
1980	126,642	272,673
1985	303,378	623,553
1990	687,151	1,095,412
1995	1,750,206	2,243,308

Tarapore Committee

The Tarapore committee is a committee set up by the Reserve Bank of India under the chairmanship of former RBI deputy governor S.S. Tarapore to "lay the road map" to capital account convertibility.

The five-member committee recommended a three-year timeframe for complete convertibility by 1999-2000.

In March 2006, the Finance Minister of India, P. Chidambaram said that the Central government was "within striking distance" of implementing the committee's report.

- During partition, the federal reserve was split by the British Raj to aid India and Pakistan separately. Some claim that Pakistan has never gotten its share to date, which is incorrect. On January 19, 1948, Pakistan received its share of 56 Crores Rupees bullion. Apart from that, Nizam of Hyderabad illegally transferred the funds for the state of Hyderabad to Pakistan, and Pakistan has not yet repaid these funds. Nawab of Junagarh fled with 3 Crore cash, which was government property. When it looked like the British would help India get that money back, the Pakistani government helped Nawab flee to Europe with the money using Pakistani government planes. One of the planes refuelling at Beirut crashed in the Aegean Sea and money was declared lost. This story has led to several modern treasure hunts in that area.

Bibliography

Adams, D. W. and Fitchett D. A.: *Informal Finance in Low-Income Countries*, Westview, Boulder, 1992.

Agnew, John: *Mastering Space, Hegemony, Territory and International Political Economy*, Routledge, New York, 1995.

Alexander, M. Counts: *Worm's Eye View: Interviews with Women of the Grameen Bank*, Results Educational Fund, Washington D.C., 1992.

Ana, Revenga: *The Impact of Mexico's Retraining Program on Employment and Wages*, The World Bank, Washington, D.C., 2000.

Atiur, Rahman: *Demand and Marketing Aspects of Grameen Bank: A Closer Look*, Grameen Bank, Dhaka, 1986.

Avery, Byllye: *Breathing Life into Ourselves: The Evolution of the National Black Women's Health Projects*, Seal Press, Seattle, 1990.

Bakker, Isabella: *The Strategic Silence: Gender and Economic Policy*, Zed Books, London, 1994.

Balkin, Steven: *A Grameen Bank Replication: The Full Circle Fund of the Women's Self-Employment Project of Chicago*, WestviewPress, Bangladesh, 1993.

Batres, Gioconda: *Executive Director, Sery Crecer*, Personal communication, Costa Rica, 1993.

Bayes, A. and Akhter, R.: *Village Pay Phones and Poverty Reduction: Insights from a Grameen Bank Initiative in Bangladesh*, Center for Development Research, ZEF. Bonn, 1999

Beattie, Valerie: *Analysis of the Results of a Survey on Sexual Violence in the UK*, Cambridge, U.K., 1992.

Beneria, Lourder and Martha Roldan: *Crossroads of Class and Gender*, University of Chicago Press, Chicago, 1987.

Beneria, Lourdes and Shelley Feldman: *Unequal Burden: Economic Crises, Persistent Poverty and Women's Work*, Westview Press, Boulder, 1992.

Berenguer, Ana Maria: *Alternativas Decade la Medicine Legaly Experiencias Sobre la Violencia Intrafamilar*, Corporacion Case de la Mujer, Colombia, 1988.

Bhatt, N. and Tang, S. Y.: *The Problem of Transaction Costs in Group Based Microlending: An Institutional Perspective*, World Development, 1998.

Bobadilla, Jose: *World Development Report Project Team*, World Bank, Washington, D. C., 1993.

Bruneforth: *Investing in the Future: Financing the Expansion of Educational Opportunity in Latin America and the Caribbean Montreal*, UNESCO Institute for Statistics, Canada, 2004.

Busto, Miren Aduncion: *BDZ;: La Tranquila Adiccion de Santiago, Santiago*, Corporacion de Saludy Politicas Sociales, Chile, 1991.

Calavan, Kay and Muhammad Yunus: *The Grameen Bank Project, in Mann, Charles K, Merilee S Grindle and Parker Shipton*, Kumarian Press, Hartford, 1989.

Camp, Jean L. and Anderson, Brian L.: *Grameen Phone: Empowering the Poor through Connectivity*, The Magazine on Information Impacts, 1999

Caufield, Catherine: *Masters of Illusion. The World Bank and the Poverty of Nations*, Henry Holt, New York.1996.

Chatterjee, Meera: *Indian Women: Their Health and Economic Productivity*, World Bank Discussion, Washington, D.C. 1990.

Chernin, Kim: *The Obsession: Reflections on the Tyranny of Slender*, Harper and Row, New York, 1981.

Clay, Jason W.: *The Spoils of Famine: Ethiopian Famine Policy and Peasant Agriculture*, Cultural Survival, Cambridge, 1998.

Collins, J and Lear, J: *Chile's Free Market Miracle: A Second Look*, Food First, Oakland, 1995.

Danaher, Kevin: *50 Years is Enough: The Case Against the World Bank and the International Monetary Fund,* South End Press, Boston, 1994.

Duale, S.: *The Karawa Health Zone Project,* The World Bank, Washington, D.C. 1991.

Durongdej, S. and L. Tokmoh: *Effect of Weight Gain Feedback on Pregnancy Outcome,* International Center for Research on Women, Washington, 1990.

Elmar, Altvater, Kurt Hubner and Jochen Lorentzen: *The Poverty of Nations: A Guide to the Debt Crisis — From Argentina to Zaire,* Zed Books, London, 1991.

Fauveau, V.: *Matlab Maternity Care Program,* World Bank, Washington, D.C. 1991.

Feifer, Chris: *Maternal Health in Jamaica,* World Bank, Washington, D.C. 1990.

Filmer, D.: *If You Build It, Will They Come? School Availability and School Enrollment in 21 Poor Countries,* The World Bank, Washington, D.C., 2004.

Fuglesang, A. and Chandler, D.: *Participation as Process: What we can Learn from Grameen Bank, Bangladesh,* Norwegian Ministry for Development Cooperation, Norway, 1987.

Goetz, A. and Sen Gupta, R.: *Who Takes the Credit? Gender, Power and Control over Loan use in Rural Credit Programs in Bangladesh,* World Development, 1996.

Griffiths, Marcia: *Status of the NHED Component,* USAID, New Delhi, 1989.

Gurgland, M., Pederson, G. and Yaron, J.: *Outreach and Sustainability of Six Rural Financial Institutions in sub-Saharan Africa,* World Bank, Washington, DC. 1994.

Hall, A. J., B.M. Greenwood, and H. Whittle: *Practice in Developing Countries,* Edward Arnold, London, 1990.

Hashemi, S., Shuler, S. and Riley, A.: *Rural Credit Programs and Women's Empowerment in Bangladesh* World Development, 1996.

Hermann, Carol B., and Sambe Duale.: *Improving Maternity Care Services in the Karawa Health Zone of Zaire,* The International Center for Research on Women, Washington, 1990.

Hofmeyr, G. J.: *Breech Presentation and Abnormal Lie in Late Pregnancy,* Oxford University Press, Oxford, 1989.

Hossain, Mahabub: *Credit for the Alleviation of Rural Poverty: The Grameen Bank in Bangladesh,* BIDS, Dhaka.1988

Israel, Arturo and Heaver, Richard, and: *Country Commitment to Development Projects,* World Bank Discussion, Washington, D.C. 1986.

Joan, Jacobs: *Fasting Girls: The Emergence of Anorexia Nervosa as a Modern Disease,* Harvard University Press, Cambridge, 1988.

Joekes, Susan and Anne Weston: *Women and the New Trade Agenda,* UNIFEM, New York, 1994.

Judith, Brown and Jacquelyn, C.: *Sanctions and Sanctuary: Cultural Perspectives on the Beating of Wives,* West view Press, Colo., 1992.

Kayani, R. and Dymond, A.: *Options for Rural Telecommunications Development,* The World Bank, Washington, 1997.

Khandker, S. and Khalily, B.: *The Bangladesh Rural Advancement Committee's Credit Programs,* The World Bank, Washington, 1996.

Khandker, Shahidur and Zahed, Khan: *Grameen Bank: Performance and Sustainability,* World Bank, Washington, D.C., 1995.

Krasovec, K., and Mary Ann Anderson: *Maternal Nutrition and Pregnancy Outcomes: Antropometric Assessment,* PAHO Scientific Publication, Washington, 1991.

Lopez, Alan D.; *Causes of Death: An Assessment of Global Patterns of Mortality Around 1985,* World Health Organization, Geneva, 1990.

Madeley, John: *Giving Credit where it's Due: Banking on the Landless in Bangladesh,* Ideas and Action, 1984.

Miller, B. A. and Leonard, K. E.: *Intra and Intergenerational Aspects of Serious Domestic Violence and Alcohol and Drugs,* National Institute of Justice, Washington, 1988.

Omar, Rahman, Chris Feifer, and Deanna Ashley: *High Risk Pregnancies at Maternal Health Services in Jamaica,* Prepared for the World Bank, California, 1991.

Onimode, Bade: *The IMF, the World Bank, and African Debt. Social and Political Impact,* Zed Press, London, 1989.

Puri, Shivani and Ritzema, Tineke: *Migrant Worker Remittances, Micro-finance and the Informal Economy: Prospects and Issues,* International Labour Organization Social Finance Unit Working, 1999.

Quinones, B. and Remenyi, J.: *Creating the Vision: Microfinancing the Poor in Asia Pacific,* Asia Pacific Development Centre, Kuala Lumpur, 1997.

Rawlings, L. B. and Rubio, G. M.: *Evaluating the Impact of Conditional Cash Transfer Programs: Lessons from Latin America,* The World Bank, Washington, D.C., 2003.

Ray, Jaynta Kumar: *A Case Study of the Grameen Bank of Bangladesh,* University Press, Dhaka, 1987.

Revenga, A.: *The Impact of Mexico's Retraining Program on Employment and Wages,* The World Bank, Washington, D.C., 2000.

Rooney, M. and Tinker, A.: *Programming for Safe Motherhood,* World Bank, Washington, 1992.

Royston, E., and Armstrong, S.: *Preventing Maternal Deaths,* World Health Organization, Geneva, 1989.

Siddique, K.: *An Evaluation of the Grameen Bank Operation,* National Institute of Local Government, Dhaka, 1984.

Taylor, K. W. and Thapa, G. B.: *Best Practice of Banking with the Poor,* Brisbane, Australia, 1995.

Temple, Frederick D.: *Thoughts on Globalisation and Development Policy,* The Independent, Dhaka, 1999.

Ugalde, Juan Gerardo: *Sindrome do la Mujer Agredida,* San Jose, Coata Rica, 1988.

Wahid, Abu: *The Grameen Bank: Poverty Relief in Bangladesh,* Westview, Boulder, 1993.

Wellenius, B. and Saunders, R., Warford, J.: *Telecommunications and Economic Development,* International Bank for Reconstruction and Development, Washington, 1994.

Wigg, David: *The Quiet Revolution, World Bank Development Essay,* The World Bank, Washington, DC. 1993.

Wood, Geoffrey and Iffath A Sharif: *Who Needs Credit? Poverty and Finance in Bangladesh,* Zed Books, 1997.

Yaron, Jacob: *Successful Rural Finance Institutions, Agriculture Policies Division,* World Bank, Washington, DC. 1991.

Yunus, Muhammad: *Credit for Self Employment: A Fundamental Human Right,* Grameen Bank, Dhaka, 1987.

——————: *The Grameen Bank: Experiences and Reflections,* Grameen Bank, Dhaka, 1991.

Index

D

E

F

I

❑❑❑